Strengthening the African American Educational Pipeline

Strengthening the African American Educational Pipeline

Informing Research, Policy, and Practice

Edited by
Jerlando F. L. Jackson

Foreword by
Gloria Ladson-Billings

State University of New York Press

Published by
State University of New York Press, Albany

For information, address State University of New York Press,
194 Washington Avenue, Suite 305, Albany, NY 12210-2384

Production by Michel Haggett
Marketing by Anne M. Valentine

Library of Congress Cataloging-in-Publication Data

Strengthening the African American educational pipeline : informing research, policy,
and practice / edited by Jerlando F. L. Jackson ; foreword by Gloria Ladson-Billings.
        p. cm.
    Includes bibliographical references and index.
    ISBN-13: 978-0-7914-6987-3 (hardcover : alk. paper)
    ISBN-13: 978-0-7914-6988-0 (pbk. : alk. paper)
    1. African Americans—Education (Higher)   2. Educational equalization—
United States.   I. Jackson, Jerlando F. L., 1973–

LC2781.S746 2007
378.1'982996073—dc22

                                                                    2006007118

Contents

Acknowledgments   vii

Foreword   ix
     Gloria Ladson-Billings

Preface   xiii
     William B. Harvey

Introduction

A Systematic Analysis of the African American Educational   1
Pipeline to Inform Research, Policy, and Practice
     Jerlando F. L. Jackson

PART I: PRE-K–12 SCHOOLS

Chapter 1

The Forgotten Link: The Salience of Pre-K–12 Education and   17
Culturally Responsive Pedagogy in Creating Access to Higher
Education for African American Students
     Tyrone C. Howard

Chapter 2

Teaching in "Hard to Teach in" Contexts: African American   37
Teachers Uniquely Positioned in the African American
Educational Pipeline
     Jennifer E. Obidah, Tracy Buenavista, R. Evely Gildersleeve,
     Peter Kim, and Tyson Marsh

Chapter 3

Bringing the Gifts That Our Ancestors Gave: Continuing the 53
Legacy of Excellence in African American School Leadership
Linda C. Tillman

PART II: HIGHER EDUCATION

Chapter 4

Descriptive Analysis of African American Students' Involvement 73
in College: Implications for Higher Education and Student
Affairs Professionals
Lamont A. Flowers

Chapter 5

The Status of African American Faculty in the Academy: 97
Where Do We Go From Here?
Barbara J. Johnson and Henrietta Pichon

Chapter 6

A National Progress Report of African Americans in the 115
Administrative Workforce in Higher Education
Jerlando F. L. Jackson and Brandon D. Daniels

PART III: SOCIAL INFLUENCES

Chapter 7

Securing the Ties That Bind: Community Involvement and the 141
Educational Success of African American Children and Youth
Mavis G. Sanders and Tamitha F. Campbell

Chapter 8

How African American Families Can Facilitate the Academic 165
Achievement of Their Children: Implications for Family-
Based Interventions
Jelani Mandara and Carolyn B. Murray

Chapter 9

Addressing the Achievement Gap in Education with the Use of 187
Technology: A Proposed Solution for African American Students
Jeffrey G. Sumrall and Ramona Pittman

Conclusion

Reconceptualizing the African American Pipeline: New Perspectives 197
from a Systematic Analysis
Jerlando F. L. Jackson

About the Contributors 211

Index 217

Acknowledgments

FROM THE PECAN ORCHARDS TO THE IVORY TOWERS: ACKNOWLEDGMENTS OF THOSE WHO STRENGTHENED MY EDUCATIONAL PIPELINE

The journey from Ashburn, GA, to Madison, WI, is a long road. These two places are worlds apart, not only with regards to the approximate 17-hour drive by car totaling 1,031 miles but also in regards to opportunity as it relates to education and social mobility. Ashburn, also known as the Peanut Capital of the World, has an estimated population of 4,435 compared to the population of the Madison area, which is approaching approximately 400,000 people. Ashburn's small population is comprised of 65.2% African Americans, compared to 5.8% in Madison. The average income for residents in Ashburn is $18,702, while Madison has an average income of $41,941. Approximately 38% of Ashburn residents have a high school diploma or equivalent, 15.8% with some college or an associate's degree, 5.4% with a bachelor's degree, and 5.3% with a graduate degree. In contrast, Madison's residents collectively have more bachelor's (27.3%) and graduate degrees (20.9%) than Ashburn residents with high school diplomas. Lastly, the racial thermometer and social climate of Ashburn nicely registers within the conservative beliefs and ethos of the Deep South. Though Madison sits squarely in the Heartland of America, it refreshingly has cultivated a liberal community of thoughts, beliefs, and actions. Needless to say, these two worlds are in stark contrast.

My traversing these worlds was made possible by a community of committed individuals, those who unselfishly gave of themselves to give me an opportunity at success broadly defined. I would first like to thank Berta Mae and Minor Louis (Sonny Boy) Cushion who fought to desegregate the Turner County

School District for my mother (Dorothy Jackson). She became the first African American student to attend the Turner County School District and later became the first African American cheerleader. I would be remiss if I did not thank Queen Ester Hudson and Lucious Cushion for raising my mother to be a committed and caring person, who in turn did the same for me. Also, I would like to thank Aretha and Will Jackson for working diligently with my father (Jerry Jackson) to make sure he graduated from high school so he could join the army. My father joining the army represented the turning point for my family, which led to a life that presented more opportunities for success. After my father's basic training, we relocated temporarily to Germany and finally to the Fort Benning/Columbus, GA, area where I lived until leaving for college.

I would like to thank the following individuals who took special interests in my development: McBride Elementary School (Mrs. Brownloe); E. A. White Elementary School (Mr. Ingram); Faith Middle School (Mrs. Hildebrand, who unintentionally participated in strengthening my educational pipeline because she scheduled a meeting with my mother to tell her that I would not graduate from high school. That meeting changed my life—from that point forward, I took my education serious. In fact, it motivated me to prove her wrong. As a result, not only did I receive the college preparatory diploma but went on to eventually receive a Ph.D.); W. H. Spencer High School (Vincent K. Rosse, Dr. Linda Skinner, Mrs. Janet Patresek, and Mrs. Dorothy Aniton); Edgewood Baptist Church (Reverend Dr. Howell); University of Southern Mississippi (Drs. Hong, Wooten, Fraschillo, and the Kappa Iota Chapter of Kappa Alpha Psi Fraternity Incorporated); Auburn University (Dr. James C. Brown, who shaped my understanding of the field of higher education); and Iowa State University (Drs. George A. Jackson, Larry H. Ebbers, Daniel C. Robinson, Walter H. Gmlech, John H. Schuh, and Mack Shelley). I also would like to thank the following individuals for their support throughout my educational process: LaShonda Irby, Chuck and Christie Odum, Larry Nelson, Linda Collier, Charlotte and Ronnie Jordan, and Tometta Walker. Lastly, as certainly not least, I would like to thank my Lord and savior—Jesus Christ.

For the many others who strengthened my educational pipeline, I thank you as well. It is because of the individuals mentioned above that I have been afforded the opportunity to work as a professor at one of America's most elite institutions, the University of Wisconsin-Madison. As I drive home from work every day to the suburbs of Madison, I cannot help but think how far I have come from the trailer home on the side of a dirt road that leads to the Pecan Orchards in Ashburn, GA. *I do hope that I too one day can serve to strengthen the education pipeline for someone else.*

Foreword

Entering the Pipeline:
The Pre-K–12 Challenge to Equally
Prepare Students for Higher Education

An interesting exercise to perform with undergraduate students in a diverse classroom is to ask them to describe how they got their first job. More often than not, middle-income students relate an experience where a family member or family friend helped them get a job. "My dad is a manager at such-and-such firm, and he got me a job filing," or, "My uncle owns a business, and he has hired me every summer since high school." On the other hand, working-class students—often students of color—report that their first job came as a result of answering "help wanted" signs in windows, perusing the newspaper want ads, or walking into an establishment and filling out an application. The point of the exercise is to demonstrate that even with something as simple as a first job, some people are already advantaged by birth. The same thing applies to accessing a college or university education.

My own journey to college was very serendipitous. No one in my immediate family had ever attended college, and I was entirely dependent on the "kindness of strangers." My high school college guidance counselor and members of my church provided me with some ideas, but for the most part I was making selections in the dark. I chose two local schools (that I did not really want to attend) and two historically Black colleges. Additionally, because of my grades, I was being offered admittance to a number of schools that seemed desperate to increase their diversity. I ultimately chose one of the historically Black schools without realizing that I had been admitted to an Ivy League school (I still do not think I would have chosen that school). However, my point is that

I did not know enough about the differences in schools to make an informed decision. I was more eager to go away to school than I was to consider what schools had to offer.

I do not think my experience was particularly different from those of most working-class, first-generation African American students who were considering college. Many of my classmates went to a local historically Black college. Another group commuted uptown to a large, state-affiliated university. But a significant number did not attend college at all. Many of the male students were drafted and sent off to Southeast Asia to fight in the Vietnam War. Still another group found its way to the workforce to fill the many retail, entry-level clerical, and civil service jobs that a major metropolitan area could provide. In the mid 1960s, it was possible to have a decent life without a college education.

Fast-forward to 2007. Even entry-level jobs that lead to a career require some postsecondary education or training. Most of the newly created jobs are in the service industry. These are minimum-wage jobs with few if any fringe benefits. These are the jobs that far too many African American youths find themselves competing for—jobs that rarely lead to real careers or provide a living wage. With these prospects, it would seem only logical that more African American youths would choose to attend college.

The facts that stand in the way of the logic of a college education deal with the failure of many African American students to complete high school. Although the graduation rate seems to be improving, graduation rates from traditional comprehensive high schools are flat. The improvement in graduation rates comes from the increasing number of students completing high school via the general equivalency diploma (GED) and other alternatives.

The problem in the pipeline for African American students is the failure of many of them to receive an adequate secondary education that will prepare them for college. Plenty of attention has been focused on the failure of high-profile Division IA colleges and universities to provide football and basketball scholarship athletes with a real education and the likely chance to graduate. African Americans comprise a large proportion of these student athletes. The unspoken problem is that at far too many Division IA colleges and universities, the graduation rate of African American student athletes exceeds that of African American students in the general student population.

Another pipeline issue is financial. Many African American students are likely to economize on a college education by starting out in two-year community or technical colleges. Unfortunately, what looks like a good strategy can become a trap for many students. Instead of transitioning to a four-year college, far too many students move into two-year terminal programs such as dental hygiene, physician's assistant, or accounting. While there is nothing wrong with these fields, they rarely provide the flexibility that graduates will need if the job market is saturated with people in these fields. Unlike a college degree that may provide multiple pathways to a variety of careers, many two-year degrees close off career possibilities.

In *Strengthening the African American Educational Pipeline*, Jerlando F. L. Jackson has brought together outstanding scholars who, through empirical evidence, explore the challenges of recruiting more African American youths to postsecondary education that results in the four-year degree. These scholars examine the multiple factors that thwart African American youths from pursuing, four-year college and university education. They also look at individual, institutional, and social forces that in turn help us understand what the numbers really mean.

Colleges and universities that bemoan the fact that fewer African American students apply to and gain acceptance on their campuses would be wise to look at this volume as part of a systematic attempt to reverse the trend of shrinking numbers of African American collegians (particularly on predominantly White campuses). To prime the pump of the pipeline it will be necessary to look further than the local high school. African American students' middle-income White counterparts begin their college planning early. By being born into families where the adults are college graduates, White middle-income students have a set of resources that makes the question of college not one of "if" but of "when." Their parents' resources are both social and material capital. They know how to ensure that they enroll in college preparatory courses, attend higher-quality high schools, and avail themselves of enrichment opportunities that prepare them for the collegiate experience.

Most of this discussion has focused on those African American students who might be headed for postsecondary education. However, another source of the pipeline problem for students who desire a college education, but find themselves woefully underprepared, resides in the juvenile justice system. Increasing numbers of African American youths are finding themselves removed from the educational pipeline because they are serving time in prison. These youths rarely figure in our calculations, but I believe it is important for us to look carefully at the way many young adults have become "throwaway" people.

If creating a strong democracy relies on maintaining a viable economic infrastructure, then we must commit ourselves to preparing all students to take advantage of postsecondary education that enhances their economic, social, and civic opportunities. This means that whether or not students decide to go to college, they are *prepared* to go to college. Precollegiate education should be about opening opportunities, not closing them off.

This volume provides an important window to the pipeline problem. It also offers some viable solutions. If we do the work it challenges us to do, then we hope that the next generation will have no need for a book that calls for strengthening the pipeline.

Gloria Ladson-Billings
University of Wisconsin

Preface

Maximizing Higher Education Attainment

The Critical Factor to Improving African American Communities

About a year ago, I assumed the responsibility for organizing a national meeting that examined issues faced by women of color in the higher education arena. As preparation for the meeting, I had the extraordinary pleasure of finding myself involved in a three-way discussion with Ruth Simmons and Johnnetta Cole, the preeminent African American higher education administrators in the nation. As might be expected, both of these insightful leaders expressed serious concern about the status of African American men and women in the academy, and they heartily proclaimed the need to dramatically increase their representation throughout the matrix of colleges and universities—from Brown to Bennett—and at all levels, from students to presidents.

Their observations take on increasing salience with each passing day. Even though there have been substantial and heartening overall increases in the total enrollment of African American students in institutions of higher education over the past three decades, the rate at which they complete high school and subsequently enroll in college continues to lag behind that of White students. African American faculty representation in predominantly White colleges and universities continues to be pitifully small, and in those institutions, appointments of African Americans at the top levels of academic administration remain rare and noteworthy events.

Strengthening the African American Educational Pipeline is a must read, because the contributors present a vivid analysis of the situation that African Americans are facing in the educational realm. The section of the book particularly focused on higher and postsecondary education will hopefully inspire creative approaches to resolve some of the problematic conditions that African Americans confront as they negotiate their way through the nation's postsecondary institutions.

For students, college and university campuses are incubating environments and developmental laboratories—or at least they should be. Thus student involvement is a necessary, but not sufficient, condition for student success. Just like their counterparts from other races, African American students have tended to achieve at a higher rate academically and fare better emotionally when they have operated in settings where their sense of identity and self-concept has been affirmed.

It is important to recognize that there are three distinct kinds of institutions that enroll African American students as they pursue higher education. According to 2001 data, there were 1,756,864 African American students enrolled in the nation's colleges and universities, and the nation's two-year community colleges had the largest concentration with 763,432. In the four-year predominantly White institutions, enrollment figures for African American students were 754,614, while 238,638 students matriculated in the historically Black colleges and universities. The good news is that the number of students enrolled is at an all-time high. The not-so-good news is that far too many of these students are leaving their chosen institutions without completing their selected academic programs and earning degrees.

There are several potentially problematic implications to having a plurality of African American postsecondary students enrolled in two-year colleges. First, students who begin their careers at these institutions are less likely to earn a baccalaureate degree than those who start their postsecondary education at a four-year college or university. Second, the spectrum of institutional supports and resources available, such as the student affairs professionals to whom Lamont Flowers refers in his chapter, is probably not as broad in the two-year college settings as in the four-year institutions. Third, substantial numbers of the African American students in two-year institutions are the first in their families to attend college, and students of all races who are in that category have more difficulty earning a degree than do students whose parents have attended college.

These observations are not intended to diminish but rather to emphasize the significance of developing and maintaining a supportive campus climate at all institutions of higher learning. An environment that is nurturing and facilitative, whether a two- or four-year setting, is certainly more likely to enhance student participation and performance than one that is debilitating and contentious. However, Flowers's proposition that student affairs professionals assume sole, or even primary, responsibility for improving the campus climate, to my mind places an inappropriate amount of the burden on one group of academic professionals.

Clearly, student affairs professionals play an important role in the higher education arena. Indeed, in a previous publication, I have referred to them as the "conscience" of the campus. But while they are an appropriate subgroup to lead the efforts to make the atmosphere at their respective institutions a welcoming one for all students, discussions regarding these matters *must* include appropriate and relevant persons from a variety of departments and units. Faculty and academic administrators also have major responsibilities to make appropriate contributions and modifications to the campus environment so that it promotes not only access but also success for African American students.

To that end, increasing the numbers of African American faculty at both the predominantly White two- and four-year institutions remains a critical and frustrating concern. During the period 1993–2001, the percentage of African American faculty in colleges and universities across the country increased by only one-half of 1%, from 4.7 to 5.2%. During that time frame, when the number of faculty positions available increased by over 65,000, just over 6,000 African Americans were hired into these positions, a slightly smaller figure than that for Hispanics and less than half the number of Asian Americans hired. The relative significance of these puny figures is further highlighted by the realization that over half of the African American faculty are employed at the nation's historically Black colleges and universities.

Barbara J. Johnson and Henrietta Pichon offer a cogent exploration of the circumstances of African American faculty in the academy. They point out the debilitating aspects of the culture in predominantly White institutions that must be faced and overcome in order for African American faculty to be successful in these settings. Certainly the numbers of African Americans in the graduate school pipelines need to be substantially increased, but the continued underrepresentation of African American faculty in predominantly White institutions cannot be attributed solely to the availability of candidates. Even in fields where there is a reasonable pool of potential African American faculty from which to select, they are usually conspicuous by their absence in the professorial ranks of predominantly White colleges and universities.

Both structural and attitudinal impediments can be identified within the academic workplace that can result in African Americans not receiving faculty appointments. The subjective manifestations of the search process, where committee members frequently seek to "clone" themselves via the new hires, and the imprecise and relative value given to particular research areas of interest, are examples of factors that result in African Americans being screened out of the pool of finalists for positions. It should come as no surprise then that there are some African American faculty who choose to work in the historically Black colleges and universities, both to avoid racism as well as to make a contribution to their communities. Nevertheless, in order to dispel lingering racist stereotypes regarding the intellectual aptitude of African Americans, to enrich the learning experiences of students of all races, to enhance the depth and quality of the institutions, and to broaden the leadership pool of the larger society, it is imperative that significant increases occur in the numbers of African American faculty in the nation's predominantly White colleges and universities.

The underrepresentation of African American faculty is echoed at the top administrative levels of postsecondary institutions. In 2004, only 157 of the

nation's 2,474 four-year colleges and universities had an African American as
president or chancellor. When the 102 historically Black colleges and universities are subtracted from this number, the resulting figure of 55 means that
African Americans occupy the top administrative position in slightly more
than 2% of the predominantly White institutions around the country. The situation is somewhat better at the two-year college level, where 101 out of 1,422
chief executive officers, or about 7%, are African Americans.

At 9.4%, the figure for African Americans holding full-time administrative appointments in positions other than president or chancellor appears more
encouraging than in other areas in the academy, but in this particular cohort,
there is no differentiation by title and level of authority. As a result, the catchall
nature of such a broad categorical grouping masks the disturbingly small representation of African Americans in the senior or management levels of the administrative structures. Further, those African Americans who do hold
administrative appointments are more likely to be found in the student services
sector of the institutions than in academic units, research administration, or fiscal affairs, areas that usually have more power and influence.

Jerlando F. L. Jackson and Brandon D. Daniels, in their examination of the
African American administrative workforce in higher education, offer an engagement, retention, and advancement model that should assist colleges and
universities in their quest to increase their representation in this category of
employees. The model identifies a number of steps that institutions of higher
education can take to increase their representation of African Americans in colleges and universities. The actions that they propose are positioned against the
backdrop of a changing set of demographics that will result in increasing numbers of African Americans in the overall population, and hopefully in the academy as well, as we move further into the twenty-first century.

Even as a small number of African Americans move to new heights in the
economic and political sectors of the society, the vast majority of folks in our
community continue to struggle, and struggle to continue. Educational attainment has certainly been the most significant of the few avenues that have been
available to us that point toward the prospect of a better life. However, the current hard-edged and mean-spirited nature of the political climate in the nation
should be sending a warning message to African Americans about the critical
importance of ensuring that the individuals who are moving through the educational pipeline are receiving quality instruction and future-oriented content,
as well as a meaningful social and historical perspective.

There is much to be done. It is critical that we identify gaps in the instructional process, and then act collectively to see that they are being filled. We
must use the benefits of technology to recreate the sense of connectedness of
the "village," even without its physical boundaries, so that our children can be
motivated, encouraged, and inspired to reach the apex of their talents and abil-

ities. Above all else, we must mobilize all of the resources within our community to celebrate, rather than denigrate, academic achievement. At a time when a four-year degree is becoming the prerequisite for reaching middle-class status, this level of achievement should be seen as the rule, not the exception.

At this moment in time, African Americans have reached the highest level of academic and intellectual attainment since our arrival on these shores. What a tragedy and a travesty it would be if we do not take advantage of those achievements for our collective betterment. From the pre-K to postgraduate experiences, our needs are great—but so are our talents. It is time to put them to use.

William B. Harvey
University of Virginia

Introduction

A Systematic Analysis of the African American Educational Pipeline to Inform Research, Policy, and Practice

Jerlando F. L. Jackson

Inequality, disparate representation, and denied access to opportunity are key challenges that have long plagued African Americans in their pursuit of education in the United States. These challenges have been well documented in the annals of history, chronicling the less than desired treatments in K–12 schools and universities. These three challenges have not been limited to African American students but African American professionals as well. Although African Americans constituted 33.5 million or 12% of the U.S. population in 2000, they participate in education at a lower rate. For example, of the students attending higher education institutions in 2000, 11% were African Americans. While the disparity in participation has narrowed to 1% for African Americans in higher education, the attainment gap remains a substantial challenge. In turn, most of the discussions in education focused on research and policy are hard pressed not to have a major agenda item centered on improving the conditions for African Americans.

Decades of research have described the dismal educational conditions for African Americans (e.g., Hoffman, Llagas, & Snyder, 2003; Nettles & Perna, 1997), coupled with federal legislation targeted at improving these conditions (e.g., TRIO Programs), however, the results have been slow and insignificant. Now we are operating in an era when affirmative action is losing support, targeted and preferential programs are under attack, and federal support for specific groups is being downsized. The key question remains: What systemic set of strategies is necessary to improve the conditions for African Americans throughout the educational pipeline? In this book we attempted to address this question by examining the status and recent progress of African Americans at critical stages in the educational pipeline. In addition, our goal was to provide appropriate implications for consideration by policy makers charged with addressing these issues, to advance the knowledge base for researchers concerned about African American education, and to provide praxis-based information to improve educational practice.

1

In the early 1960s, Coleman's *Equality of Educational Opportunity* provided large-scale empirical evidence of the underachievement of African Americans in education. *Equality of Educational Opportunity*, also known as the Coleman Report, resulted from Section 402 of the Civil Rights Act of 1964:

> The Commissioner shall conduct a survey and make a report to the President and the Congress, within two years of the enactment of this title, concerning the lack of availability of equal opportunities for individuals by reason of race, color, religion, or national origin in public educational institutions at all levels in the United States, its territories and possessions, and the District of Columbia. (Coleman, Campbell, Hobson, McPartland, Mood, Weinfield, & York, 1966, p. 548)

The product became the second largest social science research project in history, with Project Talent being the largest. Approximately 570,000 K–12 students in America were tested, along with 60,000 school teachers, and detailed information on 4,000 schools was collected.

Reactions to the report were less than settled, with supporters arguing that "it is the most important source of American education ever produced" (Mosteller & Moynihan, 1972, p. 4). Meanwhile, critics (e.g., Bowles & Levin, 1968) noted that it was not methodologically sound, thus raising more questions than it answered. While these findings were potentially flawed, they were relevant to African Americans' participation in education. Several key findings prefaced perennial challenges for the education of African Americans. Nationwide median test scores in 1965 for first- and twelfth-grade students described and documented the achievement gap between African Americans and Whites. In addition, the report documented that the absence of key educational tools and interventions in homes and communities for African American students contributed greatly to their underachievement in schools.

Moreover, findings of the Coleman Report indicated that African American students were more likely to be taught by African American teachers. In conjunction, the report noted that teachers who instruct African American students tended to be less well credentialed than those who instruct White students. School counselors for African American students were less involved in their professional association, thus lagging behind in current knowledge compared to the school counselors for White students. Lastly, the disparate enrollment of African American students in higher education institutions was well documented in the report. Of the African American students enrolled at institutions of higher education, they were largely concentrated at institutions with less prestige and fewer resources. It is difficult to understand the current status of African Americans in education without examining their historical struggle over access to education.

HISTORICAL CONTEXT FOR THE
EDUCATION OF AFRICAN AMERICANS:
FROM SLAVERY TO THE TWENTIETH CENTURY

African Americans' plight regarding education in the United States has been a unique journey (Anderson, 1988). African Americans represent the only immigrant group to be legally denied access to education. Their conspicuous journey in education began prior to their ancestors being brought to America. Slave masters deliberated over the type and scope of training that Africans would need to be adequate slaves in America (Woodson, 1919). These slave masters believed that the slaves could not be enlightened without developing a thirst for liberation, which would make it far more difficult to exploit these new people. The majority of southern slaveholders adopted this philosophy and decided that African Americans should not be educated.

In 1661, slavery was legalized in Virginia, with other southern colonies to follow soon thereafter. Accordingly, teaching slaves to read or write was deemed illegal because it was thought to be a deterrent to slavery. While the Quakers were the first settlers of the American colonies to offer African Americans the same educational and religious opportunities as Whites, many Catholic churches were instrumental in providing education for African Americans, even within the confines of slavery (Woodson, 1919). In addition, many African American slaves were astute enough to teach themselves how to read and write. For instance, Phillis Wheatley in 1761 taught herself how to read in 16 months around age 8 (Nott, 1993).

The first African Free School was founded in New York City by the Manumission Society in 1787. By 1824, seven African Free Schools were funded by the city, such that free education for all African American children was available in New York City. In 1834, White students at Oberlin College (Ohio) voted to admit African American and women students. Lincoln University (Pennsylvania) was founded in 1854, making it the first historically Black institution specifically for college-level education. By 1870, 21% of newly freed African Americans were literate. Edward A. Bouchet received his Ph.D. in physics from Yale University in 1876, thus becoming the first African American to be awarded a doctoral degree from an American university.

Alexander Crummel established the American Negro Academy, the first national association of African American intellectual leaders in 1897. In 1907, the Jeanes Foundation, the Negro Rural School Fund (later known as the Anna T. Jeanes Fund), was established, making it the first fund with the sole purpose of improving rural public education for African American children in the South. Atlanta University was established in 1929 as the first African American institution solely for graduate and professional education. While not a complete history, the previous section does provide a description of the initial years for African Americans in education.

KEY POLICY TOOLS FOR
AFRICAN AMERICAN EDUCATION

In order to understand the level of participation that African Americans currently have in education, policy tools require attention. Policy tools are critical, because they are the elements in policy design that cause individuals to do something they would not otherwise do with the intention of modifying behaviors to solve public problems or attain policy goals (Baker, 2001; Fastrup, 1997). Moreover, policy tools have implications in public policy designs because they direct the ways in which individuals are treated. These tools are designed to change behavior through several distinct mechanisms, each of which carries significant symbolic and instrumental connotations. The authoritative perspective on policy tools assumes that without the explicit or even implicit threat of other sanctions, individuals will not treat all groups equitably. Accordingly, what follows are policy tools, broadly defined, that affected African American education.

In 1865, the U.S. Freedman Bureau was established by Congress to assist newly freed slaves with food, medicine, jobs, contracts, legal matters, and education. The bureau subsequently established over 4,000 schools for African Americans. The U.S. Congress passed the Morrill Act II in 1890, which led to the founding of historically Black land-grant institutions. The *Plessy v. Ferguson* decision in 1896 upheld that states have the constitutional authority to provide "separate but equal" accommodations for African Americans. One of the more significant early admission cases that forced states to establish separate professional programs for African Americans occurred in 1938, *Missouri ex rel. Gains v. Canada*.

Frederick D. Patterson, president of Tuskegee Institute, conceived of the United Negro College Fund (UNCF), which was incorporated in 1944. The UNCF's purpose was to enhance the quality of education for historically Black colleges and universities (HBCU) students, provide scholarships, raise operating funds, and provide technical assistance for member institutions. In *McLaurin v. Oklahoma State Regents for Higher Education* (1950), the courts found that the state must treat students of color equal to or the same as White students in all aspects of education and services provided. Subsequently, the Supreme Court, in *Sweatt v. Painter* (1950), made it clear that when programs are not equal, it is a violation of the Equal Protection Clause. This decision was based on an evaluation of whether the legal education program at Texas State University for Negroes (TSUN) School of Law (later relocated to Texas Southern University) was equal to the program at the University of Texas Law School.

Thurgood Marshall, who was at the time special council of the National Association for the Advancement of Colored People (NAACP), argued the *Brown v. Board of Education, Topeka, Kansas*, case in front of the Supreme Court in 1954. The Supreme Court concluded that racial segregation in public schools violates the Fourteenth Amendment of the U.S. Constitution. The decision ultimately forbids racial segregation in public schools, thus providing students of color with the opportunity to attend the same public schools as White students. On the higher education level, *Frasier v. UNC Board of Trustees* (1955) represented a significant victory for African American students who were denied admission to colleges and universities on the basis of admission policies that admitted Whites only. Subsequently, in *Cooper v. Aaron* (1958), the Supreme Court ruled, based on constitutional rights, that children are not to be discriminated against in schools' admissions because of race or color.

In 1964, affirmative action policies were instituted based on the Civil Rights Act. In accordance, President Lyndon B. Johnson signed Executive Order 11246 supporting affirmative action policies and practices. The Civil Rights Act specifically exempted higher education from its jurisdiction. In the following year, Title III of the Higher Education Act stipulated aid for "strengthening developing institutions." Historically Black colleges and universities were well positioned to take advantage of these additional federal resources. The same year, the Office of Economic Opportunity started the Head Start programs, designed to address the education, health and nutrition, and social needs of low-income children and their families. As result of Title IV, Section 402, of the Civil Rights Act of 1964, James Coleman's study *Equality of Education Opportunity*, often referred to as the "Coleman Report," was conducted. Policy implications from these findings resulted in busing as a means for addressing segregation, and tracking, which inadvertently led to re-segregation.

The National Association for Equal Opportunity in Higher Education (NAFEO) was founded in 1969 primarily as a public policy advocate to address the interests of HBCUs. Due to the *Adams v. Richardson* (1973) case, the U.S. Department of Health, Education, and Welfare (HEW) was established with an affirmative obligation to enforce its duties under the Civil Rights Act of 1964 with respect to education programs that receive federal funds. The Black Mississippians' Council of Higher Education filed a class action suit, *Ayers v. Waller* (later known as *Ayers v. Fordice*), in 1975. The group requested that the state enforce Title VI of the Civil Rights Act of 1964. When the suit was filed by HEW, it was named *United States v. Fordice*. The U.S. Supreme Court in 1992 ordered the state of Mississippi to dismantle its dual system of higher education. In *Regents of the University of California v. Bakke* (1978), the Supreme Court ruled that colleges and universities may administer carefully designed admissions programs that to some extent take race and ethnicity into account to foster diversity of their student bodies. At the same time, the court held that quotas and set-asides in admissions were illegal. In 1986, it decided the only ruling on de facto segregation and faculty assignment schemes in *Wyant v. Jackson Board of Education*, stating that seniority could be considered but race could not. The American Council on Education in Washington, DC, established the Office of Minorities in Higher Education in 1987.

PROBLEMATIZING THE AFRICAN AMERICAN EDUCATIONAL PIPELINE

When used in reference to education, the pipeline metaphor elicits various responses. For the most part, while some may be impartial, two camps have developed in response to the metaphor: supporters and critics. Supporters tend to find legitimacy in the use of the term as a heuristic tool to help explain the representation of a group across a large and complex enterprise such as education (e.g., Cole & Barber, 2003; Kulis, Chong, & Shaw, 1999; Kulis, Sicotte, & Collins, 2002). Meanwhile, critics tend to view the term as limited and less representative of the experiences of underrepresented populations (e.g., Bowen & Bok, 1998; Cross, 1994). Some critics (e.g., Bowen & Bok, 1998; Malveaux, 1995) have offered alternative metaphors (e.g., shape of the river and merry-go-rounds). In the context of this book, the educational pipeline metaphor is used to describe and depict critical stages in the educational process for African Americans, both as students and professionals. As such, this metaphor permits key decision makers (e.g., researchers, policy makers, and practitioners) to examine the identified stages to determine where additional attention and interventions may be needed (Bowen & Rudenstine, 1992; Turner, Myers, & Creswell, 1999). In short, the metaphor was retained for this book because it provides clear stages for interventions to improve the conditions for African Americans in education.

In the final chapter, I present an enlarged and a more tangible understanding of the pipeline metaphor for African Americans in education. This discussion extends the pipeline metaphor and attempts to provide direct connections to African American participation, attainment, and outcomes in education. This is done by drawing on knowledge from applied science. This field provides excellent guidelines and terminology to depict an enlarged understanding of the African American educational pipeline as a "free-flowing" pipe. In doing so, this new conceptualization of the pipeline encompasses the dynamic nature, multiple and parallel lines of progression, various end points, blocked passages, cracked surfaces, and nonlinear status often attributed to African American participation in education.

NATIONAL CONTEXT OF THE PARTICIPATION, ATTAINMENT, AND OUTCOMES FOR AFRICAN AMERICANS IN THE EDUCATIONAL SYSTEM

To provide a context for examining African American participation, attainment, and outcomes in education, this section highlights national-level data at key stages of the educational pipeline. The enrollment of African Americans in preschool declined 5.4% between 1991 and 1999 (see Table 1). During this 9-year period, African American preschool enrollment decreased from 182,133 in 1990 to 172,388 in 1999. In contrast, African American students' participation in elementary and secondary schools increased 13.7% from 1990 to 1999. In 1990, African American elementary and secondary school enrollment constituted 6,800,805 and 7,731,405 in 1999. High school completion rates for African American students increased slightly (3.6%) during the time of data collection. Specifically, African American students equaled 19,136,040 in 1990 and 19,817,201 in 1999.

TABLE 1

Distribution of African American Students in Pre-K–12 Schools

Category	1990	1999	Change
Preschool			
Total	182,133[a]	172,388	−5.4%
Elementary/ Secondary School			
Total	6,800,805	7,731,405	13.7%
High School Completion			
Total	19,136,040	19,817,201	3.6%

Note: [a] represents 1991. Enrollment counts for preschool total enrollments were based on the number for each year: 1,239,000 in 1991 and 1,214,000 in 1999. Enrollment counts for elementary and secondary school students were based on the number for each year: 41,217,000 in 1990 and 46,857,000 in 1999. High school completion counts were based on the number for each year: 24,852,000 in 1990 and 26,041,000 in 1999.

The participation of African Americans in professional positions in pre-K–12 schools is a critical aspect of the educational pipeline (see Table 2). African Americans who held teaching posts in pre-K–12 schools increased 10.4% from 1990 to 1999. Overall, African Americans accounted for 221,102 in 1990 and 244,035 in 1999. When examining these data more closely, the majority of African Americans held teaching positions in public schools. For example, African American teachers in public schools constituted 211,640 in 1990 and 227,505 in 1999. In addition, African American teachers in private schools equaled 9,462 in 1990 and 16,530 in 1999.

Data on school principals show that African Americans' participation increased 45.9% from 1990 to 1999. More precisely, there were 7,413 African American principals in 1990 and 10,813 in 1999. When taking into account sector (public versus private), as with teachers, the majority of African American school principals were employed at public schools. In 1990, African Americans held 6,770 of the principal positions at public schools and 9,239 in 1999, whereas, at private schools African Americans held 643 of the principal positions in 1990 and 1,574 in 1999.

Overall, the enrollment of African Americans at colleges and universities increased 38.8% from 1990 to 2000 (see Table 3). African American undergraduate enrollment was 1,247,000 in 1990 and 1,730,000 in 2000. When considering gender, African American females outnumbered African American males as undergraduates. The percentage of African Americans securing bachelor's degrees increased 70.3% between 1990 and 2000. In 1990, African Americans completed 65,341 bachelor's degrees and 111,307 in 2000. Regarding gender, African American females earned almost twice the number of bachelor's degrees compared with males.

TABLE 2
Distribution of African American Professionals in Pre-K–12 Schools

Category	1990	1999	Change
School Teachers			
Total	221,102	244,035	10.4%
Public	211,640	227,505	
Private	9,462	16,530	
School Principals			
Total	7,413	10,813	45.9%
Public	6,770	9,239	
Private	643	1,574	

Note: Employment counts for school teachers were based on the number for each year: 2,915,773 in 1990 and 3,451,315 in 1999. Employment counts for school principals were based on the number for each year: 102,770 in 1990 and 110,021 in 1999.

TABLE 3
Distribution of African American Students in Higher Education

Category	1990	2000	Change
Undergraduate Enrollment			
Total	1,247,000	1,730,000	38.8%
Men	485,000	635,000	31.1%
Women	762,000	1,095,000	43.6%
Bachelor's Degree			
Total	65,341	111,307	70.3%
Men	26,956	38,103	41.4%
Women	41,013	73,204	78.5%
Master's Degree			
Total	16,139	38,265	137.1%
Men	5,709	11,568	102.6%
Women	10,430	26,697	156.6%
First Professional			
Total	3,575	5,416	51.5%
Men	1,672	2,110	26.2%
Women	1,903	3,306	73.7%
Doctoral Degree			
Total	1,003	1,604	59.9%
Men	417	587	40.8%
Women	586	1,017	73.5%

Note: Enrollment counts for undergraduate total enrollments were based on the number for each year: 13,819,000 in 1990 and 15,312,000 in 2000. Bachelor's degree completion counts were based on the number for each year: 1,081,280 in 1990 and 1,244,171 in 2000. Master's degree completion counts were based on the number for each year: 328,645 in 1990 and 468,476 in 2000. First professional degree completion counts were based on the number for each year: 71,515 in 1990 and 79,707 in 2000. Doctoral degree completion counts were based on the number for each year: 37,527 in 1990 and 40,744 in 2000.

Master's degree completion rates for African American students more than doubled between 1990 and 2000. Collectively, African Americans secured 16,139 master's degrees in 1990 and 38,265 in 2000, which amounted to a 137.1% increase. During this time frame, master's degree completion rates increased 102.6% for African American males and 156.6% for African American females. Over a 10-year period (1990–2000), African Americans obtaining first professional degrees increased from 3,575 to 5,416, a 51.5% increase. The growth by gender was as follows: African Americans females increased by 26.2%, and African American males increased by 73.7%. The percentage of African Americans earning doctoral degrees between 1990 and 2000 increased by 59.9%. Total growth went from 1,003 in 1990 to 1,604 in 2000. More growth occurred for African American females (73.5%) during this time period than for African American males (40.8%).

African Americans holding faculty positions between 1990 and 2000 increased 39.8% (see Table 4). Specifically, in 1990 there were 23,225 African American faculty and 29,222 in 2000. During the time of data collection, African American females' representation increased at a higher rate (65.9%) than African American males (26.7%). The increase resulted in parity between African American males and females in the professoriate. African Americans holding higher education administrative positions increased 19.1% between 1990 and 2000. There were 11,796 African American administrators in 1990 and 14,047 in 2000. Between 1990 and 2000, African American females in administrative positions increased 36.0%, while African American males increased only 2.7%. As a result, African American females outnumbered African American males in administrative positions by 2000. African Americans holding university CEO positions increased 20.3% between 1993 and 2003. In 1993, African Americans held 177 of the university CEO positions and 213 in 2003. When considering gender, African American females increased 77.1%, while African American males only increased 6.3%. Even with the sizeable increase, African American males still outnumbered African American females in university CEO positions.

In summarizing data from the 1990s, African American pre-K–12 student participation saw a decline in preschool enrollment, a moderate increase in elementary and secondary school enrollment, and a modest improvement in high school completion. As pre-K–12 professionals, African Americans realized sig-

TABLE 4

Distribution of African American Professionals in Higher Education

Category	1990	2000	Change
Full-Time Faculty			
Total	23,225	29,222	39.8%
Men	12,483	14,660	26.7%
Women	10,742	14,562	65.9%
Full-Time Admin.			
Total	11,796	14,047	19.1%
Men	5,997	6,160	2.7%
Women	5,799	7,887	36.0%
University CEOs			
Total	177[a]	213[b]	20.3%
Men	142	151	6.3%
Women	35	62	77.1%

Note: Employment counts for full-time faculty were based on the number for each year: 514,662 in 1990 and 571,599 in 2000. Employment counts for full-time administrators were based on the number for each year: 137,561 in 1990 and 158,270 in 2000. [a] represents 1993 and [b] represents 2003. University CEO counts were based on the number for each year: 2,802 in 1993 and 3,191 in 2003.

nificant growth as school principals. Additionally, African Americans experienced moderate growth as schoolteachers. In both cases, the majority of the growth occurred in public schools. The 1990s saw much wider access and participation for African Americans in higher education compared to enrollment and attainment growth in pre-K–12 schools. It is likely that this is due in large part to the marked participation growth that African Americans experienced in pre-K–12 schools in the 1970s and 1980s. Considerable growth occurred in the higher education workforce for African Americans at several levels (e.g., faculty, administrators, and presidents). A significant share of this growth could be attributable to the participation level of African American women.

OVERVIEW OF THE BOOK

The sections of this book parallel the organization of the educational pipeline (i.e., pre-K–12 schools and higher education). The final section examines the importance of the social and technical context and its influence on the African American educational pipeline. While on the surface these sections may seem disconnected, the connections among them are essential considerations for examining the success of the African American educational pipeline. The conditions of education in pre-K–12 schools are critical in determining African Americans' readiness for postsecondary education, and they serve as building blocks for success. As African Americans' participation and success rates increased marginally compared to their counterparts, concerned groups (e.g., parents, policy makers, and researchers) continued to seek remedies to benefit individuals in this ethnic and racial category. Clearly, the multitude of problems encountered by African Americans throughout the educational pipeline requires examination across sectors.

In chapter 1, Tyrone C. Howard examines the performance of African American students on various student achievement factors and provides recommendations for how schools and teachers can improve the overall educational experiences for these students. In chapter 2, Jennifer E. Obidah, Tracy Buenavista, R. Evely Gildersleeve, Peter Kim, and Tyson Marsh explore the experiences of African American teachers who work in "hard-to-teach-in" contexts. The authors focus on African American teachers in large urban school districts (e.g., Los Angeles and New York City). African Americans in school leadership positions in K–12 schools are the subjects of chapter 3. Linda C. Tillman in this chapter explores the historical context and key roles of school principals in shaping the policy agenda for the education of African American children.

In chapter 4, Lamont A. Flowers uses longitudinal data to examine African American students' involvement in college. In chapter 5, Barbara

J. Johnson and Henrietta Pichon provide a comprehensive review of research on African Americans faculty in higher education. They explore African Americans' participation in graduate school and its impact on the professoriate. Chapter 6 provides a national portrait for African Americans in leadership positions at colleges and universities. Here Jerlando F. L. Jackson and Brandon D. Daniels report national-level data on important characteristics for African Americans in both academic and student affairs administration.

In chapter 7, Mavis G. Sanders and Tamitha F. Campbell problematize the intersection between community involvement and educational success for African American students. In chapter 8, Jelani Mandara and Carolyn B. Murray describe the importance of the role African American families play in facilitating academic achievement in their children. In chapter 9, Jeffrey G. Sumrall and Ramona Pittman explain how technology can be used to help address the achievement gap for African American students.

In closing, the goals of this book are (1) to provide a longitudinal and systemic perspective on the African American educational experience that offers a status report on the progress made since *Brown* and *Fordice*; (2) to examine the trends and challenges encountered by African American students and professionals as their participation widens in an era where multiple educational reforms are competing for limited resources; and (3) to identify and share the lessons learned across institutional components of the pipeline and to both broaden and deepen the understanding for effective practice and policy. In doing so, a systemic understanding of the African American educational pipeline should emerge.

REFERENCES

Adams v. Richardson, 351 F.2d 636 (D.C. Cir. 1972); 356 F.2d 92 (D.C. Cir.1973); 480 F.2d 1159 (D. C. Cir. 1973).

Anderson, J. A. (1988). *The education of Blacks in the south*. Chapel Hill: University of North Carolina Press.

Baker, B. D. (2001). Measuring the outcomes of state policies for gifted education: An equity analysis of Texas school districts. *Gifted Child Quarterly, 45*(1), 4–15.

Bowen, W. G., & Bok, D. (1998). *The shape of the river: Long-term consequences of considering race in college and university admissions*. Princeton, NJ: Princeton University Press.

Bowen, W. G., & Rudenstine, N. L. (1992). *In pursuit of the Ph.D*. Princeton, NJ: Princeton University Press.

Bowles, S., & Levin, H. M. (1968). The determinants of scholastic achievement: An appraisal of some evidence. *Journal of Human Resources, 3*(1), 3–24.

Brown v. Board of Education of Topeka, 347 U.S. 483 (1954).

Cole, S., & Barber, E. (2003). *Increasing faculty diversity: The occupational choices of high-achieving minority students.* Cambridge, MA: Harvard University Press.

Coleman, J. S., Campbell, E. Q., Hobson, C. J., McPartland, J., Mood, A. M., Weinfeld, F. D., & York, R. L. (1966). *Equality of educational opportunity.* Washington, DC: U.S. Department of Health, Education, and Welfare.

Cooper v. Aaron, 358 U.S. 1 (1958).

Cross, T. (1994). Black faculty at Harvard: Does the pipeline defense hold water? *The Journal of Blacks in Higher Education, 4,* 42–46.

Fastrup, J. C. (1997). Taxpayers and pupil equity: Linking policy tools with policy goals. *Journal of Education Finance, 12*(1), 69–100.

Frasier v. UNC Board of Trustees, 134 F. Supp. 589 (1955).

Hoffman, K., Llagas, C., & Snyder, T. D. (2003). *Status and trends in the education of Blacks.* Washington, DC: National Center for Educational Statistics.

Hopwood v. Texas, 861 F. Supp. 551 (WD Tex. 1994).

Kulis, S., Chong, Y., & Shaw, H. (1999). Discriminatory organizational contexts and Black scientists on postsecondary faculties. *Research in Higher Education, 40*(2), 115–148.

Kulis, S., Sicotte, D., & Collins, S. (2002). More than a pipeline problem: Labor supply constraints and gender stratification across academic science disciplines. *Research in Higher Education, 43*(6), 657–691.

Malveaux, J. (1995). Education pipeline or merry-go-round? *Black Issues in Higher Education, 12*(16), 40.

McLaurin v. Oklahoma State Regents, 339 U.S. 637 (1950).

Mosteller, F., & Moynihan, D. P. (Eds.). (1972). *On equality of educational opportunity.* New York: Random House.

Nettles, M. T., & Perna, L. W. (1997). *The African American education databook volume II: Preschool through high school education.* Fairfax, VA: Frederick D. Patterson Research Institute.

Nott, W. (1993). From "uncultivated barbarian" to "poetical genius": The public presence of Phillis Wheatley. *Melus, 18*(3), 21.

Plessy v. Ferguson, 163 U.S. 537 (1896).

Regents of the University of California v. Bakke, 438 U.S. 265 (1978).

State of Missouri Ex Rel. Gains v. Canada, 305 U.S. 337 (1938).

Sweatt v. Pianter, 339 U.S. 629 (1950).

Turner, C. S. V., Myers, Jr. S. L., & Creswell, J. W. (1999). Exploring underrepresentation: The case of faculty of color in the Midwest. *The Journal of Higher Education, 70*(1), 27–59.

United States v. Fordice, 112 S. Ct. 2727 (1992).

Woodson, C. G. (1919). *The education of the negro prior to 1861: A history of the education of colored people of the United States from the beginning of slavery to the civil war* (2nd ed.). Washington, DC: The Associated Publishers.

Wygant v. Jackson Board of Education, 476 U.S. 267 (1986).

Part 1

_____

Pre-K–12 Schools

Chapter 1

The Forgotten Link

The Salience of Pre-K–12 Education and Culturally Responsive Pedagogy in Creating Access to Higher Education for African American Students

Tyrone C. Howard

The academic achievement and social adjustment of African American students in K–12 schools has been the subject of conceptual and empirical research over the past three decades (Ford, 1996; Hale-Benson, 1982; Hopkins, 1997; Irvine, 1990; Ladson-Billings, 1994; Polite & Davis, 1999; Noguera, 1996; Ogbu, 2003). Much of this research has been concerned with the identification of effective strategies and skills for teaching and learning, and the creation of a knowledge base that may offer ways to improve the educational aspirations of African American students. More recently, over the past decade, a number of scholars have called for investigations on racial disparities that exist in higher education. This research has focused on access for African American and other racially diverse students into colleges and universities (Chang, 1999). Some have cited the poor graduation rates of African American students (JBHE, 2004a) and the lack of African American students in professional and graduate programs across the country (Allen, 1992).

While research examining African American students in higher education is critical, many of these studies fail to acknowledge the important role that pre-K–12 education plays in preparing African American students for postsecondary education. In this chapter, I contend that pre-K–12 education, and more specifically effective teachers in pre-K–12 school settings, has become the "forgotten link" in discussions regarding the educational pipeline for African American students. The premise behind this chapter is that the distribution of African American students in higher education in many ways is a direct result of their preparation in pre-K–12 education for scores of African American students. Moreover, in this chapter, I contend that until significant improvements are made in the area of teaching at the pre-K–12 level, the state of education for

African American students and their dismal participation in higher education will continue.

The purpose of this chapter is threefold. The first section will highlight educational trends for African American student performance in pre-K–12 schools over the past three decades, as well as the important improvements in achievement data for African American students, but it will also examine the persistent achievement disparities. The second section will examine the critical role that effective teachers, and more specifically culturally responsive teaching, can play in addressing the underachievement of African American students in schools. It will highlight research on effective teachers and culturally responsive teaching for African American students. This area of research is critical because it examines the efficacy of classroom teachers and culturally centered pedagogical practices that have been successful in addressing achievement trends for African American students in schools.

More importantly, I contend that classroom teachers are one of the most important links between students' academic potential and their actual academic success. Thus evaluating the research on effective teachers for African American students is crucial, because it helps establish a knowledge base of useful ideologies, practices, and skills that will have implications for educators of African American students in pre-K–12 schools. Finally, I will offer recommendations for effective research and practice concerning African American students. While a plethora of theory and practice (e.g., Foster, 1994, 1995; Gay, 2000; Ladson-Billings, 1994) has informed educators about improving the achievement of African American students, the underachievement remains. Therefore, there remains a need for exploring new paradigms and frameworks to examine the persistent underachievement for many African American students in pre-K–12 schools.

THE STATE OF AFRICAN AMERICAN
PRE-K–12 EDUCATION

The notion of an educational pipeline provides the perfect metaphor for looking at the African American educational experience in the United States. The idea of a pipeline in its most basic definition is that it is a mechanism that allows the successful matriculation of any material, object, or individual to pass through a particular area to another. The matriculation through the pipeline is contingent upon each of the areas of the pipe to be unobstructed and working in proper order, which allows for a free-flowing exchange from point to point. In many ways, the educational experiences for many African American students reveal a pipeline that has been severely obstructed by poor schooling, historical injustices, and racial inequities (Anderson, 1988; Darling-Hammond, 2004; Kozol, 1991; Siddle Walker, 1996). The state of education for many African American students merits immediate attention if the pipeline is to ever allow a greater transference of individuals to matriculate from one end of the pipeline (pre-K–12) to the opposite end (higher education and beyond) to become a reality.

Research examining the educational pipeline for African American students has been much needed as the achievement data (e.g., standardized test scores and grade point averages) for African American students have revealed that many of them lag behind most other ethnic groups in almost all levels of academic achievement (NCES, 2003b). For researchers whose works are concerned with African American students, the dismal educational state of African American achievement is alarming, but not surprising. Previous research has made it abundantly clear that many African American students attending U.S. schools are not faring well in their quest to become academically successful (Shujaa, 1994; Steele, Perry, & Hilliard, 2004). A multitude of statistics underscores the severity and persistence of academic underachievement and social maladjustment of African American students in pre-K–12 schools. For example, over the past decade, the majority of African American students in the fourth, eighth, and twelfth grades did not reach grade-level proficiency in vital subject areas such as reading, mathematics, history, and science (Wirt, 2000). In addition, less than one-quarter of African American students were at or above grade level in these same subject matter areas. Furthermore, fewer than 3% performed at advanced levels in these areas (Wirt, 2000).

To add further clarity to the state of pre-K–12 education for African American students, consider the fact that African American students currently make up approximately 17.1% of the nation's student population, yet they make up a disproportionate number of students receiving special education and remedial services. African American students make up approximately 26% of students nationwide identified as educable mentally retarded, 34% of students diagnosed with serious emotional disorders, and 33% of students identified as trainable mentally retarded, or developmentally delayed (Harry & Anderson, 1999; Ford, Grantham, & Bailey, 1999). The disproportionate representation of various ethnic groups in special education has been documented by a number of scholars (e.g., Harry & Anderson, 1999). However, it is clear that no other group has been more adversely affected by disproportional special education placements than African American students in general and African American males in particular (Ford, 1996; Noguera, 1996; Price, 2000). Thus to effectively create a viable educational pipeline from pre-K–12 to higher education for African American students, it is important to identify useful program practices and policies that have proven success in helping them achieve academically.

SHORT- AND LONG-TERM DATA ON
AFRICAN AMERICAN STUDENT ACHIEVEMENT

Achievement data for African American students over the past three decades convey a mixed picture regarding students' performance. An analysis of National Assessment of Educational Progress (NAEP) data from 1970 to 2000 showed that African American students have increased levels of attending and completing high school and college, increased levels of parental involvement in their education, and upward trends in math and reading achievement (NAEP, 1999; Jenks & Phillips, 1998). These data convey a positive outlook on the achievement of African American students. These trends cannot be disputed, as the relative outlook for African American students has improved considerably over the past three decades compared to African American education data pre-1960. To be clear, the post-civil rights racial climate for African American students is a stark contrast to the pre-civil rights climate, wherein many African American students encountered overt racism, were excluded from better financed schools, and were frequent victims of discrimination in many of the nation's newly desegregated schools (Foster, 1997; Irvine & Irvine, 1983; Oakes, 1985; Siddle-Walker, 1996).

The improvement in the achievement of African American students over the past three decades can be somewhat deceiving given the fact that the achievement gap between African American and White students decreased from 1970 to 1990 (Mullis, Dorsey, Foertsch, Jones, & Gentile, 1991). For example, in 1960, approximately 20% of African American adults had completed high school, in comparison to the 79% who had completed high school in 2002 (U.S. Department of Education, 2003). Moreover, school dropout rates for African American students have decreased sharply, and the number of African American students attending colleges and universities has increased considerably (Anderson, 1988; Carter & Wilson, 1993). Thus the message, some would argue, is that substantial progress has been made in the education of African American students, so examinations of their underachievement are not necessary. It is this general premise that opponents of affirmative action and other race-based policy initiatives used in their stance for more merit-based rewards and admissions (D'Souza, 1995). However, the NAEP data also revealed a disturbing side to the achievement of African American students, one that shows that despite the significant gains that have been made by African American students over the past century, other groups have made steady gains as well, thus keeping the achievement gap intact. Therefore, while the gap has narrowed since 1970, African American students still score 75% lower than Whites on most standardized tests, and they score significantly lower on tests that claim to measure scholastic aptitude and intelligence (Jenks & Phillips, 1998).

Reiterating the earlier point regarding the achievement data of African American students, scores of African American students have significantly improved (Mullis, et al. 1991). However, what is most disturbing is that in light of these improvements over the past three decades, African American students still lag behind all major[1] ethnic groups on most academic indices. Therefore, any thorough and critical examination of the educational pipeline for African American students must shed light on the relative underachievement of African American students in comparison to other groups—in essence, the same individuals with whom they will ultimately compete against for enrollment slots in colleges and universities and subsequent labor and employment opportunities. One area that speaks to the viability of a healthy pipeline for any group of students is the enrollment in high-stakes classes that provides an entrée to college and university eligibility. Oakes's (1985) work has shown how many African American and other students of color are placed into low-status and non advanced placement (AP) classes early in their academic careers, thus significantly hampering their opportunities for being college eligible. The most recent U.S. Department of Education data reinforce Oakes's contention. In 1998 and 2000, African American students were less likely than White, Asian American, or Latino students to take AP courses in mathematics, science, or foreign language (NCES, 2003b).

The exclusion from high-stakes classes all but assures the fact that African American students will be among the lowest groups represented at most colleges and universities. The underrepresentation of African American students in high-stakes classes helps clarify data from the College Board that showed that White students are twice as likely as African American students to take the SAT I or SAT II (JBHE, 2004b). Even more disturbing are the achievement discrepancies in SAT II mean scores between African American and White students. According to the College Board, African American students have a mean score of 521 in biology, compared to 595 for White students, 534 in writing, compared to 619 for White students, and a median score of 519 in math, compared to 606 for White students (JBHE, 2004b). These achievement disparities begin to provide a clear understanding as to how and why the educational pipeline for African American students begins to show seemingly irreparable breakdown during the pre-K–12 years and remains increasingly weak, thus producing paltry numbers in postsecondary education.

As African American students enter kindergarten, the NCES data begin to provide discouraging portrayals of the schooling experience for African American youths. The U.S. Department of Education highlighted early childhood data from a longitudinal report titled "The Condition of Education, 2000." These data showed that African American students were the least likely of any other ethnic group to be identified as "persistent on tasks," least likely to be viewed as "eager to learn," and were identified as the group of students who paid the least attention in class. These data revealed that approximately half of the African American kindergarten students studied paid attention in class, while close to 40% of them were labeled "nonpersistent" on academic tasks, and not eager to learn. One can only begin to infer the implications that these labels will have on the future achievement of African American students.

To highlight additional data that explain the increasing disparities involving African American students, one needs to look no further than subject matter competence. A close examination of reading achievement data offers insight into how the educational disparities begin to surface early in the schooling process. The NAEP data from 1999 showed that at age 9, African American students lagged behind White students by a mean score of 36 points in 1971 (NAEP, 1999). Over the next 30 years, the reading achievement for African American 9-year-olds improved, yet in 1999 the gap between African American students still had a mean that was 35 points lower than White students, thus a decrease of a single point compared to 1971. Moreover, Latino students began to show better performance than African American 9-year-olds over the same period. Most troubling with these achievement data in the area of reading is the fact that the longer African American students remain in school, the wider the gap in comparison to White students (NAEP, 1999). The NAEP data also showed that African American high school seniors, on average, read and do math only as well as White eighth graders.

Reading proficiency in particular has obvious importance to the overall academic success for any group of students. A multitude of research suggests that when students struggle with reading proficiency, this has the potential for a critical carryover effect into other subject matters (National Reading Panel, 2000; Rasinski, 2004). A comprehensive understanding of reading proficiency is not limited to the casualty of merely reading the written word. If students' reading proficiency is not at grade level, then they may be excluded from legitimate participation in the production of texts, the creation of new knowledge, and the application of information into a recognizable schema, whether in reading, writing, science, math, or social studies (Duke, 2004). Thus to view reading proficiency in a context that does not recognize its salience to other subject areas and overall academic proficiency is to omit key consideration in the overall academic underachievement for many African American students.

The examination of academic underachievement for African American students is undoubtedly a complex and multifaceted problem. Any attempts to provide meaningful intervention must include a critical analysis of factors such as family structure and support, school funding, curriculum and instruction, educational policies, institutional racism, teacher and administrator roles and attitudes, social constructions of race and poverty, community development, legal rulings, and other social, political, historical, and economic forces that shape the nature of schools and students' learning potential (Darling-Hammond,

2004; Knapp & Wolverton, 1994). Obvious space limitations will not allow for an investigation of all of these areas, thus the following section of this chapter will center on one of the more important features in the reversal of under-achievement, and that is the role that teachers play in the education of African American students.

TEACHING AND AFRICAN AMERICAN STUDENTS

It goes without saying that the role classroom teachers have played in the educational experiences of African Americans is a long and rich one. Dating back to the pre-*Brown* era and racially segregated schools, the important roles of teachers have been well documented (Anderson, 1988; Foster, 1997; Siddle-Walker, 1996). Many of these accounts offer insight into the important roles that teachers have played in helping African American students attain high academic achievement, even during the most hostile of social conditions. Siddle-Walker (1996) discussed effective teachers in segregated schools in her work by stating that

> the phrase most frequently used by teachers to describe their task is that it was their responsibility to be certain that every child "reached his or her "highest potential." The term seems to captures their commitment to push students to perform as well as they were intellectually capable of performing. They believed this type of push—giving other children what you would want for your own—was the basis of good teaching and of a good program. (p. 158)

The essence of these early accounts of African American teachers describes dedicated, concerned, and committed educational providers. Equally as important is the notion that many of these teachers employed a pedagogy that was centered on students' cultural and social capital, and the community context in which their schools were situated (Irvine & Irvine, 1983). It is critical to note the characteristics of these teachers because some theorists argue that the *Brown* decision, and the subsequent decline of African American teachers, signaled a significant shift in the quality of education for African American students. Irvine and Irvine (1983) argued that

> the effect was that new mostly white teachers were placed in all black schools in which they did not want to work. One can only speculate about the quality of the instructional programs in black schools which are characterized by teachers assigned to schools against their will ... and teachers who perceive their work site as unacceptable. (p. 418)

Despite the loss of African American teachers, effective teaching has still persisted since the *Brown* decision. My contention is that there is a pressing need to examine pedagogical practices and philosophies of education and teaching of teachers who are having success educating African American students. Teaching is an important unit of analysis because it represents the most immediate point of contact with students (Dreeben, 1987; Darling-Hammond, 2004). Although numerous efforts have called for new legislation in schools, reform policies to improve student performance, and high stakes testing to increase school accountability, it remains clear that all of these measures ultimately come back to teachers' ability to enact them in the classroom. Therefore, an examination of the research on effective teaching represents an important ingredient in creating educational equity for African American students.

CULTURE AND TEACHING

Although a teacher's race might appear to be a prevailing factor in the successful education of African American students, a more important factor is the concept of culture and all of its manifestations in the teaching and learning process. A number of researchers have maintained that culturally relevant, or culturally responsive, teaching may offer African American students a more equitable opportunity for school success (Gay, 2000; Howard, 2001; Ladson-Billings, 1994). Culturally relevant pedagogy has also been described as a philosophical orientation and a set of teaching practices that enables students to pursue academic success while maintaining cultural integrity (Gay, 2000; Howard, 2001; Ladson-Billings, 1994; Shade, Kelly, & Oberg, 1997). Gay (2000) asserts that culturally relevant pedagogy uses "the cultural knowledge, prior experiences, frames of reference, and performance styles of ethnically diverse students to make learning more relevant to and effective [for students]. . . . It teaches *to and through* strengths of these students. It is culturally *validating and affirming*" (p. 29, emphasis in original).

A number of studies have been conducted to assess the extent to which culturally relevant teaching can help promote academic development among African American students. For example, Lee (1995) examined the efficacy of signifying, a form of social discourse in the African American community, as a scaffold for teaching African American high school students core skills in literary interpretation. She hypothesized that teachers who demonstrated the ability to signify and had prior knowledge about social discourse, values, and themes on which instructional texts were based would positively influence the ability of African American students to interpret fiction. Lee attributed student improvement to schema theory, which asserts that when analogies are used to connect unfamiliar information with existing schemata, it places unfamiliar information within a recognizable context. She maintained that this familiarity often leads to better comprehension and high mastery of skills. Lee concluded that there is a need to further analyze classroom environments wherein teachers create learning strategies out of metacognitive experiences involving the analysis of culturally specific texts and culturally familiar experiences.

Ladson-Billings's (1992) research examined culturally relevant teaching in an attempt to understand what teachers did to develop literacy among African American learners. Her qualitative findings revealed six key principles or tenets: (1) Students whose social, political, and cultural futures are most tenuous become intellectual leaders of the classroom; (2) Students are apprenticed into a learning community rather than taught isolated and unrelated skills; (3) Students' real-life experiences are legitimated as part of the "official curriculum"; (4) Teachers and students participate in a broad conception of literacy that includes both literature and orature; (5) Teachers and students are collectively involved in a struggle against the status quo; and (6) Teachers involved in a broad conception of curriculum are cognizant of themselves as political beings. Ladson-Billings has suggested that teachers' role with African American students becomes a political process designed to improve various facets of their day-to-day living situations. Thus literacy development, as well as other academic areas, should focus on discussions, debates, analysis, and investigation of content, people, and issues relevant to life-giving and life-sustaining circumstances in students' communities.

Ladson-Billings's (1994) work *The Dreamkeepers,* which summarized a three-year ethnographic study of eight effective teachers of African American students, also highlighted the importance of teachers understanding students' cultural capital. Ladson-Billings based her construct of culturally relevant pedagogy on three broad propositions: (1) conceptions of self and others; (2) social relations; and (3) conceptions of knowledge. In their conception of self and others, culturally relevant teachers see themselves as part of the community and see teaching as a way of giving back to that community. These teachers have high expectations for students, help students make connections between their community and national and global identities, and view teaching as "pulling knowledge out" of students.

The social relations aspect of culturally relevant teaching includes teachers who demonstrate a connectedness with all students, encourage collaborative learning in order to create a community of learners, and establish fluid teacher-student relations that extend beyond the classroom and into the community. Ladson-Billings states that culturally relevant conceptions of knowledge include teachers who encourage students to view knowledge critically, as something continuously recreated and recycled. In addition, teachers construct their notion of excellence based on student diversity and individual differences. Also noteworthy in Ladson-Billings's work was the fact that one of her expert teachers was

White, yet she still was able to effectively teach African American students, thus dispelling the idea that only African American teachers can effectively teach African American students.

Howard's (2000) study revealed that elementary teachers who employed culturally relevant teaching practices helped African American students' reading proficiency improve significantly over the course of one academic year. Howard's research discovered teachers employing four key pedagogical principles that led to improved academic performance: (1) holistic instructional strategies; (2) culturally consistent communicative competencies; (3) skill-building strategies; and (4) teaching as an art form. Howard's work found that equally as important to the improvement of African American students was a firm belief that teachers had in their students' academic potential, and the undying commitment that they had as teachers to ensure that students maximized their potential. Moreover, these findings revealed the importance of situating the teaching of core academic skills within a culturally familiar context.

The use of incorporating students' cultural capital is consistent with Ball's (1995) research on effectively utilizing text design patterns that students bring to the classroom to help literacy development for African American elementary school students. Ball asserted that teachers should allow students from culturally diverse backgrounds to use their preferred methods of expression as a building block for bridging home and community-based experiences with academic-based texts and content. Moreover, Ball stated that students' ways of expression should be viewed as a rich resource of knowledge that all students should attempt to understand in order to broaden their capacity to express ideas in various ways. Ball's findings had important implications for reading development, because of the importance of storytelling in reading. Methods of expression and communication have critical ties to the effectiveness of storytelling, decoding, and students' reading comprehension.

Gay (1994) has argued that culturally grounded instruction as a form of multicultural pedagogy is an appropriate strategy for improving the schooling experience for African American and other marginalized student populations. She suggests five major themes that pedagogical principles can be based on, which could improve instruction for culturally diverse and at-risk students: (1) *universal literacy,* which includes the teaching of basic skills within a culturally familiar context, and the teaching of critical thinking skills to solve problems related to ethnic and cultural diversity; (2) *scholarly truth,* which entails teaching students about the contributions of culturally diverse individuals and wherein knowledge is culturally pluralistic; (3) *equity and excellence,* where appropriate sensitivity is given to cultural diversity, and positive ethnic identities have beneficial effects on the academic achievement of culturally diverse students; (4) *developmental appropriateness,* which means teaching styles are centered on the understanding of different cultural learning styles, and educational experiences match students' development levels; and (5) *teaching the whole child*, which includes the teaching of cultural style-shifting skills, and a concern for the child beyond academic competence.

Nasir's (1997) work examined the relationship between identity and schooling in the area of mathematics proficiency for African American adolescents. Building on the students' knowledge of dominoes, Nasir's qualitative and quantitative findings were that in practices such as dominoes, mathematical goals arise in the context of activity—when math concepts became a normalized and mandatory part of a particular activity. Nasir (2000) found similar types of connections between culture and learning when she explored how the practice of basketball afforded different levels of engagement of statistical thinking and reasoning for African American males. In short, Nasir suggests that when students' cultural experiences and contributions are not recognized as being valuable parts of the learning process, then they may assume that their poor performance is a result of race-based failure. Thus Nasir makes an important call for linking classroom learning goals to essential learning goals.

The research around effective teaching for African American students has revealed that teachers must be able to connect to students' cultural context if they are to help them academically. Moreover, teachers must develop the ability to constructively develop an understanding of how students' personal, social, and cultural realities coexist with their cognitive processing and academic goals. The educational pipeline for African American students will not improve until teachers become aware of the manner in which out-of-school factors influence in-school processes. Perry and others (2003) argued that "learning is fundamentally contextual . . . there are extra social, emotional, cognitive, and political competencies required of African American youth" (p. 4). Previous work in culturally centered teaching has also suggested that students must have a working knowledge of the communities in which schools are situated. Foster (1995) posits that a similar background between students and teachers does not guarantee productive, fluid, or uncomplicated relationships between them. Yet she maintains that teachers who have a cultural solidarity with the schools and the students they teach, can effectively link classroom content to students' experiences and community issues built on familiar cultural patterns and incorporate culturally compatible communication patterns.

RESEARCH IMPLICATIONS

The research on effective teaching for African American students highlights the cogent role that culture plays in the learning process. The call for cultural responsiveness in the teaching and learning of African American students rests on the belief that many African American students face the unenviable decision of choosing between academic prowess and cultural competence. Culturally responsive teaching enables the pursuit of high academic achievement to occur within a culturally affirming learning environment, which does not require students to compromise their cultural integrity. Ford's (1996) research with gifted African American students revealed that many of them intentionally underachieved in order to show cultural allegiance to their peers over the desire to show their academic competence. The students from Ford's study continually stated that being smart in schools required the adoption of many European American cultural norms. Responses such as the ones provided by students in Ford's study are consistent with the earlier research by Fordham and Ogbu (1986), who found that many African American students equated academic success with "acting White."

These studies suggest that educators must be willing to listen to students' accounts of how classroom culture is shaped, and how it frequently is diametrically opposed to the cultural characteristics that many African American students possess. An increasing amount of research has uncovered students' accounts of how they put forth more effort, are more engaged in learning, and are more receptive to teachers when the learning environments are closely linked to their day-to-day sociocultural realities (Miron & Lauria, 1998; Nieto, 1994; Phelan, et al., 1994). Equally important is that culturally responsive teaching must engage students with classroom content, create an environment conducive to high achievement, and most importantly must be culturally respectful and academically rigorous. Nonetheless, there remains a pressing need for more research that examines how school culture is shaped, who is placed on the margins by that culture, and the effects on students' academic achievement.

One of the consistent themes in much of the research on culturally responsive teachers has been investigating teacher practices. Several scholars have suggested that student perspectives about culturally responsive pedagogy become an important aspect of the paradigm (Gay, 2000; Howard, 2001a). These calls are warranted given the unique perspective that students have of their own educational experiences, and the inexplicable manner in which their voices have been silenced in much of the dialogue. There is also a need to study out-of-school practices to identify how they may link to in-school content. Much like Nasir's (2000) findings, there are rich subtexts that emanate from students' everyday practices that can offer important implications for classroom teachers. Lastly, there is a need to problematize the complexity of culture from student and teacher standpoints. Culture remains a misunderstood yet critical concept in the teaching and learning process for all students. Future modes of inquiry about culture and teaching must offer deeper levels of analysis on how culture is shaped and how it influences cognitive development, motivation, and other learning-centered areas of development.

The intent of this chapter was to help contribute to the knowledge base of effective teaching and teachers for African American students by way of culturally responsive teaching. While much of the research on culturally responsive teaching continues to emerge, there remains a pressing need for additional empirical research capturing the various elements of the practice. The existing literature is rich but still needs research across different grade levels and subject matters and teachers from different racial, gender, and cultural backgrounds and from practitioners who are in more challenging classroom situations. There is also a need for large-scale studies that examine culturally responsive teaching. One of the limitations of previous research on culturally responsive teaching is that relatively small sample sizes were utilized. Researchers who are concerned with the area of culturally responsive teachers should consider different methodological approaches that may offer new theoretical considerations.

POLICY IMPLICATIONS

The challenge of educating African American students requires a multi-pronged approach. Issues pertaining to teacher practice and curriculum reform, and normative beliefs about them, are essential. However, what must be clear is that policy initiatives also play an important role in the process. Most germane to the conversation of reversing the underachievement of African American students is the fact that policy initiatives must recognize the vital need for African American students to have consistent access to qualified, competent, and experienced teachers (Darling-Hammond, 2004). The history of African American education is replete with accounts of inequity in funding and sub-par schooling frequently mandated by legislation (Anderson, 1988; Taylor & Piche, 1991). Historical accounts of funding inequities should be at the forefront of policy efforts designed to erase age-old discrepancies in funding and create equitable schools. A number of studies have documented the dearth of teachers in low-income and minority schools (NCES, 1997; Howard, 2003; Dreeben, 1987). This research revealed that the frequent cry of a teacher shortage in the nation's schools is more of a problem for distribution than absolute numbers. These findings would seem to suggest that many teachers avoid teaching in culturally diverse and low-income schools (e.g., places where African American students are most likely to attend).

Thus policies must be enacted that provide incentives for experienced and exemplary teachers to teach in more challenging school settings, where their skills and knowledge can have a more significant effect by teaching low-achieving students. Moreover, mandates must consider the fact that African American students, and other students from low-income and diverse backgrounds, are more likely to come into contact with underqualified and out-of-subject area teachers than their counterparts (Darling-Hammond, 2000). Policy recommendations concerned with reversing school underachievement for any population should take several factors into account. First, ensure that low-performing schools are provided quality teachers, effective administrators, and improved facilities. Second, give serious attention to the curriculum being used in schools. Highly scripted curriculum programs have come under heavy criticism for removing teacher autonomy and failing to take into account students' developmental differences. Third, consider the effects of high-stakes testing. Policy mandates must investigate the usefulness of high-stakes testing and determine if this contributes to increased student learning. Moreover, ongoing teacher training and development should be a constant at school sites where low achievement has become the norm. The sobering reality in many schools today is that various policy initiatives may not be able to mandate normative beliefs that current and future teachers have toward educating African American students. The "no child left behind" legislation, for all of the criticism that it has received, appears to address one major area with regard to teacher quality, and that is ensuring that every student is educated by a qualified and credentialed teacher. This is an important first step, however, what also must be examined are the degrees to which "credentialed" or "qualified" teachers are well equipped with the necessary knowledge, skills, and attitudes to effectively teach across racial, cultural, linguistic, and social class differences.

PRACTICE IMPLICATIONS

While there are a number of research implications contained in studies discussed in this chapter, there are also practical implications that offer promise for classroom practice. The following design principles offer strategies that can be used to help promote the academic development of African American students. While the list is not exhaustive, it offers several pedagogical approaches based on the findings from the studies discussed in this chapter:

- *Recognition of nonmainstream methods of discourse.* Language plays an essential role in the communicative and literacy development for African American students. Teachers should recognize that any attempts to invalidate or denigrate the use of non-standard English may have detrimental effects on the academic and literacy development of African American students. Negative depictions of language and discourse patterns used by many African American students can be interpreted as negative portrayals of the families, homes, and communities to which they belong. Teachers should acknowledge and respect the use of African American discourse patterns and communication styles. They can help African American students by having explicit dialogue about the appropriateness of standard and non-standard English, and they can help students understand the value of code switching.

- *Skill acquisition.* Improving the educational aspirations of African American students not only requires the infusion of ethnically and culturally relevant content in the curriculum but also the explicit development of essential academic skills necessary for reading and math development. Teachers should not assume that exposure to multicultural content alone will improve academic proficiency. Teachers should have high expectations for students and should establish attainable goals and objectives. They should also present students with developmentally appropriate content with clear objectives, meaningful activities, and multifaceted evaluations. Teachers may consider incorporating activities that are consistent with the students' way of knowing and learning and should have reliable evaluation methods to gauge the students' level of comprehension. Other tools that may help in this area include being sensitive to students' individual cognitive processes, having students provide verbal explanations of how, where, and why new skills and concepts are used, peer tutoring, and multiple forms of assessment.

- *Engaged pedagogy.* The manner in which information is presented can be a powerful tool in the learning process. Once teachers have a command of the subject knowledge, the method of instruction should be dynamic, engaging, and relevant to the students. Even when using rigidly designed, prescriptive curriculum, teachers should still be mindful of methods of delivery. They should convey an authentic level of concern and care to their students about their academic development and implement a coherent curriculum that is articulated across grade levels. Moreover, there must be a sincere belief in student potential, and student failure must not be an option.

- *African American cultural knowledge.* Teachers working with African American students can increase their chances for success if they possess knowledge and understanding of various aspects of African American culture. Critical features to understand could include language, methods of interaction, motivational strategies, ways of caring, displays of respect and disrespect, value of family, and collaboration. The use of content and instruction consistent with these types of knowledge and cultural realities can help create congruence between home lives and school content. Teachers with limited knowledge about African American culture and history should become familiar with information that helps explain the origin and purpose of certain cultural practices and the role that education has historically played in these communities. Cultural knowledge can be acquired through various types of literature on African American culture or can be gained from genuine exposure and interaction with African Americans.

Given the troubling state of education for many African American students, examinations about access to higher education should investigate what is happening at the pre-K–12 level. The current condition of teaching has caused many African American students in pre-K–12 schools to question the overall care, commitment, and concern that their teachers have for them and their education (Howard, 2003). If the quality of the educational pipeline for African American students is to improve, then comprehensive analyses of pre-K–12 schools must not be limited to the quality of teaching. While teaching has obvious importance in the education success of all students, equally as critical are the roles of school principals and guidance counselors, the quality of the curriculum, the effects of high-stakes testing, adequate resources, examination of access to high-track classes, and the role of parents and community. The continuous downward spiral for scores of African American students in pre-K–12 and higher education should be of serious concern for researchers and practitioners involved in equity related work in education. As previously stated, the condition of the educational pipeline cannot afford to be investigated in separate components without acknowledging the important connection that each part of the educational continuum influences the other. This chapter has attempted to bring to the forefront what seems to have become the "forgotten link" in the higher education discussion concerning African American students, the salience of pre-K–12 education.

NOTE

1. Major ethnic groups constitute African American, Asian American, Latino, Native American, and White.

REFERENCES

Allen, W. R. (1992). The color of success: African American college student outcomes at predominately White and historically Black public colleges and universities. *Harvard Educational Review, 62,* 26–44.

Anderson, J. A. (1988). *The education of Blacks in the South, 1860–1935.* Chapel Hill: University of North Carolina Press.

Ball, A. (1995). Text design patterns in the writing of urban African American students in multicultural settings. *Urban Education, 30*(3), 253–289.

Brown, M. C., & Davis, J. E. (Eds.) (2000). *Black sons to mothers: Compliments, critiques, and challenges for cultural workers in education.* New York: Peter Lang.

Carter, D., & Wilson, R. (1993). *11th annual status report on minorities in higher education*. Washington, DC: American Council on Education.

Chang, M. J. (1999). Does racial diversity matter? The educational impact of a racially diverse undergraduate population. *Journal of College Student Development, 40*, 377–395.

Darling-Hammond, L. (2000). *Solving the dilemmas of teacher, supply, demand, and quality*. New York: National Commision on Teaching and America's Future.

Darling-Hammond, L. (2004). What happens to a dream deferred? In J. A. Banks & C. A. M. Banks (Eds.), *Handbook of research on multicultural education* (2nd ed., pp. 607–630). San Francisco: Jossey-Bass.

Dreeben, R. (1987). Closing the divide: What teachers and administrators can do to help Black students reach their reading potential. *American Educator, 11*(4), 28–35.

D'Souza, D. (1995). *The end of racism: principles for a multiracial society*. New York: Free Press.

Duke, N. K. (2004). The case for informational text. *Educational Leadership, 61*(6), 40–43.

Ford, D. Y. (1996). *A study of underachievement among gifted, potentially gifted, and talented students*. Storrs: University of Connecticut, National Research Center on the Gifted and Talented.

Ford, D. Y., & Harris, J. J. (1999). *Gifted multicultural education*. New York: Teachers College Press.

Ford, D. Y., Grantham, T. C., & Bailey, D. F. (1999). Identifying giftedness among African American males: Recommendations for effective recruitment and retention. In V. C. Polite & J. E. Davis (Eds.), *African American males in school and society* (pp. 51–67). New York: Teachers College Press.

Fordham, S., & Ogbu, J. (1986). African American students' school success: Coping with the "burden of 'acting White.'" *Urban Review, 18*, 176–203.

Foster, M. (1991). Constancy, connectedness, and constraints in the lives of African American women teachers. *National Association of Women's Studies Journal, 3*(2), 70–97.

Foster, M. (1994). Effective Black teachers: A literature review. In E. R. Hollins, J. E. King, & W. C. Hayan (Eds.), *Teaching diverse populations: Formulating a knowledge base* (pp. 225–241). Albany: State University of New York Press.

Foster, M. (1995). African American teachers and culturally relevant pedagogy. In J. A. Banks & C. A. M. Banks (Eds.), *Handbook of research on multicultural education* (pp. 570–581). New York: Macmillan.

Foster, M. (1997). *Black teachers on teaching*. New York: The New Press.

Gay, G. (1994). *At the essence of leaving: Multicultural education*. West Lafayette, IN: Kappa Delta Pi.

Gay, G. (2000). *Culturally responsive teaching*. New York: Teachers College Press.

Hale-Benson, J. E. (1982). *Black children: Their roots, culture, and learning styles*. Baltimore: Johns Hopkins University Press.

Harry, B., & Anderson, M. G. (1999). The social construction of high-incidence disabilities: The effect on African American males. In V. C. Polite & J. E. Davis (Eds.), *African American males in school and society* (pp. 34–50). New York: Teachers College Press.

Hopkins, R. (1997). *Educating Black males: Critical lessons in schooling, community, and power*. Albany: State University of New York Press.

Howard, T. C. (2000). Reconceptualizing multicultural education. In M. C. Brown & J. E. Davis (Eds.), *Black sons to mothers: Compliments, critiques, and challenges for cultural workers in education* (pp. 155–172). New York: Peter Lang.

Howard, T. C. (2001a). Powerful pedagogy for African American students: A case of four teachers. *Journal of Urban Education, 36*(2), 179–202.

Howard, T. C. (2001b). Telling their side of the story: African American students' perceptions of culturally relevant pedagogy. *Urban Review, 33*(2), 131–149.

Howard, T. C. (2003). Who receives the short end of the shortage?: America's teacher shortage and implications for urban schools. *Journal of Curriculum and Supervision, 18*(2), 142–160.

Irvine, J. J. (1990). *Black students and school failure: Policies, practices, and prescriptions*. New York: Greenwood Press.

Irvine, J. J., & Irvine, R. W. (1983). The impact of the desegregation process on the education of Black students: Key variables. *The Journal of Negro Education, 52*(4), 411–422.

Jenks, C., & Phillips, M. (1998). *The Black-White test score gap*. Washington, DC: Brookings Institutions Press.

Journal of Blacks in Higher Education (JBHE). (2004a). The persisting racial gap in college student graduation rates. *JBHE, 45*, 77–85.

Journal of Blacks in Higher Education (2004b). The worsening of the Black-White gap on SAT II achievement tests. *JBHE, 42*, 48–50.

Knapp, M. S., & Wolverton, S. (1994). Social class and schooling. In J. A. Banks & C. A. M. Banks (Eds.), *Handbook of research on multicultural education* (2nd ed., pp. 656–681). San Francisco: Jossey-Bass.

Kozol, J. (1991). *Savage inequalities*. New York: Crown.

Ladson-Billings, G. (1992). Liberatory consequences of literacy: A case of culturally relevant instruction for African American students. *Journal of Negro Education, 61*(3), 378–391.

Ladson-Billings, G. (1994). *The dreamkeepers: Successful teachers of African American students*. San Francisco: Jossey-Bass.

Lee, C. D. (1994). A culturally based cognitive apprenticeship: Teaching African American high school students skills in literary interpretation. *Reading Research Quarterly*, 30(4), 608–630.

Lee, C. D. (1995). Signifying as a scaffold for literary interpretation. *Journal of Black Psychology*, 21(4), 357–381.

Miron, L. F., & Lauria, M. (1998). Student voice as agency: Resistance and accommodations in inner-city schools. *Anthropology & Education Quarterly, 29*(2), 189–213.

Mullis, I. V., Dorsey, J. A., Foertsch, M. A., Jones, L. R., & Gentile, C. A. (1991). *Trends in academic progress: Achievement of U.S. students in science, 1969–70 to 1990, mathematics, 1973–1990, reading, 1971–1990, writing, 1984–1990.* (Prepared by Educational Testing Service.) Washington, DC: U.S. Department of Education, Office of Educational Research and Improvement.

Nasir, N. (2000). Points ain't everything: emergent goals and average and percent understandings in the play of basketball among African American students. *Anthropology and Education Quarterly; 31*(3), 283–305.

Nasir, N. S. (2002). Identity, goals, and learning: Mathematics in cultural practice. *Mathematical Thinking and Learning, 4*(2&3), 211–245.

Nasir, N. S., & Saxe, G. B. (2003). Ethnic and academic identities: A cultural practice perspective on emerging tensions and their management in the lives of minority students. *Educational Researcher, 32*(5), 14–18.

National Assessment of Educational Progress (NAEP). (1999). *Reading report card for the nation and states.* Office of educational research and improvement. Washington, DC: U.S. Department of Education.

National Center for Educational Statistics (NCES). (1997). *America's teachers: Profile of a profession.* Washington, DC: U.S. Department of Education.

National Center for Education Statistics (NCES). (2003a). *Mathematics 2003 major results: Subgroup results for the nation.* Washington, DC: U.S. Department of Education. Institute of Education Sciences.

National Center for Education Statistics (NCES). (2003b). *Status and trends in the education of Blacks.* Washington, DC: U.S. Department of Education. Institute of Education Sciences.

National Reading Panel. (2000). *Teaching children to read: An evidence-based assessment of the scientific research literature on reading and its implications for reading instruction. Reports of the subgroups.* Washington, DC: National Institute of Child Health and Human Development.

Nieto, S. (1994). Lessons from students on creating a chance to dream. *Harvard Educational Review, 64*(4), 392–426.

Noguera, P. (1996). Responding to the crisis of Black youth: Providing support without further marginalization. *Journal of Negro Education, 65*(1), 37–60.

Oakes, J. (1985). *Keeping track: How schools structure inequality*. New Haven, CT: Yale University Press.

Ogbu, J. U. (2003). *Black Americans in an affluent suburb: A study of academic disengagement*. Mahwah, NJ: Lawrence Erlbaum.

Perry, T., Steele, C., & Hilliard III, A. (2003). *Young, gifted and black: Promoting high achievement among African American students*. New York: Beacon Press.

Phelan, P., Yu, H. C., & Davidson, A. L. (1994). Navigating the psychosocial pressures of adolescence: The voices and experiences of high school youth. *American Educational Research Journal, 31*(2), 415–447.

Polite, V. C. (1994). The method in the madness: African American males, avoidance, schooling, and chaos theory. *Journal of Negro Education, 60*(30), 345–359.

Polite, V. C., & Davis, J. E. (Eds.) (1999). *African American males in school and society: Practices and policies for effective education*. New York: Teachers College Press.

Price, J. N. (2000). *Against the odds: The meaning of school and relationships in the lives of six African American men*. Westport, CT: Ablex.

Rasinski, T. (2004). Creating fluent readers. *Educational Leadership, 61*(6), 46–51.

Shade, B. J., Kelly, C., & Oberg, M. (1997). *Creating culturally responsive classrooms*. Washington, DC: American Psychological Association.

Shujaa, M. J. (Ed.). (1994). *Too much schooling, too little education: A paradox of Black life in White societies*. Trenton, NJ: African World Press.

Siddle-Walker, V. S. (1996). *Their highest potential*. Chapel Hill: University of North Carolina Press.

Taylor, W. T., & Piche, D. M. (1991). *A report on shortchanging children: The impact of fiscal inequity on the education of students at risk*. Prepared for the Committee on Education & Labor, U.S. House of Representatives. Washington, DC: Government Printing Office.

U.S. Department of Education, National Center for Education Statistics. (1998). *Digest of Education Statistics*. Washington, DC.

U.S. Department of Education, National Center for Education Statistics. (1999). *Digest of Education Statistics*. Washington, DC.

U.S. Department of Education, National Center for Education Statistics. (2000). *Digest of Education Statistics*. Washington, DC.

U.S. Department of Education, National Center for Education Statistics. (2003). *Digest of Education Statistics*. Washington, DC.

Wirt, J. G. (2000). *The condition of education, 2000*. Washington, DC: National Center for Educational Science.

Chapter 2

Teaching in "Hard to Teach in" Contexts

African American Teachers Uniquely Positioned in the African American Educational Pipeline

Jennifer E. Obidah, Tracy Buenavista,
R. Evely Gildersleeve, Peter Kim, and Tyson Marsh

According to a census report supplement to the March 2002 United States Current Population Survey, out of the general population of 288 million North Americans, 36 million (12.5%) were African American. While highly concentrated in the southern region of the United States, the African American community is also centered within America's metropolitan areas inside major cities. Over half (51.5%) of African Americans resided in urban communities, defined as regions having a population higher than 100,000 residents within a given metropolitan area (U.S. Census Bureau, 1990). Given this high concentration of African Americans within urban America, it is important to examine African American education in metropolitan centers. Of the 97,623 (K–12) public schools in the United States located within 17,140 school districts, African American students comprised 7.9 million (16.6%) of the school population (NCES, 2002a). While African Americans comprised 12.5% of the general population, African American students were highly concentrated in American public schools, at 16.6% nationally. In metropolitan areas, these students also comprised a large portion of the overall 24% of students living below the poverty line within metropolitan areas (NCES, 2002b).

Today, as in the past, the majority of African American teachers in the teaching workforce are instructing in areas where they serve the largest number of African American students. Among the 2.7 million teachers in America's public schools, only 214,000 (7.8%) were African American (NCES, 2002a). However, while this is an extremely small percentage of the national teaching force, the majority of these teachers are teaching in urban communities with high numbers of African American students. Data from the two largest school districts of the nation are offered to illustrate this point.

The New York City School District serves more than 1 million students and is the largest school district in the nation (New York State Education Department, 2002). According to the New York State Education Department, 372,214 students (34.9%) in the district are African American. African American teachers employed within the New York City School District comprise 39% of the teaching force in this district (New York State Education Department, 2002). In the Los Angeles Unified School District, which serves a total of 746,852 students (California Department of Education, 2002), there are 90,541 (21.1%) African American students. African American teachers comprised 14% of teachers employed in this school district. The percentages of African American teachers in these two districts are twice (in Los Angeles) and almost five times (in New York) the national percentage of African American teachers mentioned earlier. Clearly, African American teachers are concentrated in the same urban communities as African American students. As such, in a discussion of African American teachers and the African American education pipeline, it is important to situate this discussion in the urban, inner-city public school context, often referred to as a "hard to teach in" context.

This chapter discusses the role of African American teachers in the educational pipeline for African American students. In the first section of this chapter, we elaborate on the "hard to teach in" contexts where African American teachers have historically taught and continue today in the profession. Specifically, we describe the challenges faced by these teachers who teach in the midst of the difficult social and ecological conditions coupled with the proliferation of state and federal education reform policies shaping the education of African American students. We argue that from a history of such conditions emerged a culturally produced pedagogy utilized by African American teachers to teach African American students. We assert that despite historical segregation and discriminatory practices that placed African American teachers in schools serving a predominantly African American student population, these teachers also employ a teaching philosophy that significantly influences why they choose to teach in these areas. We conceptualize these teachers' path to teaching in theories of culture production (Willis, 1977) and an African American philosophy of achievement (Perry, Steele, & Hilliard, 2003). In effect, we argue that African American traditions, which shape the teaching philosophy of African American teachers, more accurately account for their positionality in the African American educational pipeline. We conclude this chapter with recommendations that assert the importance of reinforcing the presence of African American teachers in schools where the majority of the students are African American in light of their teaching roles based in the African American tradition.

THE "HARD TO TEACH IN" CONTEXTS WHERE AFRICAN AMERICAN TEACHERS TEACH

In this section we contrast the "hard to teach in" contexts where African Americans teachers have honed their teaching craft historically and today. Today, "hard-to-teach-in" refers to the urban context where the majority of African American teachers teach and African American students attend school. Historically, "hard to teach in" referred primarily to segregated schools in the South where this same population (teachers and students) attended school.

"Hard-to-Teach-In" Urban Context

Urban centers of metropolitan cities often suffer from debilitating social conditions such as poverty and its associated dysfunctions. When considering the political context, urban areas have a dwindling tax base and low voter turnout. As it relates to economic stability, there are high unemployment rates, limited employment opportunities, limited or no access to upwardly mobile jobs, low educational attainment among residents, and, consequently, while on the social level, high rates of substance abuse, crime, and violence (Anyon, 1997, Kozol, 1991, Jencks & Peterson, 1991). Previous research suggests that these challenges affect schools located in these metropolitan centers of urban cities. Often these challenges are discussed only in relation to the education of students. Here we discuss these contextual considerations in relation to their impact on African American teachers' ability to effectively educate African American students. Along with their students, African American teachers contend with poor working conditions, lack of materials and resources, and other structural barriers resulting from adverse economic, social, and political circumstances in urban centers, ultimately affecting the teaching and learning at these schools.

For example, in an expert report for the ongoing case against the California State Department of Education, *Williams v. State of California*, Robert Corley (2002) defined school conditions as various aspects of the school environment, including functionality, cleanliness, and the amount of "crowding" of people and access to personal health facilities such as bathrooms and drinking facilities. In describing the schools cited in the case, he reports their "unusually poor" conditions (versus normal conditions) such as overcrowded classrooms, dirty facilities and/or equipment, and the presence of large external distractions such as traffic and noise. Although all schools experience to some degree negative environmental conditions, unusually poor conditions are distinct in that they are chronic problems that are severe and persist. Other scholars argue that these unusually poor conditions plague urban schools and compromise the educational environment for participants in these schools (Anyon, 1997; Darling-Hammond, 2002; Lipman, 1995; Oakes, 1985).

Along with dilapidated facilities, teachers in urban schools also deal with an overwhelming lack of resources, such as textbooks, classroom supplies, and technological equipment (e.g., computers). Appropriate academic resources afford greater teaching and learning opportunities in school (Oakes, 2002). However, many urban schoolteachers often report lacking every kind of teaching and instructional material, in particular, textbooks. African American teachers, as do many of the teachers in schools where they are not provided with the necessary materials to do their job, often use a substantial amount of their personal monies to buy classroom supplies (Darling-Hammond, 1997).

Additionally, many urban schools are falling behind more affluent schools in terms of providing access to computers and the Internet. While 65% of all schools provide Internet access to teachers and students, only 50% of urban schools report having this access (U.S. Department of Education, NCES, 1997). Textbooks, access to technology, and other instructional materials are essential to teaching and learning because they provide access to the knowledge and skills deemed essential by state and national standards. All of these structural barriers contribute to the creation of a "stressful setting" for teaching and learning (Darling-Hammond, 2002). Unfortunately, it is this stressful setting that characterizes the urban school environment where many African American teachers work to educate a large portion of the African American student population. Ironically, the dire circumstances found in most urban schools today are relatively similar to the conditions under which African American teachers taught in segregated schools in the South.

"Hard to Teach in" Context of the South

Prior to the 1954 landmark ruling against school desegregation in *Brown v. the Board of Education, Topeka, Kansas*, African American teachers were *the* teachers of African American students. They taught in segregated schools located in the southern region of the United States. Foster (1997) reported census data from the mid-nineteenth century, when between 1890 and 1910 (soon after the 1896 *Plessy v. Ferguson* case establishing segregation) the number of African American teachers quadrupled from 15,100 to 66,236. In 1940, just prior to the overturn of the *Plessy* ruling, Foster (1997) wrote that of the 63,697 African American teachers in the United States, 75% of them "were employed in the 17 southern and border states" (p. xxv).

Regarding the conditions of these schools, they often existed under the poorest circumstances. Except for a few of these schools that were well maintained because of the strengths of the communities in which they were located

(Siddle-Walker, 1992), the majority of these schools were housed in poor facilities, were overpopulated (since one school often served large counties), and were
severely lacking in textbooks and other academic materials (Anderson, 1988;
Foster, 1997, 1990; Irvine & Irvine, 1983; Stanford, 1995). In summary, for
African American teachers as well as African American students, over the history of American public education policy makers have often provided inade-
quate facilities and resources to the educational pipeline of African Americans.
Because of the history of unequal education, poor working conditions, and lack
of sensitivity to their culture, historically and today, the African American community and African American teachers have engaged in the cultural production
of a teaching philosophy. African American teachers were the champions in
maintaining the right to an education, and this determination undergirds the
philosophy of teaching established in the African American tradition.

TEACHING IN THE AFRICAN AMERICAN TRADITION
THEORETICAL FRAMEWORKS

W. E. B. DuBois, in his seminal work *The Souls of Black Folk* (1986), outlines the
identity struggle among African Americans in America that resulted from a history of slavery coupled with a persistent denial of access to education. DuBois
wrote that after the Voting Rights Act of 1870, African Americans began to see
a new vision of liberty: "Slowly but steadily, in the following years, a new vision
began. It was the ideal of 'book-learning.' Here, at last, African Americans
seemed to have discovered the mountain path to Canaan, the biblical land of
freedom" (p. 19). African Americans saw education as being vital to freedom from
institutionalized slavery and the key to attaining full citizenship in America.

However, all the while believing in and striving for the American educational ideal, African Americans were simultaneously operating from an acute
awareness of mainstream America's institutionalized rejection of them as full
participants in this society. Thus although African Americans are aware of
themselves as American citizens, their status as oppressed beings is a constant
challenge to perceptions of themselves as full and equal participants in this society. In this struggle to maintain their human dignity, African Americans have
been engaged in a process of "culture production" (Willis, 1977).

Willis (1977) defined culture production as "the active, collective use and explorations of received symbolic, ideological, and cultural resources to explain,
make sense of, and positively respond to 'inherited' structural and material conditions" (p. 123). From the perspective of culture production, all cultures, including
those of oppressed groups, are viewed as cultures in and of themselves, not simply cultures that arise in opposition to domination. Willis's important conception
provides a theoretical lens for examining the legitimate cultural resources of

racially and socioeconomically oppressed people. Oftentimes the cultural traditions of these groups are perceived by mainstream cultures merely as responses
to these groups' oppressed status. However, culture production challenges this
perception. It affirms agency as the primary existence lived by African Americans
and other oppressed groups in the face of a reactionary existence.

Culture production also affirms African Americans' development of cultural resources that are separate from received symbolic, ideological, and cultural
forces, which maintain their status as dominated beings. The role of African
American teachers from this perspective then encompasses transmission of cultural resources to African American students that act in opposition to debilitating schooling processes to which many African American students are
subjected. Thus a struggle is embedded in the African American teacher's role:
the teacher is obligated to maintain the standards and ideals of the dominant
culture operant in the schooling process. However, simultaneously, embedded in
the teacher role as defined in the African American tradition, the teacher also
has to combat the subverted limitations of mainstream standards on African
American students. Perry, Steele, and Hilliard (2003) further elaborated on this
African American philosophy of schooling and the consequent teacher role.

In a critical analysis of the establishment of an African American education philosophy, Perry posited a philosophy comprised of the following elements: education for freedom, racial uplift, citizenship, and leadership. Perry
asserted that in lieu of the uncontested reality of unequal educational opportunity afforded African Americans in the pre-civil rights era of America's history,
African Americans worked intentionally to oppose the ideology of Black[1]
intellectual inferiority. She notes that,

> in addition to being sites of learning, [Black segregated schools] also
> instituted practices and expected behaviors and outcomes that not
> only promoted education—an act of insurgency in its own right—but
> also were designed to counter the ideology of African American intel-
> lectual inferiority and ideologies that saw African Americans not
> quite equal and as less than human. Everything about these institu-
> tions was supposed to affirm Black humanity, Black intelligence, and
> Black achievement. (p. 88)

In this context of resistance emerged teachers and principals who coupled
their grassroots intellectualism learned in the African American tradition with
their academic certification as teachers, to develop a pedagogy that encom-
passed curricular, behavioral, and ritualistic practices "designed to counter the
status of African Americans as a racial caste group" (p. 89). Perry gave one example of this type of pedagogy in the African American ritualistic exhortation

of "hold your head up high, throw your shoulders back, walk like you are somebody," historically used by African American teachers in the South with their students. This exhortation conveyed to Perry and other students that they should "carry themselves as if we were free, asking us to refuse to allow our social location, our positional identity, to find expression in our bodies" (p. 90). Perry noted that this and similar exhortations comprised some of the rituals sustained during the northern and western African American migrations from the southern parts of the United States. She argues that, in effect,

> what the Black community did was to organize intentional educational communities, collectively constituted "as-if" communities, imaginary communities that were capable of modeling possibilities. One can call historically Black schools "figured universes," or more precisely counterhegemonic figured communities. (p. 91)

Similar rituals are discussed in the experiences of African American teachers (Foster, 1997; Ladson-Billings, 1994) and their connections to their communities (Siddle-Walker, 1996).

In her ethnographic study of an African American high school in the segregated South, Siddle-Walker (1996) gave a historical account of how the Caswell County community in North Carolina worked together to ensure the successful academic achievement of its students. In keeping with Perry's conception of an African American pedagogy encompassing curricular, behavioral, and ritualistic practices, Walker noted, for example, that the school's clubs and assemblies were organized as an integral part of the school's educational plan. The weekly chapels and assemblies were a focal point for club planning and provided opportunities for students to display their talents. Teachers were actively involved in these student-centered activities. In effect, the teachers and administrators believed in the possibility and importance of all students reaching their highest potential, and as such, they assumed multiple roles in the school. These roles required their participation in a behavioral and ritualistic practice that took into account both the students' circumstances and the needs of the race.

Perry asserted the institutionalization of this philosophy because:

> it was a central meaning system that informed institutional life in these schools and to which its participants would to a greater or lesser extent be socialized. This philosophy was explicitly articulated, regularly ritualized, and passed on in formal public events (assemblies, graduations, May Day celebrations, etc.). . . . Stories and narratives concretized the enactment of this philosophy over time. (pp. 93–94)

A review of several texts supports Perry's assertion of a philosophy that was institutionalized. This philosophy utilized by African American teachers manifests in a variety of practices: teachers as mentors support students' navigation of the school system (Irvine, 1990); teachers help African American students (particularly those from low socioeconomic backgrounds who were also identified as underachieving) develop their self-concept (King, 1993); teachers are available to students beyond the regular school hours; teachers work to dispel myths of African American students' racial inferiority and incompetence (Adair, 1984); teachers develop unique pedagogies that relate school knowledge to students' academic, economic, political, social, and cultural lives (Delpit, 1995); and teachers negotiate the social and political structures of schools to ensure African American students' rights and access to a quality education (e.g., more African American students in gifted rather than special education programs; more African American students graduating from high school rather than being suspended and expelled) (Meier, Stewart, & England, 1989). We argue that it is these institutionalized rituals, behaviors, and practices comprising the African American philosophy of achievement that primarily influence African American teachers' decisions to follow African American students in the education system. That is, African American teachers exercise a cultural calling by teaching where African American students are enrolled.

Similarly, King (1993) highlights the critical factors that influenced African American teachers to pursue a career in teaching, including the "lack of role models for youth," the "need for minority teachers," the "poor conditions of minority communities," and their "interest in a service occupation" (p. 484). These factors place African American teachers in the position of providing their services, primarily mentoring and leadership skills, to the disenfranchised sections of their respective communities. In assuming the position of public servants, African American teachers would expect to address a void in such communities and make a difference.

The research of contemporary African American scholars lends support to a teacher role steeped in the African American tradition. These scholars have published extensively on the need for culturally relevant teaching based in a pedagogy that empowers students intellectually, socially, emotionally, and politically, a pedagogy that allows African American students to choose academic excellence yet still identify with Africans and African Americans (e.g., Lisa Delpit, James Banks, Geneva Gay, Jacqueline Irvine, and Gloria Ladson-Billings). Ladson-Billings (1994) and Irvine (2002), among others, identify the importance of employing culturally based instructional practices that assist African American students in navigating the public education system.

In summary, African American teachers who embrace and define their teacher role in the African American tradition have an expanded view of their role in the lives of African American children, and this explains, in large part, why the majority of African American teachers choose to teach where the majority of African American students attend school. However, African American teachers are greatly affected by issues unique to their position in the teaching force, which provides an added dimension of their teaching contexts as "hard to teach in." These issues evolve in particular from the impact of how and why African American teachers have been historically and continue to be undervalued in their chosen profession.

AFRICAN AMERICAN TEACHERS
A QUESTION OF VALUE

Throughout the history of African Americans in the American education system, African American teachers have been hired primarily to teach African American students. Prior to 1954, in the southern states, it was the law under a segregated system of African American education. However, as argued by Walker (1996), segregated schools also served as anchors of school communities. Walker's research is based on a framework by Bullock (1967), which focused on the unintended consequences of intentional neglect, which in the case of her book was the unification of a community to provide an exemplary education for its African American children in a segregated high school.

At the heart of Walker's ethnography is an assertion that as an integrated fabric of the community, the school she studied was culturally contextualized within the African American community it served, and the learning that it provided was mutually constituted by the cultural practices of the community. Schooling, at the level of the community, was individualized. There was investment in the students' learning and the school's success from all members of the school community. These were some of the unintended consequences of school segregation. Importantly, African American teachers were highly valued in this professional context.

Ironically, in the South, African American teachers thrived as professionals. They were the largest sector of educated people within the segregated African American communities, they were well regarded and respected in their communities, and they enjoyed unrestricted job opportunities in the sense that they could teach all grades and all subjects in their schools. As such, working in segregated schools and establishing a much sought after right to an education for African American students produced the philosophical approach to teaching discussed earlier, as well as a positive sense of being valued by the community served by these teachers.

In contrast was the reception given to African American teachers in the North and West. Foster (1997) elaborated on how much African American teachers were devalued in the northern segregated context. In the northern states, though no legal enforcement existed, it was the practice to hire Black teachers to teach only in schools serving primarily Black students. Foster (1997) wrote that:

> as more blacks migrated to Northern cites, the school systems adopted policies that resulted in the de facto segregation of black pupils and teachers. In cities such as Philadelphia, Boston, New York, and Chicago it was customary to assign black teachers to predominantly black schools or to restrict them to particular grades (usually elementary). . . . Between 1932 and 1948 the number of black teachers doubled, but the pattern of segregation was firmly established. (p. xxv)

Moreover, although African American teachers were assigned to teach in predominantly Black schools, these teachers were often not the majority of the teaching force in these schools and hardly ever comprised members of the governing bodies (such as members of school boards and other administrative roles). And across northern and western states, African American teachers had a very difficult time securing employment in their profession.

Thus African American teachers entered the teaching profession in both de jure (in the South) and de facto (in the North) segregated contexts, with their role, both chosen and assigned, identified with the express purpose of educating African American students. However, viewing the African American teaching force from a historical perspective, in areas other than the South, African American teachers were undervalued in the profession. We contend that the value of these teachers needs to be examined and critiqued as one of the areas of improving the recruitment and retention of these teachers in the teaching force today, particularly in light of the unique philosophy of teaching that they potentially bring to the education of African American students. We conclude this chapter with recommendations to this effect.

African American Teachers in the African American Education Pipeline Recommendations for Their Retention and Recruitment

In 2004, the education community celebrated the fiftieth anniversary of the landmark Supreme Court case, *Brown v. Board of Education*. Hailed as a triumph for African American education, *Brown* set out to desegregate schools. It was a legal, structural shift that disrupted schooling in America. *Brown* was public acknowledgment that not all children were receiving equal education under the law. It is often lauded as the first major federal action that produced cycles of reform that continued over the duration of the twentieth century.

However, fifty years after *Brown*, America's schools are almost as segregated as they were in 1954 (Orfield, 2001). Orfield (2001) points out that segregated, high-poverty communities have become a way of life in America. He asserts that in metropolitan areas housing remains seriously segregated, and most current segregation is between school districts of differing racial composition, not within individual districts as it was historically. Nowhere is this segregation more apparent than in urban schools, where the majority of African American students attend school and African American teachers teach.

The preceding pages of this chapter attempted to highlight the crucial role that African American teachers play in the maintenance of the African American educational pipeline. African American teachers were historically the primary teachers of African American students. In this context they constructed a teaching philosophy embedded in the African American tradition of achievement. Their craft was honed in the process of establishing education in the African American community after decades of denied access. This unique pedagogical approach to teaching evidences the crucial role that these teachers play in the education of African American students. We conclude this chapter with recommendations in the areas of improving salaries and job status for all teachers, especially African American teachers working in the hard-to-teach-in educational contexts. We urge the reexamination of educational policies that inhibit African American teachers' ability to effectively educate African American children in the African American tradition of achievement. Finally, we assert the need for African American teachers to be valued in the educational system. These recommendations can be employed to reinforce the presence of African American teachers in the African American educational pipeline.

Improving Salaries and Job Status

Many scholars assert the importance of recruiting and retaining African Americans into the teaching profession (Cole, 1986; Cooper, 1986; Dupre, 1986; Garibaldi, 1986; Hudson & Holmes, 1994; King, 1993; Smith, 1988; Wilson, 1988, Witty, 1986). With regard to issues that might prevent African Americans from pursuing a career in teaching, King (1993) found that deterrents included the low prestige and low salary, poor working environments, attraction of more prestigious careers, and lack of preparation for the job. In addressing the lack of prestige associated with teaching, it is critical that teacher education programs begin to improve the perceived status of the profession.

A potential method of countering this perception is to expand the pool of potential teacher education students through outreach and recruitment efforts, which is done in other professions. This effort can begin as early as junior high school. As stated by Garibaldi (1986), "Students should be introduced to the teaching profession in the junior high school years and encouraged to consider it as a career" (p. 395). Just as professions such as law and business are promoted through high school courses and programs are offered through debate and business, teacher education programs should work with high schools in creating courses and programs that can begin to develop students' interests and perceptions on the values of teaching and teachers. In addition, teacher education programs can begin to more aggressively recruit undergraduates at career and graduate school fairs as do other disciplines. Finally, through the creation of undergraduate minors and majors in education, teacher education programs can begin to cultivate the teachers of tomorrow.

REEXAMINE EDUCATIONAL POLICIES THAT SUBVERT THE AFRICAN AMERICAN PHILOSOPHY OF ACHIEVEMENT

The proliferation of state and federal educational reforms such as the No Child Left Behind Act (NCLB) undermines the goals and aspirations that have historically attracted African Americans into the profession. In the tradition of the *A Nation At Risk Report*, such policies embrace standardization and high-stakes testing, and they employ a one-size-fits-all approach to education. For example, according to the NCLB, each state must assess its schools based on state-approved standards that follow guidelines from the U.S. Department of Education. This translates into a high-stakes testing-based curriculum, where teachers must teach students to perform on standardized examinations rather than be foremost concerned with pedagogy and learning (Darling-Hammond, 2002). Additionally, state and federal policies also play a role in shaping perceptions of African American teachers' self-efficacy. As demonstrated by Macrine (2003), such policies hurt teachers, as they can "strip teachers of their decision-making role" (p. 204).

This approach to teaching contradicts the underlying principles of the African American philosophy of achievement and hinders the work of African American teachers who enter the profession with the intent of affecting the lives of students beyond the goal of improving their test scores. These reform initiatives impede these teachers' creativity, energy, and personal commitment to teaching. For the African American teachers who stay in the profession, many of them find it far easier to reap rewards in urban schools by following traditional methodologies of teaching that may not effectively serve the needs of African American students than to face the discord resulting from introducing new and creative means of transforming the intellectual development of these students. As such, we recommend that educational policies be examined in terms of their detrimental effect on African American teachers' ability to effectively educate African American students and, consequently, these teachers' desire to remain in the teaching profession.

Value African American Teachers As Professionals

There currently exists a paucity of research on the significance of valuing African American teachers on their rates of recruitment and retention in the teaching force. However, being valued is an important element in developing efficacy. According to Lee (2002), feelings of efficacy must be reinforced in pre-service and in-service African American teachers. Lee argues that teacher educators and practitioners should work to develop methods of improving feelings of efficacy among aspiring African American teachers. Such methods could include increasing the number of African Americans in decision-making roles (e.g., principals, district administrators, and school board members).

In addressing this concern it is critical that current methods of measuring teacher ability and content knowledge be reconsidered and restructured to ensure that such measures are not culturally biased and actually serve the purpose of measuring teacher ability (Hudson & Holmes, 1994; King, 1993; Cole, 1986; Cooper, 1986; Dupre, 1986; Garibaldi, 1986). These methods might be improved if they were to consider which qualities and knowledge potential teachers possess and how they might be valuable in particular communities with unique needs, in this case, the African American community.

In conclusion, as demonstrated earlier, it is evident that African American teachers chose the profession in hopes of providing a service to their respective communities. In addition, they seek to bring their lived experiences to the profession, as they share many commonalties with their African American students. If curriculum restrictions enforced through the standardization and application of a one-size-fits-all educational policy prevent African American teachers from applying their knowledge and experience in the classroom, then the career aspirations of African American teachers are undermined. As a result, we must begin to critically reflect on educational policies that prevent African American teachers from bringing their "intelligence, expertise, and commitment" to the profession (King, 2003). In doing so, we must include African American teachers in the federal, state, and local district policy decision-making processes (Hudson & Holmes, 1994; King, 1993).

NOTE

1. African American and Black will be used interchangeably in this chapter.

REFERENCES

Adair, A. (1984). *Desegregation: The illusion of Black progress*. Lanham, MD: University Press of America.

Anderson, J. D. (1988). *The education of Blacks in the south, 1860–1935*. Chapel Hill: University of North Carolina Press.

Anyon, J. (1995). Race, social class, and educational reform in an inner-city school. *Teachers College Record, 97*(1), 69–95.

Anyon, J. (1997). *Ghetto schooling: A political economy of urban educational reform*. New York: Teachers College Press.

California Department of Education. (2002). *California public schools—District reports*. Sacramento: California Department of Education.

Cole, B. P. (1986). The Black educator: An endangered species. *The Journal of Negro Education, 55*(3), 326–334.

Cooper, C. C. (1986). Strategies to assure certification and retention of Black teachers. *The Journal of Negro Education, 55*(1), 46–55.

Corley, R. (2002). *The condition of California school facilities and policies related to those conditions*. Expert report prepared for *Williams v. State of California*.

Darling-Hammond, L. (1997). *The right to learn: A blueprint for creating schools that work*. San Francisco: Jossey-Bass.

Darling-Hammond, L. (1999). *New standards, old inequalities: The current challenge for African-American Education*. New York: National Urban League.

Darling-Hammond, L. (2002). Access to quality teaching: An analysis of inequality in California's public schools. Expert report prepared for *Williams v. State of California*.

Delpit, L. (1995). *Other people's children: Cultural conflict in the classroom*. New York: New Press.

Du Bois, W. E. B. (1986). *The souls of Black folk*. New York: Library of America.

Dupre, B. B. (1986). Problems regarding the survival of future Black teachers in education. *The Journal of Negro Education, 55*(1), 56–66.

Earthman, G. I. (2002). *The effect of the condition of school facilities on student achievement*. Expert report prepared for *Williams v. State of California*.

Foster, M. (1990). The politics of race: Through the eyes of African American teachers. *Journal of Education, 172*, 123–141.

Foster, M. (1997). *Black teachers on teaching*. New York: The New Press.

Garibaldi, A. M. (1986). Sustaining Black educational progress: Challenges for the 1990s. *The Journal of Negro Education, 55*(3), 386–396.

Hudson, M. J., & Holmes, B. J. (1994). Missing teachers, impaired communities: The unanticipated consequences of *Brown v. Board of Education* on the African American teaching force at the precollegiate level. *The Journal of Negro Education, 63*(3), 388–393.

Irvine, J. J. (1990). Beyond role models: An examination of cultural influences on the pedagogical perspectives of Black teachers. *Peabody Journal of Education, 66*(4), 51–63.

Irvine, J. J. (2002). *In search of wholeness: African American teachers and their culturally specific classroom practices.* New York: Palgrave/St. Martin's Press.

Irvine, R., & Irvine, J. (1983). The impact of the desegregation process on the education of Black students: Key variables. *Journal of Negro Education, 52*, 410–422.

Jencks, C., & Peterson, P. E. (1991). *The urban underclass.* Washington, DC: The Brookings Institution.

King, S. H. (1993). Why did we choose teaching careers and what will enable us to stay?: Insights from one cohort of the African American teaching pool. *The Journal of Negro Education, 62*(4), 475–492.

Kozol, J. (1991). *Savage Inequalities: Children in America's schools.* Crown Publishers.

Ladson-Billings, G. (1994). *The dream keepers: Successful teachers of African American children.* San Francisco: Jossey-Bass.

Lee, G. H. (2002). The development of teacher efficacy beliefs. In J. J. Irvine (Ed.), *In search of wholeness: African American teachers and their culturally specific classroom practices* (pp. 33–45). New York: Palgrave.

Lipman, P. (1995). Bringing out the best in them: The contribution of culturally relevant teachers to educational reform. *Theory into Practice, 34*(3), 202–206.

Macrine, S. L. (2003). Imprisoning minds: The violence of neoliberal education or "i am not for sale!" In K. J. Saltman & D. A. Gabbard (Eds.), *Education as enforcement: The militarization and corporatization of schools* (pp. 203–211). New York: Routledge Falmer.

McLaughlin, M., & Talbert, J. (1990). Constructing a personalized school environment. *Phi Delta Kappan, 72*(3), 230–235.

Meier, K. J., and Stewart, J. & England, R. E. 1989. *Race, class, and education: The politics of second generation discrimination.* Madison: University of Wisconsin Press.

National Center for Educational Statistics (NCES). (2002a). *Condition of education: Educational background of teachers.* Washington, DC: Author.

National Center for Educational Statistics (NCES). (2002). *Condition of education: Racial/Ethnic distribution of public school students.* Washington, DC: Author.

New York State Education Department. (2002). New York, the state of learning: Statistical profiles of public school districts. New York: Author.

Oakes, J. (1985). *Keeping track: How schools structureinequality.* New Haven, CT: Yale University Press.

Oakes, J. (2002). Access to textbooks, instructional materials, equipment, and technology. Expert report prepared for *Williams v. State of California.*

Olsen, B., & Kirtman, L. (2002). Teacher as mediator of school reform: An examination of teacher practice in 36 California restructuring schools. *Teachers College Record, 104* (2), 301–324.

Orfield, G. (2001). *Schools more separate: Consequences of a decade of resegregation.* Cambridge, MA: The Civil Rights Project.

Perry, T., Steele, C., & Hilliard III, A. (2003). *Young, gifted and Black: Promoting high achievement among African American students.* New York: Beacon Press.

Rist, R. C. (1972). Planned incapacitation: A case study of how not to teach Black teachers to teach. *The Journal of Higher Education, 43*(8), 620–635.

Siddle-Walker, E. V. (1992). Falling asleep and failure among African American students: Rethinking assumptions about process teaching. *Theory into Practice, 31*(4), 321–327.

Siddle-Walker, V. (1996). *Their highest potential: An African American school community in the segregated south.* Chapel Hill: University of North Carolina Press.

Smith, A. W. (1988). Maintaining the pipeline of Black teachers for the twenty-first century. *The Journal of Negro Education, 57*(2), 166–177.

Stanford, G. C. (April 1995). *African American pedagogy: Needed perspectives for urban education.* Paper presented at the annual meeting of the American Educational Research Association, San Francisco.

U.S. Census Bureau. (1990). *Federal register notice.* Washington, DC: Author.

U.S. Census Bureau. (2002). *Demographic supplement to the current population survey.* Washington, DC: Author.

United States Department of Education, National Center for Educational Statistics (NCES). (1997). *The condition of education.* NCES ED 407 766. Washington, DC: United States Department of Education, National Center for Educational Statistics (NCES).

U.S. Elementary and Secondary Schools Act. "No Child Left Behind." (2002).

Ware, F. (2002). Black teachers' perceptions of their professional roles. In J. J. Irvine (Ed.), *In search of wholeness: African American teachers and their culturally specific classroom practices* (pp. 33–45). New York: Palgrave.

Willis, P. (1997). *Learning to labor: How working class kids get working class jobs.* New York: Columbia University Press.

Wilson, R. (1988). Recruiting and retaining minority teachers. *The Journal of Negro Education, 57*(2), 195–198.

Witty, E. P. (1986). Teacher testing and assessment. *The Journal of Negro Education, 55*(3), 358–367.

Chapter 3

Bringing the Gifts That Our Ancestors Gave

Continuing the Legacy of Excellence in African American School Leadership

Linda C. Tillman

There is a tradition of excellence in the discourse on African American[1] school leadership. At times, this has been obscured by factors that disproportionately affect African Americans in K–12 schools, such as desegregation (Orfield & Lee, 2004; Tillman, 2004), poor student achievement (Williams & Parker, 2003), and challenges that often characterize urban districts such as underfunding, poverty, illiteracy, and violence (Hunter & Brown, 2003). Despite these factors, African American school leaders have played key roles in shaping the policy agenda for the education of African American children in schools. Alongside African American teachers, African American principals and superintendents have been in the forefront of the struggle to educate African American children in the pre- and post-desegregation eras of public schooling.

While African American administrators at all levels have been instrumental in supervising the education of African American students, this chapter will focus on K–12 African American school principals. I will present a historical overview of African Americans in K–12 school leadership, discuss current demographics of African American K–12 principals, and explore factors that affect access to the principalship for African Americans. The discussion will then shift to three areas that are critical to creating and sustaining an African American K–12 leadership pipeline: (1) recruiting, selecting, and training African Americans for the principalship; (2) mentoring African Americans for the principalship; and (3) retaining African American principals. I will conclude the chapter with implications for practice and several policy recommendations.

A HISTORICAL PERSPECTIVE OF
AFRICAN AMERICAN SCHOOL LEADERSHIP

The terms *school administration* and *school leadership* are often used inter-changeably[2] within the K–12 literature base. The Contemporary frameworks have focused on the various administrative and leadership styles (Bolman & Deal, 1997; Leithwood & Duke, 1999; Lomotey, 1994), administrative and leader-ship functions (Farkas, Johnson, & Duffett, 2003; Leithwood & Riehl, 2003), alternative perspectives on school administration and leadership, such as spiri-tuality (Dantley, 2001), leadership for social justice (Dantley & Tillman, 2005), and diversity in educational administration and leadership (González, 2002; Tillman, 2002b, 2003). While some of these frameworks are inclusive of the perspectives of African American school leaders (see, for example, Alston, 1999; Jones, 2003; Lomotey, 1994), much of the theoretical and empirical literature on school leadership has failed to consider the unique history and present-day contributions of African American school leaders.

Researchers (i.e., Valverde & Brown, 1988; Banks, 1995) have noted that African American perspectives on school leadership are an underresearched, underdeveloped, and undervalued topic in the discourse on school administra-tion and leadership. Additionally, recent reports such as *Rolling Up Their Sleeves: Superintendents and Principals Talk About What's Needed to Fix Public Schools* (Farkas, Johnson, & Duffet, 2003), *Who Is Leading Our Schools?: An Overview of School Administrators and Their Careers* (Gates, Ringel, Santibañez, Ross, & Chung, 2003), and *Preparing School Principals: A National Perspective on Policy and Program Innovations* (Hale & Moorman, 2003) tend to be nar-rowly scripted discussions of what school leadership is and the desired charac-teristics and skills of individuals who serve as school leaders. The focus and content of these reports indicate a privileging of voice that often excludes the theoretical and practical knowledge of African American school leaders.

A tradition of excellence in the education of African Americans can be traced back to African American school leaders who helped build schools and secure funding and other resources, interacted with the African American com-munity, and worked as advocates for equitable and accessible education for African American children (Edwards, 1996; Pollard, 1997; Siddle-Walker, 2000). According to Pollard (1997), the work of African American school lead-ers was critical to building and operating schools for African American children and dates back to the 1860s. Pollard also notes that the educational philosophies of African American school leaders typically reflected those of an African American community that believed education was the key to enhancing the life chances of its children. A system of education for African Americans could be found in both public and private schools where African American leaders served dual but complementary roles as administrators and activists.

Siddle-Walker (2000) notes that African American principals were central figures in segregated schooling and in the African American community. These individuals served as connections to and liaisons between the school and the community. African American principals encouraged parents to donate resources to the schools, helped raise funds for schools, and served as models of servant leadership as well as professional role models for teachers and other staff members. African American principals also served as instructional leaders in these segregated schools. As instructional leaders, African American principals not only provided a vision and direction for the school staff but also transmitted the goals and ideals of the school to a philanthropic White power structure. As liaisons to the White community, African American principals often requested funding, resources, and other forms of support for these all-Black schools. Siddle-Walker cites Rodgers's (1967) analysis of African American principals in which he describes them as superintendents, supervisors, family counselors, financial advisors, community leaders, employers, and politicians. Almost 40 years later, many of these same characteristics can be used to describe African American principals, particularly those who work in large urban school districts. Indeed, their jobs are multifaceted and require the application of a combination of professional, personal, social, economic, and political skills (Blackman & Fenwick, 2000).

The tradition of excellence in African American school leadership was dramatically changed by desegregation, particularly in the South. While some African American principals retained their positions after the historic *Brown v. Board of Education* decision, generally desegregation had a devastating impact on African American school leaders (Ethridge, 1979; Pollard, 1997; Valverde & Brown, 1988; Tillman, 2004; Yeakey, Johnston, & Adkison, 1986). Ethridge (1979) noted that 1954 to 1965 was the most devastating period for Black principals. During this time, Whites believed that Black children had not learned in part because Black principals had not been effective in assuring that these children were educated. Expert witnesses in court cases argued for the dismantling of all-Black schools and replacing Black principals with White principals. For example, between 1954 and 1965, the states of Oklahoma, Missouri, Kentucky, West Virginia, Maryland, and Delaware closed most of their all-Black schools, and more than 50% of the African American principals in these states were dismissed. Ethridge (1979) concluded that "Thousands of educational positions which would have gone to Black people in the South under a segregated system have been lost for them since desegregation" (p. 231).

Clearly, one of the unintended consequences of the *Brown* decision and the subsequent desegregation of America's schools (particularly those schools in the South) was the loss of Black principals. The firing of African American principals led to the silencing of voices and exclusion of specific racial, social, and cultural perspectives that were critical to the education of Black children.

Not only were positions lost in the numerical sense, but more importantly there was a loss of a tradition of excellence, a loss of leadership as one of the foundations of the Black community, and a loss of the expertise of these educators who were committed to the education of Black children. Present challenges in K–12 schooling that disproportionately affect African American children necessitate a return to this tradition of excellence. From a pipeline perspective, more African American school leaders are needed at the forefront of the current struggle to educate African American children. The pipeline must be strengthened so that African American principals are active participants in the development, interpretation, and implementation of policy initiatives that can enhance the educational achievement of African American children.

REPAIRING THE CRACKS IN THE PIPELINE

African Americans are severely underrepresented within the principalship ranks, and the racial and ethnic makeup of K–12 leadership remains predominantly White. A 2006 National Center for Educational Statistics report indicates that in the 2003–2004 school year, there were approximately 10,000 African American public school principals, representing 11% of all public school principals. Additionally, a RAND Education report (Gates, et al., 2003) notes that compared to dramatic increases in the number of female principals, increases in the number of principals of color were more limited, particularly compared to the number of students of color in the population. Thus while the nation as a whole, and K–12 education in particular, has become more racially and ethnically diverse, the field of educational leadership remains underdiversified. While the African American K–12 student population is currently 17% (Orfield & Lee, 2004), African Americans represent only 11% of all public school principals.

Valverde and Brown (1988) discussed the underrepresentation of African Americans and other ethnic minorities in school leadership in the *Handbook on Research on Educational Administration*. In their chapter "Influences on Leadership Development among Racial and Ethnic Minorities," the authors stated, "Changing demographic trends have accelerated the need for recruiting, preparing, and placing minority candidates in administrative positions" (p. 153). They also posed a question that is still being asked today: "How can more minorities be recruited into, and be appropriately prepared in, administration programs?" (p. 153). Valverde and Brown argued that the recruitment and selection of talented individuals from all racial and ethnic groups was needed to improve the effectiveness of schooling and to expose educators to diverse perspectives. They also argued that these objectives could be accomplished by increasing the numbers of African American and other administrators of color and improving efforts in colleges and universities to increase the enrollment of African American and other students of color in educational administration programs. Hale and Moorman (2003) noted that a 1987 University Council for Educational Administration (UCEA) study identified the lack of minorities in educational leadership as a problem area in the field. More than a decade after the 1987 UCEA report, these same points are being discussed by scholars who are members of the UCEA (González, 2002; Tillman, 2002b, 2003). According to Michelle Young, executive director of the UCEA, the organization remains predominantly White, and less than 5% of the faculty members are African American. Additionally, Young notes that in 2004 fewer than 30 African American faculty and 20 African American students regularly attended the UCEA annual meeting. While the UCEA is not the only K–12 leadership organization, it does represent a significant number of student professionals, faculty, and K–12 administrators.[3] Thus the lack of diversity in principal preparation programs and in leadership organizations can be linked to the underrepresentation of African Americans as K–12 school principals.

Reports mentioned earlier in this chapter (Farkas, Johnson, & Duffett, 2003; Gates, et al., 2003) do not specifically address the underrepresentation of African Americans as school leaders; rather, the issue of the underrepresentation of African Americans in school leadership is subsumed under the category of women and people of color. The failure to investigate, discuss, and pose solutions for the underrepresentation of African Americans as a specific group continues to position this issue as unimportant in the broader discourse on school leadership and ultimately student achievement. As I mentioned earlier, this narrowly scripted version of school leadership is usually presented from a "majority administrator's" perspective.

These same reports (e.g., Farkas, Johnson, & Duffett, 2003; Gates, et al., 2003) also point to a principal shortage. But according to Fenwick (cited in Education Writers Association, 2002), school districts have overlooked a talented pool of potential leaders, many of them African Americans. African American leadership candidates typically complete administrative preparation programs and are more likely to hold master's and doctoral degrees than their White counterparts; however, they are less likely to be selected for administrative positions (Blackman & Fenwick, 2000). While some districts contain a critical mass of African American principals (usually large urban school districts with majority African American student populations), the profession remains predominantly White and male.

When considering these issues from a pipeline perspective, several factors directly affect African Americans. First, the traditional route to the principalship is via teaching, and 99.3% of all principals have been teachers (Hale & Moorman, 2003). The current shortage of African American teachers (Gay & Howard, 2000) directly affects the numbers of African Americans entering the principalship. The shortage of African American teachers and administrators is particularly acute in urban school districts that serve large numbers of African American students. As Obidah et al. (chapter 2) correctly pointed out, the majority of African American teachers work in urban school districts. However, as Gay and Howard (2000) note, African Americans continue to be underrepresented in the teaching workforce overall (7%), and this underrepresentation is most acute in urban school districts. According to Gay and Howard (2000), a significant number of veteran teachers were expected to retire in 2005, and a high percentage of these teachers are African American. Additionally, these authors note that it will be difficult to replace these African American teachers "because there are so few students of color enrolled in teacher education programs" (p. 3). Jacqueline Jordan Irvine concurs that there is a severe shortage of African American teachers. She also notes that while some African Americans enter the teaching profession via special programs such as "Teach for America" and "Pathways to Teaching," these individuals usually leave the profession approximately 3 years after beginning their teaching careers. According to Irvine, given the attrition rates of these teachers, such programs cannot be viewed as viable alternatives to replacing those African American teachers who will retire over the next several years.[4]

Valverde (2003) cites a 1996 National Education Association report on urban school districts titled *Status of the Public Schools*, detailing the shortages of African American teachers and principals in relation to the African American student population. The following statistics are particularly telling:

- In 1993, there were 14.8% African American students compared to 9% African American teachers.
- In 1996, the number of African American students increased to 16.6%, while the number of African American teachers decreased to 7.3%.
- In 1994, there were 16.6% African American students compared to 10.8% African American principals.

These statistics point to the imperative for increasing the numbers of African Americans who choose teacher education as a college major, enter the profession and choose to teach in urban school districts with large numbers of African American students, and remain in the profession. Research indicates that many African American teachers leave the profession within 3 to 5 years after being hired (Gay & Howard, 2000). Many of these individuals pursue careers in other fields such as business, engineering, and higher education—fields that are now employing increasing numbers of persons of color.

Second, from a pipeline perspective, African American leaders are needed to supervise the education of African American students, to prepare these students for postsecondary education, and to help African American students increase their life chances socially, emotionally, and academically. The presence, expertise, and influence of African American leaders are directly connected to African American student achievement, cultural and community norms, and the discourse on and implementation of policies that advantage rather than disadvantage African American students.

Barriers to the principalship for African Americans are an additional pipeline consideration. Since African Americans represent only 11% of all public school principals, it appears that they may encounter barriers that do not typically exist for White principals. These barriers include ineffective recruiting efforts, hiring practices that are based on a White male standard, the lack of socialization and mentoring, and professional challenges that affect the retention of African American principals (Gates, et al., 2003). In the next section I will discuss three approaches to increasing the numbers of African Americans who are recruited, selected, and trained for the principalship.

REPAIRING THE PIPELINE
CREATING A CRITICAL MASS FOR
RECRUITING, SELECTING, AND TRAINING
AFRICAN AMERICANS FOR THE PRINCIPALSHIP

The majority of African Americans who hold administrative certification are credentialed through university preparation programs, thus the recruitment of African American candidates for the principalship can begin in university leadership preparation programs. Faculty can work with school districts to focus recruitment efforts and strategies on attracting African Americans who have the interest, ability, and qualifications for leadership positions in K–12 schooling. Such strategies should include not only collaborating with school districts to identify potential candidates but *encouraging* interested master's and doctoral students to pursue leadership positions. Collaborations with school districts can be particularly helpful in identifying African Americans who may be interested in school leadership but who have not received the appropriate information or been encouraged to pursue these positions. Given the underrepresentation of African Americans in K–12 school leadership nationally, university faculty can be instrumental in assisting school districts in identifying these potential candidates. Universities can and should play a critical role in helping school districts build a critical mass of African Americans who aspire to the principalship. This type of collaboration is consistent with the goals and objectives of administrative preparation programs to identify and train a more racially and ethnically diverse group of school leaders.

African Americans who aspire to the principalship should be encouraged to participate in professional development activities such as principal leadership academies. University leadership preparation programs have been criticized for curricula that lack practical applications to the real world of schooling (Farkas, Johnson, & Duffett, 2003; Hale & Moorman, 2003). Thus additional professional preparation in leadership academies can provide African Americans with a more extensive knowledge base and a variety of experiences specifically designed to assist principals in developing the skills and dispositions needed to become effective leaders in today's schools (Hale & Moorman, 2003; National Association of Elementary School Principals, 2003; Richard, 2001). Principal leadership academies may be particularly important for African Americans who aspire to the principalship and who are likely to lead in challenging urban districts. Principal academies such as the Harvard Principals Center, the California School Leadership Academy, and the Danforth Educational Leadership Program provide principals with training, support, and mentoring. Participation in principal academies can provide opportunities to interact with colleagues from a variety of school districts with similar as well as different characteristics and to bridge the gaps between espoused theory and actual practice.

The importance of leadership training that will ultimately benefit African American students cannot be overemphasized. One aspect of school leadership that is particularly important to African American student achievement is an understanding of federal and state educational policies. In this vein, African American principals must be trained to implement the mandates of policies such as No Child Left Behind (NCLB), which is specifically designed to address educational inequities experienced by disadvantaged students and students of color. As a professor of educational leadership and policy studies, I have found that many African Americans who aspire to the principalship are underprepared to discuss the specifics of the NCLB legislation and what must be done to meet its goals and objectives. While this lack of knowledge is not specific to African Americans, I would argue that it is this group that *must* be prepared to interpret how educational policy such as NCLB can benefit African Americans. Everett Thomas,[5] a retired African American principal, is an NCLB consultant. According to Thomas, African American principals must have a basic understanding of the legislation, including the long-range goals and objectives of their school. Thomas notes that African American principals may also have to implement multiple strategies for achieving the goals of NCLB, since many districts lack the necessary funding to carry out the mandates. That is, even while many of the goals and objectives of NCLB will be extremely difficult to achieve without necessary funding, administrators will still be held accountable for the academic success of their students. Finally, Thomas notes that African American principals must develop effective strategies to work with all parents, including those parents who are unempowered and disadvantaged in many of the same ways as their children. According to Thomas, parents are the "difference makers," and African American administrators must work to establish positive relationships with parents if they are to make NCLB advantageous for African American children.

Mentoring African Americans for the Principalship

While the recruitment and training of African American candidates for school leadership are important, it is also important that they are given continued support in the form of mentoring. African Americans must be given opportunities for purposeful and long-term mentoring relationships with practicing administrators who are willing to help prepare them for the oftentimes challenging environment of K–12 education. Specifically, principals and other administrators who mentor future African American leaders must be willing to help them develop strategies to work with the entire school community that includes teachers, students, parents, community members, and school support staff. This is particularly important when African American principals work in large urban districts that are often characterized by student underachievement, underfunding, few resources, and external factors such as poverty and violence (Valverde, 2003). In addition, such districts are often measured against a White, middle-class norm of student achievement, even while many African American students in these districts have historically been underserved and undereducated.

Socialization to the norms of the profession and mentoring should begin early in one's career, preferably as a teacher. According to Yeakey, Johnston, and Adkison (1986), "The proper socialization processes for aspiring administrators begin during the period of teaching, for it is principals and other key administrators who provide the latitude for prospective candidates to progress" (p. 121). Additionally, it is often the case that African Americans are selected for administrative positions later in their careers than their White counterparts and thus have shorter administrative careers (Pollard, 1997). The identification, recruitment, training, socialization, and mentoring of African American teachers who aspire to the principalship should occur early in their careers to increase the numbers of African Americans who enter the leadership pipeline. African Americans should also be encouraged and given opportunities to participate not only in professional development activities but also in culturally and racially specific leadership organizations such as the National Alliance of Black School Educators (NABSE). It is not only important that African Americans be trained to lead, but trained to lead in school districts that serve majority African American student populations, since the majority of African Americans are employed in these districts.

Retaining African American Principals

Much of what I have discussed in the previous section can also be applied to the retention of African American school leaders. Clearly, school districts must be committed to retaining African American leaders. Many of these individuals bring unique educational, racial, and cultural perspectives, and their contributions can enhance theory and practice in educational leadership. More importantly, these African Americans can help shape the lives of African American students in positive ways that will lead to their social, emotional, academic, professional, and economic excellence. School districts must implement policies and procedures to assure that African American principals are successful and remain in schools. District personnel can reassess and, if necessary, restructure how African American principals are supported. Farkas, Johnson, and Duffett (2003) indicate that the shortage of principals and the increased number of early retirements are due in part to politics and bureaucracy, unreasonable demands of standardized testing and accountability, low pay and prestige, and stressful working conditions. The authors also note that these problems will likely become more acute in large urban districts. District personnel must support African American principals by assessing their needs, helping them identify the most critical problem areas in their schools and communities, helping them implement problem-solving strategies, and facilitating mentoring arrangements that are professionally and personally rewarding. These and other types of support from school district personnel can help address the shortage and success rates of African American principals.

BRINGING OUR GIFTS
RECLAIMING THE TRADITION OF EXCELLENCE IN
AFRICAN AMERICAN SCHOOL LEADERSHIP

As I close this chapter, I am optimistic about reclaiming the tradition of excellence in African American school leadership. While some forms of African American school leadership practice and theory may be considered an alternative perspective (Lomotey, 1994; Tillman, 2002a), it is this type of leadership that is needed in the struggle to educate African American children and to enhance their life chances. Several factors must be addressed in our efforts to strengthen the African American leadership pipeline in K–12 schools.

First, the pipeline can be strengthened by recruiting more African Americans into the teaching profession and making their personal and professional development a priority. Efforts to increase the numbers of African American teachers who move into leadership positions must begin in the classroom. Given the shortage of African American teachers, school districts must consider implementing specific strategies to assure that African American teacher excellence is cultivated for school leadership. Second, the pipeline can be strengthened through collaborations between school districts and university preparation programs. Collaborations should be formed for the specific purpose of identifying, encouraging, recruiting, and training African Americans who aspire to leadership positions. Equally important is placing an emphasis on the specific ways of thinking, believing, and knowing based on African American cultural and community norms (Tillman, 2002a). African American perspectives on teaching, learning, and school leadership must be acknowledged by school district personnel as well as in university preparation programs. The acknowledgment of multiple perspectives on school leadership, as well as the role of culture in the education of Black children, should be a part of the discourse on leadership preparation.

Next, the pipeline can be strengthened by linking the achievement of African American students to school leadership. This positions African American leaders as advocates for the academic success of African American children. African American leaders must be prepared to discuss, debate, and promote policies and procedures that advantage Black students, and to challenge those policies and procedures that diminish their chances for personal and professional growth. It is typically the case that the specifics of policies such as NCLB are somewhat removed from the day-to-day responsibilities of the school site leader. However, African American principals must understand the implications of such policies for African American students at all levels. The pipeline is further strengthened when African American students achieve at their maximum potential and are positioned to participate in postsecondary education and in American society. Thus African American leaders must question how and in what ways educational policy can be used to benefit African American children.

Policy Implications

Policy recommendations for strengthening the African American school leadership pipeline focus on three major sites of educational reform: federal government, state government, and the local school district. While education is a function of the state, it is imperative that policies designed to increase the number of African Americans in the principalship pipeline be initiated at the federal level. The Department of Education must take a proactive position on this issue and develop appropriate policies for focusing attention on the shortage of African American principals. It is at this level where sufficient funds must be allocated to the states (e.g., block grants) to support the recruitment and training of African Americans who aspire to the principalship, particularly in districts where there are large numbers of African American students and where there are shortages of African American principals. Department of Education officials must actively work with state departments of education to provide funds and other forms of support to maintain programs, policies, and procedures for increasing the numbers of African American principals.

State-level activity must begin with the investigation of the specific circumstances that contribute to the shortage of African Americans in the principalship pipeline within the state. Again, this investigation should be particularly focused in urban districts with large populations of African American students. Secondly, state departments of education should develop specific, long-term policies and procedures to increase the number of African Americans in the pipeline who are recruited and trained for principal positions. States should apply for federal funds to design, implement, support, and maintain initiatives that will increase the number of African Americans in the pipeline. Additionally, a portion of these funds should be used to cultivate the leadership skills of African American teachers who aspire to the principalship. As I mentioned earlier in this chapter, the socialization process for aspiring principals should begin during their tenure as teachers. As Foster (2004) has suggested, special attention should be given to collaborating with historically Black colleges and universities (HBCUs). Many of these institutions have exemplary teacher education programs and graduate African Americans who choose teaching as a career. School districts should work with HBCUs to develop professional schools where one of the goals is to cultivate teacher skills and identify prospective leaders.

State officials should also work proactively with local school districts to implement policies and procedures to increase the number of African Americans in the principalship pipeline. Such policies could include the following:

1. *Establishing cohorts of African Americans who aspire to the principalship.* Students in the cohort would complete the requirements for principal certification at the school site or university. Cohorts offer the advantage of a supportive, collegial environment for individuals who work in similar as well as dissimilar districts. Individuals could apply through a nomination process, be recommended by the school district, or be selected through a collaborative process between the local university and a school district.

2. *Establishing a leadership academy that provides long-term, strategic, purposeful professional and personal development activities that prepare individuals for the principalship in general as well as the principalship in specific environments (e.g., urban settings).*

3. *Establishing mentoring programs that pair practicing principals with principal candidates.* Mentoring can be a critical factor in helping aspiring principals acquire the knowledge, skills, and dispositions for the principalship from both a theoretical and practice-based perspective. Mentoring can provide aspiring principals with professional, social, emotional, and cultural support.

4. *Establishing internships that provide African Americans who aspire to the principalship with purposeful experiences in districts in which they are likely to work.* Such internships should be structured to give interns release time from their teaching duties with full pay. Additionally, internships should provide incentives for both the principal candidate and the principal mentor. Mentoring internships should be structured so that they are mutually beneficial to both the practicing principal (mentor) and the principal candidate (mentee).

5. *Evaluating the leadership academies and mentoring arrangements to reassess policies and procedures.* This should be done on an annual basis as a method of determining both the effectiveness and ineffectiveness of current policies and practices. Annual evaluations can also serve as a method for addressing the general and specific needs of the participants.

6. *Using current research about the barriers and conditions that may prevent African Americans from entering the principalship pipeline.* Policy makers should apply the findings from research to assist in the implementation of policies and procedures that create opportunities to increase the number of African Americans in the principalship pipeline. Additionally, policy makers should investigate how leadership theory can be applied to practice (e.g., the realities of K–12 schooling and the principalship).

7. *Convening a representative group of practitioners, state department officials and policy makers, and university faculty to review, discuss, plan, and design effective programs that address the underrepresentation of African Americans in the principalship.* Such plans should include strategies for increasing the number of African Americans in the principalship pipeline.

8. *Initiating conversations with practicing principals as a separate group to determine the specific circumstances and factors that affect "being a principal" generally and an African American principal in particular.* Questions for discussion should include the following: What are the unique circumstances that define the principalship in urban, rural, and suburban school districts? What skills and dispositions are needed for effective leadership? What are the hiring practices in districts where the majority of African Americans will assume principalships? How can the school culture affect the work of African American principals? What external factors (e.g., socio-economic status, literacy rates, and crime) can affect the work of African American principals? What skills and dispositions are needed to facilitate the academic achievement of African American students? These and other questions are important to the socialization and mentoring of African Americans who aspire to the principalship.

The important issue of African Americans in the principalship pipeline should be linked to African American student achievement. Thus a primary reason for increasing the numbers of African American principals must be to use their expertise to establish the agenda for Black education. Hudson and Holmes (1994) suggested four strategies to "chart a new course" (p. 392) for the education of African American children. These strategies are particularly applicable to the issue of increasing the leadership pipeline. They suggest the following:

1. Exercising leadership by setting a rigorous educational agenda and high expectations for African American students;
2. engaging in community planning that connects K–12 and higher education systems in African American communities;
3. participating consistently in the formulation of state and local educational policy; and,
4. closely monitoring how and where various state and local educational polices are implemented.

Fifty years after *Brown* and 40 years after the Civil Rights Act, African American school leaders must bring their gifts, reclaim the tradition of African American excellence in leadership, and chart a new course for Black education.

NOTES

1. The terms *Black* and *African American* will be used interchangeably in this chapter.

2. I am using the terms *educational administration* and *educational leadership* interchangeably in this chapter. While it is not within the scope of this chapter to enter into a complete discussion of the similarities and differences between the two terms, it is worth noting that much of the focus in the field has turned to leadership. For a more extensive discussion of the evolution of and increased use of term *leadership* see Leithwood & Duke, 1999.

3. Personal conversation with Michelle Young, executive director of the University Council for Educational Administration, March 2, 2004.

4. Personal conversation with Jacqueline Jordan Irvine, Charles Howard Candler Professor of Urban Education at Emory University, May 29, 2004.

5. Personal conversation with Everett Thomas, former Columbus (Ohio) Public Schools principal, January 15, 2004.

REFERENCES

Alston, J. (1999). Climbing the hills and mountains: Black females making it to the superintendency. In C. Brunner (Ed.), *Sacred dreams: Women and the superintendency* (pp. 79–90). Albany: State University of New York Press.

Banks, C. M. (1995). Gender and race as factors in educational leadership and administration. In J. A. Banks & C. M. Banks (Eds.), *Handbook of research on multicultural education* (pp. 65–80). New York: Macmillan.

Blackman, M., & Fenwick, L. (2000). The principalship. *Education Week, (19)*29, 46, 68.

Bolman, L., & Deal, T. (1997). *Reframing organizations: Artistry, choice, and leadership* (2nd ed.). San Francisco: Jossey-Bass.

Dantley, M. E. (2001). *Transforming school leadership through Cornel West's notions of African American prophetic spirituality.* Paper presented at the Annual Meeting of the University Council for Educational Administration, Cincinnati, OH.

Dantley, M. E., & Tillman, L. C. (2005). Social justice and moral transformative leadership. In C. Marshall & M. Oliva (Eds.), *Leadership for social justice: Making revolutions in education* (pp. 16–30). Boston, MA: Allyn & Bacon.

Education Writers Association. (2002). Special Report. *What is good leadership?* (pp. 2–11). Washington, DC: Author.

Edwards, P. (1996). Before and after school desegregation: African American parents' involvement in schools. In M. Shujaa (Ed.), *Beyond desegregation: The politics of quality in African American schooling* (pp. 138–161). Thousand Oaks, CA: Corwin Press.

Ethridge, S. (1979). Impact of the 1954 *Brown vs. Topeka Board of Education* decision on Black educators. *The Negro Educational Review, (30)*4, 217–232.

Farkas, S., Johnson, J., & Duffett, A. (with Syat, B. & Vine, J.). (2003). *Rolling up their sleeves: Superintendents and principals talk about what's needed to fix public schools.* New York: Public Agenda.

Foster, L. (2004). Administrator and teacher recruitment and selection post-*Brown*: Issues, challenges, and strategies. *Journal of School Public Relations, 25*(2), 220–232.

Gates, S. M., Ringel, J. S., Santibañez, Ross, K. E., & Chung, C. H. (2003). *Who is leading our schools?: An overview of school administrators and their careers.* Arlington, VA: RAND Education.

Gay, G., & Howard, T. (2000). Multicultural teacher education for the 21st century. *The Teacher Educator, 36*(1), 1–16.

González, M. L. (2002). Professors of educational administration: Learning and leading for the success of ALL children. *University Council for Educational Administration Review, 64*(1), 4–9.

Hale, E. L., & Moorman, H. N. (2003). *Preparing school principals: A national perspective on policy and program innovations.* Washington, DC: Institute for Educational Leadership.

Hudson, M. J., & Holmes, B. J. (1994). Missing teachers, impaired communities: The unanticipated consequences of *Brown v. Board of Education* on the African American teaching force at the precollegiate level. *Journal of Negro Education, 63*(3), 388–393.

Hunter, R., & Brown, F. (2003). Introduction: Challenges of urban education—efficacy of urban education. In R. Hunter & F. Brown (Eds.), *Challenges of urban education and efficacy of school reform* (pp. 1–11). Oxford, UK: JAI Press.

Jones, S. N. (2003). *The praxis of Black female educational leadership from a systems perspective*. Unpublished dissertation. Bowling Green State University.

Leithwood, K. A., & Duke, L. (1999). A century's quest to understand school leadership. In J. Murphy & K. Seashore Louis (Eds.), *The handbook of research on educational administration* (2nd ed., pp. 45–72). San Francisco: Jossey Bass.

Leithwood, K. A., & Riehl, C. (2003). *What we know about successful school leadership*. Philadelphia: Laboratory for Student Success, Temple University.

Lomotey, K. (1994). African American principals: Bureaucrat/administrators and ethno-humanists. In M. Shujaa (Ed.), *Too much schooling, too little education: A paradox of Black life in White societies* (pp. 203–219). Trenton, NJ: Africa World Press.

National Association of Elementary School Principals. (2003). *Making the case for principal mentoring*. Providence, RI: Brown University.

National Center for Educational Statistics. (2006). *Digest of Educational Statistics*. Washington, DC: Government Publication Office.

Orfield, G., & Lee, C. (2004). *Brown* at 50: King's dream or Plessy's nightmare? The Civil Rights Project, Harvard University. http://www.civilrightsproject.harvard.edu

Pollard, D. (September, 1997). Race, gender, and educational leadership: Perspectives from African American principals. *Educational Policy, (11)*3, 353–374.

Richard, A. (2001). Growth of academies highlights new thinking about leadership. *Education Week, (20)*37, 1, 14, 15.

Rodgers, F. (1967). *The Black high school and its community*. Lexington, MA: Lexington Books.

Siddle-Walker, V. (2000). Value segregated schools for African American children in the South, 1935–1969: A review of common themes and characteristics. *Review of Educational Research, 70*(3), 253–285.

Tillman, L. C. (2002a). Culturally sensitive research approaches: An African American perspective. *Educational Researcher, 31*(9), 3–12.

Tillman, L. C. (2002b). The impact of diversity in educational administration. In G. Perreault & F. Lunenburg (Eds.), *The changing world of school administration* (pp. 144–156). *National Council of Professors of Educational Administration Yearbook*. Lanham, MD: Scarecrow Press.

Tillman, L. C. (2003). From rhetoric to reality? Educational administration and the lack of racial and ethnic diversity within the profession. *University Council for Educational Administration Review, 45*(3), 1–4.

Tillman, L. C. (2004). (Un)intended consequences?: The impact of the *Brown v. Board of Education* decision on the employment status of Black educators. *Education and Urban Society, (36)*3, 280–303.

Valverde, L. (2003). School leadership for 21st century urban communities. In R. Hunter & F. Brown (Eds.), *Challenges of urban education and the efficacy of school reform* (pp. 187–199). Oxford, UK: JAI Press.

Valverde, L., & Brown, F. (1988). Influences on leadership development of racial and ethnic minorities. In N. Boyan (Ed.), *The handbook on educational administration* (pp. 143–158). New York: Longmans.

Williams, D., & Parker, L. (2003). Standardized testing and assessment policy: Impact on racial minorities and implications for leadership. In R. Hunter & F. Brown (Eds.), *Challenges of urban education and efficacy of school reform* (pp. 207–220). Oxford, UK: JAI Press.

Yeakey, C. C., Johnston, G. S., & Adkison, J. A. (1986). In pursuit of equity: A review of research on minorities and women in educational administration. *Educational Administration Quarterly, 22*(3), 110–149.

Part II

Higher Education

Chapter 4

Descriptive Analysis of African American Students' Involvement in College

Implications for Higher Education and Student Affairs Professionals

Lamont A. Flowers

Few topics in student affairs and higher education have received more attention than the impact of student involvement on educational outcomes. An examination of the student affairs and higher education literature reveals an enormous amount of research that has either explored the topic of student involvement directly or used student involvement experiences as control variables in student outcomes studies (Pascarella & Terenzini, 1991, 2005). Overwhelmingly, the weight of evidence examining student involvement has suggested that participation in student activities and campus organizations enhances students' learning outcomes, cognitive development, and intellectual orientations (Astin, 1984, 1985, 1993; Baxter Magolda, 1992; Chickering & Reisser, 1993; Hernandez, Hogan, Hathaway, & Lovell, 1999; Moore, Lovell, McGann, & Wyrick, 1998; Terenzini, Pascarella, & Blimling, 1996; Terenzini, Springer, Pascarella, & Nora, 1995; Williams & Winston, 1985). Moore et al. (1998) completed a comprehensive literature review of the research on the impact of student involvement on college students and noted, "student involvement does indeed have an impact on student learning and development. Additionally, we found that the type of student involvement matters" (p. 14). This study is a prime example of the accumulated research on this topic that underscores the importance of student involvement for college students.

Research specifically examining African American student involvement has also appeared in the student affairs and higher education research literature over the years. For example, DeSousa and King (1992) found that African American and White students differed in small ways in terms of their campus involvement levels. This finding was later supported by McKay and Kuh (1994), who examined data from 12 postsecondary institutions on African American and White students who completed the College Student Experiences Questionnaire (CSEQ).

They found that student involvement levels did not differ for African American and White students. In contrast to the two previously cited studies, Watson and Kuh (1996) analyzed survey data from 799 African American and White students from four private institutions (i.e., two historically Black and two predominantly White institutions) and found that African American students at historically Black and predominantly White institutions were more likely to participate in campus-sponsored organizations than were White students.

Studies exploring the factors that impact African American student involvement have provided an additional understanding of the personal and institutional characteristics and/or experiences that enhance and detract from student involvement (Mitchell & Dell, 1992; Sutton & Kimbrough, 2001; Taylor & Howard-Hamilton, 1995). Overall, these research studies have suggested that African American student involvement is influenced by precollege characteristics, college racial composition, and students' college experiences. For example, Mitchell and Dell (1992) and Taylor and Howard-Hamilton (1995) found that involvement levels for African American students were influenced by their self-perceptions of racial identity, awareness, and self-concept. A small body of research has also sought to understand the effects of African American student involvement on students' educational outcomes. For example, McKay and Kuh (1994) found that African American student involvement that focused on academic-related experiences (e.g., using the library, experiences with faculty, and course learning experiences) yielded significant and positive effects for African American students in terms of understanding literature, philosophy, the arts, gains in intellectual and writing skills, and gains in vocational preparation. McKay and Kuh also found that African American students who were more involved in activities that centered on personal interactions with others (e.g., experiences with student acquaintances and friends) achieved higher gains on measures of personal and social development. Additionally, DeSousa and Kuh (1996) found that African American students who were involved in academic experiences on campus accrued significantly higher gains in critical thinking, understanding in science and technology, and vocational skills. Recently, Littleton (2002) analyzed qualitative data from African American students attending a small liberal arts college and found that student involvement influences student retention.

While research comparing African American and White students' involvement levels has expanded our understanding of the influence of race on campus involvement, limited research has explored differences in involvement for African American students (Fleming, 1984; Sutton & Kimbrough, 2001). However, viewed collectively, this small line of research has suggested that African American students' participation levels in clubs and organizations differ by institutional type. Thus while we know that African American students' involvement levels differ by gender and institutional racial composition, and academic experiences in college, we do not know the extent to which African American student involvement levels change during college. Toward this end, the purpose of this chapter is to determine the extent to which African American students' involvement changed during their college years. The primary objective here is to report descriptive information pertaining to African American college students' involvement on campus by class level. A secondary objective is to discuss implications for student affairs professionals and institutional policy makers as well as cite recommendations for future research based on the results of the descriptive statistical analyses.

METHOD

Theoretical Foundation

Astin's (1984) theory of student involvement serves as the theoretical foundation for this research. According to Astin, "Student involvement refers to the amount of physical and psychological energy that the student devotes to the academic experience" (p. 297). In summary, Astin's theory of student involvement can be represented by the following propositions or tenets:

1. Involvement refers to the investment of physical and psychological energy in various objects. The objects may be highly generalized (the student experience) or highly specific (preparing for a chemistry examination).
2. Regardless of its object, involvement occurs along a continuum; that is, different students manifest different degrees of involvement in a given object, and the same student manifests different degrees of involvement in different objects at different times.
3. Involvement has both quantitative and qualitative features. The extent of a student's involvement in academic work, for instance, can be measured quantitatively (how many hours the student spends studying) and qualitatively (whether the student reviews and comprehends reading assignments or simply stares at the textbook and daydreams).
4. The amount of student learning and personal development associated with any educational program is directly proportional to the quality and quantity of student involvement in that program.
5. The effectiveness of any educational policy or practice is directly related to the capacity of that policy or practice to increase student involvement.

Since Astin's theory has been advanced, several research studies have explored the effects of student involvement on student development (Hernandez et al., 1999; Moore et al., 1998). For example, Williams and Winston

(1985) utilized data from 168 students attending a postsecondary institution in the Southeast and found that students who expended effort in campus organizations and campus activities reported higher development on measures of interdependence, understanding of the importance and relevance of the educational environment, and occupational aspirations. Also, Baxter Magolda (1992) analyzed data from a 4-year longitudinal investigation consisting of more than 100 students at a public institution and found that students who were involved in extracurricular activities and out-of-class activities gained significantly higher levels of cognitive development despite their differences in learning styles and intellectual orientations.

Data

The revised third edition of the CSEQ was the primary data source for this research. The CSEQ measured the frequency and extent of student involvement in various activities in college. Since the CSEQ contained self-reported information of students' intellectual and social gains made in college and had an extensive history of use in American colleges and universities (Bauer, 1995; Decoster, 1989; Kuh & Hu, 2001; Kuh, Pace, & Vesper, 1997; Kuh, Vesper, Connolly, & Pace, 1997; Pace, 1984), it was deemed an appropriate data source for the present research.

Student Sample

The student sample consisted of 5,821 African American students (3,706 females and 2,115 males) from 212 postsecondary institutions who participated in the CSEQ data collection between 1990 and 2000. The sample consisted of 3,787 freshmen (65%) and 2,034 seniors (35%). Eighteen percent of the sample attended a historically Black institution, and 82% of the sample attended a predominantly White institution. There were 11 historically Black institutions and 201 predominantly White institutions included in the institutional sample.

Variables

In order to assess the extent to which African American student involvement changes during the college years, this research examined whether African American college freshmen and African American college seniors reported different levels of involvement in college as measured by the following CSEQ scales: Library Experiences, Experiences with Faculty, Course Learning, Art,

Music, and Theater, Student Union, Athletic and Recreation Facilities, Clubs and Organizations, and Personal Experiences. The Library Experiences scale measured students' involvement with the local or college library and their extent of interaction with library resources (e.g., they used the library as a quiet place to read or study the materials brought with them). The Experiences with Faculty scale assessed students' interactions with faculty (e.g., they talked with a faculty member). The Course Learning scale measured students' level of effort to learn course information (e.g., they took detailed notes in class). The Art, Music, and Theater scale assessed students' level of involvement in artistic and musical events and activities on campus (e.g., they visited an art gallery or art exhibit on campus). The Student Union scale measured students' degree of use of the student union on campus (e.g., they had meals, snacks, etc. at the student union or student center).

The Athletic and Recreation Facilities scale assessed students' level of participation in wellness activities, intramural sports, and sporting events (e.g., they followed a regular schedule of exercise or practice of some sport on campus). The Clubs and Organization scale measured students' level of participation in campus-based student groups (e.g., they attended a meeting of a club, an organization, or a student government group). The Personal Experiences scale assessed students' level of effort used to understand themselves as well as others (e.g., they have been in a group where everyone, including themselves, talked about their personal problems). Each CSEQ involvement scale had a response set comprised of 4-Likert type scale choices: 4 = very often, 3 = often, 2 = occasionally, and 1 = never. In the present research, the alpha reliabilities for the eight CSEQ involvement scales were the following: Library Experiences scale (.84), Experiences with Faculty scale (.88), Course Learning scale (.86), Art, Music, and Theater scale (.87), Student Union scale (.89), Athletic and Recreation Facilities scale (.91), Clubs and Organizations scale (.92), and Personal Experiences scale (.85).

RESULTS

Means and standard deviations were reported, by class level (freshmen and senior), for each item from the following CSEQ involvement scales: Library Experiences, Experiences with Faculty, Course Learning, Art, Music, and Theater, Student Union, Athletic and Recreation Facilities, Clubs and Organizations, and Personal Experiences (Kuh, Vesper, Connolly, & Pace, 1997). The differences between the freshmen and senior means (i.e., mean differences) were also reported for each item. All statistical results were reported significant at $p < .001$. Effect size estimates were computed by subtracting the freshmen mean scores from the senior mean scores and dividing the mean difference by the pooled standard deviation (Rosnow & Rosenthal, 1996). This effect size estimate measured (in standard deviation units) the practical significance of the mean differences.

Appendix A results show that freshmen and senior means differed on each item in the Library Experiences scale. In addition, seniors reported higher levels of library usage than did freshmen. The largest differences were reported by class levels for the following experiences: used the card catalogue or computer to find materials on a specific topic, used indexes (such as the Reader's Guide to Periodical Literature) to locate journal articles, developed a bibliography or set of references for use in a term paper or other report, and ran down leads and looked for further references cited in literature read. Effect size estimates for these four items were moderate in size, from .27 to .34.

Appendix B reveals that significant differences were reported for freshmen and seniors in terms of their experiences with faculty. The greatest variation in freshmen and seniors scores was reported on the following items: talked with a faculty member, visited informally and briefly with an instructor after class, made an appointment to meet with a faculty member in his or her office, discussed ideas for a term paper or other class project with a faculty member, discussed career plans and ambitions with a faculty member, had coffee, soda, or snacks with a faculty member, and worked with a faculty member on a research project. In terms of practical significance, effect size estimates for these items ranged from .26 to .42. Freshmen and senior African American students' course learning experiences were also significantly different. Appendix C shows that African American seniors were more likely than African American freshmen to report that they underlined major points in the readings, tried to see how different facts and ideas fit together, thought about practical applications of the material, and worked on a paper or project where ideas had to be integrated from various sources. The effect size estimates for these involvement experiences ranged from .26 to .40.

Appendix D reveals that several items related to experiences with art, music, and theater resulted in significant differences between freshmen and seniors; however, the magnitude of the effect size estimates was small. The only exception was the involvement item, which assessed the extent to which students visited an art gallery or art exhibit. For this item, the difference was moderate in value. African American students' experiences in the student union are found in Appendix E, where data show that African American freshmen reported significantly higher experiences in the student union than did African American seniors with respect to eating meals, attending social events, and playing games in the union. Effect size estimates for these items suggested that these differences were small. Appendix F also shows that African American freshmen reported significantly higher involvement with athletic and recreation facilities in college. Specifically, African American freshmen were more likely to set goals for their performance in some skills and used facilities in the gym for playing sports requiring more than one person. Again, effect size estimates indicated that the practical significance of these noteworthy differences was small and trivial.

Results from Appendix G indicated that African American seniors reported greater involvement and participation in clubs and organizations. For each item, all mean differences were statistically significant. More specifically, African American seniors were more likely to report that they voted in a student election, worked in some student organization or special project (a publication, student government, a social event, etc.), discussed reasons for the success or lack of success of student club meetings, activities, or events, worked on a committee, and met with a faculty adviser or an administrator to discuss the activities of a student organization. These effect size estimates were moderate (.34 to .43), suggesting that these differences were also practically significant and suggestive of substantive differences in involvement levels. Appendix H shows that only two involvement items assessing students' personal experiences resulted in significant differences between freshmen and seniors. African American seniors were more likely to report that they had elected a course that dealt with understanding personal and social behavior and read articles or books about personal adjustment and personality development. However, the effect size estimates were small for these items.

DISCUSSION

Remarking on the state of the research literature on student involvement, Moore et al. (1998), stated:

> It is imperative that the body of literature regarding student involvement continues to be developed and utilized. This research should be a factor in how universities approach program development, assessment, and budgeting issues. Further study and research will help professionals to impact students in a positive and effective manner. (p. 15)

Utilizing a similar frame of mind, I argue that more research is needed to explore African American student involvement. Along those lines, previous research examining the levels of student involvement for African American students has pointed to several individual background characteristics and various institutional integration experiences that support or hamper African American student development (Flowers & Pascarella, 2003; McKay & Kuh, 1994; Nettles, Thoeny, & Gosman, 1986; Sampel & Seymour, 1971; White, 1988; Wolfle, 1983). Taken as a whole, this line of research suggests that African American student involvement is impacted by gender, institutional type (e.g., attending a historically Black institution or predominantly White institution), perceptions of the campus climate, class level, and college major.

Among the 82 separate student involvement items used to determine the impact of class level on African American student involvement, only two of these items yielded a mean above a 3 for the freshmen students. Similarly, only six of the items yielded a mean above a 3 for seniors. These results indicate that African American students' participation levels were low to moderate across the 10-year period for which data were available. Based on Cohen's (1988) guidelines for evaluating the magnitude of effect size estimates, data in this study suggest that the practical significance of the statistical findings was also small to moderate. For example, of all of the effect size estimates calculated for this research, the highest value was .43. This evidence suggests that African American freshmen and senior involvement levels are fairly similar. Moreover, the effect size estimates indicate that during the college years, African American students' involvement does not change very much during their time on campus.

Implications for Higher Education and Student Affairs Practice

A conceptual model of African American student involvement is presented in Figure 4.1. The conceptual model is based on research that documents the impact of precollege factors on student outcomes and student development (Astin, 1993; Chickering & Reisser, 1993; Pascarella & Terenzini, 1991, 2005). The conceptual model also incorporates research that suggests that African American students experience college differently from other students and may encounter problematic social challenges on campus that may impact their retention in school and their educational experiences in college, such as their participation in academic and nonacademic activities and their involvement with institutional representatives (e.g., faculty and advisors) (Ancis, Sedlacek, & Mohr, 2000; Cabrera, Nora, Terenzini, Pascarella, & Hagedorn, 1999; Cooper, 1997; Cuyjet, 1998; Feagin, Vera, & Imani, 1996; Holmes, Ebbers, Robinson, & Mugenda, 2000-2001; Schwitzer, Griffin, Ancis, & Thomas, 1999; Solórzano, Ceja, & Yosso, 2000). Students' academic experiences (e.g., grade point average and college major) and social experiences (e.g., campus residence and work status) have also been included in the conceptual model based on several research studies exploring the impact of college on student development (Astin, 1993; Pascarella, 1985; Pascarella & Terenzini, 1991; Terenzini, Pascarella, & Blimling, 1996; Terenzini, Springer, Pascarella, & Nora, 1995; Terenzini & Wright, 1987; Tinto, 1993). Thus overall the conceptual model of

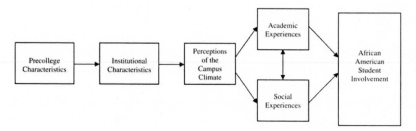

FIGURE 4.1   Conceptual Model of African American Student Involvement

African American student involvement indicates that the following categories of variables may influence the nature, magnitude, and extent of African American student involvement on campus: precollege characteristics; institutional characteristics; perceptions of the campus climate; academic experiences; and social experiences.

In recent years, student affairs researchers and professionals have been interested in learning how to design programs, implement services, and assess program performance to facilitate students' intellectual and affective development in college (Astin, 1985, 1991; Kuh, 1996, 1999; Kuh et al., 1991; Upcraft & Schuh, 1996). To further provide a systematic model that might assist student affairs professionals in creating and/or improving programs and services that support the increased involvement of African American students on campus, the conceptual model of African American student involvement may be used as a heuristic tool for student affairs researchers and student affairs professionals interested in better understanding the role of student affairs programs and services in promoting African American student involvement.

The conceptual model of African American student involvement indicates that the primary variable under the direct influence of student affairs professionals is the campus climate. While some might argue that students' perceptions of the campus climate are influenced by a variety of institutional images, students' interactions on campus, as well as students' classroom experiences and therefore student affairs professionals, may be ill equipped to facilitate positive campus climate perceptions; I would submit that student affairs professionals are in a great position to improve African American students' perceptions of the campus climate. This assertion is promulgated based on the fact that student affairs professionals represent a diverse group of advisors, counselors, and leaders from a variety of offices, divisions, program areas, and locations on campus. Thus student affairs professionals are virtually a part of most offices and instructional units on campus. As a result, the number of student affairs offices on college and university campuses ensures that all students will encounter at least one student affairs professional during their college career. As such, I contend that if higher education and student affairs professionals reflected on their role to impact the lives of all students in a positive way, they would be more likely to recognize that when they have the opportunity to meet or interact with African American students they should make the most of the experiences to ensure that African American students will leave their environment, intervention, and/or service saying, "Wow, that was a very helpful and beneficial experience." As a self-assessment tool, student affairs professionals should ask themselves, following an experience with an African American student: (1) Was the interaction meaningful? (2) Did I do everything in my power to assist this student? (3) Did I make use of all of the knowledge, skills, and talents I possess to assist this African American student in accomplishing his or her desired task? (4) What can I do next time to improve my interactions with an African American student? Responses to these questions, if posed after an experience with an African American student, will assist student affairs professionals in better serving this population and also help improve African American students' perceptions of the campus climate.

IMPLICATIONS FOR HIGHER EDUCATION AND STUDENT AFFAIRS POLICY

In light of the findings, the following recommendations are suggested for student affairs offices interested in developing policies to take into account African American students' experiences on college campuses:

1. Focus retention efforts on making African American students aware of the various student involvement experiences (e.g., student organizations, faculty experiences) that exist on campus for their development. Related to this recommendation is the view that student affairs professionals should communicate to students the potential reported effects of participation in certain activities on their academic and social development. This will require an understanding of the higher education and student affairs research literature on this topic. The reference section at the end of this chapter provides an excellent initial reading list to assist higher education and student affairs professionals in this regard.

2. Initiate exploratory data analyses to collect information on African American students' out-of-class experiences and related outcomes. This data collection system can be established using the following model:

    Phase 1—Assessment: Assess African American students' out-of-class experiences to determine the type of experiences African American students have on campus as well as the quality of those experiences. Also, be sure to assess African American students' perceptions of the campus climate.

Phase 2—Implementation: Based on the information obtained in Phase 1, develop appropriate plans to increase African American student involvement on campus or enhance the quality of those experiences, depending on the results of the data analyses.

Phase 3—Follow-up: This process includes reexamining initial data as well as collecting additional information needed to improve decision making to enhance African American college student development.

Phase 4—Modification: In this phase, programs and services are remodeled and reformed to maximize African American college s tudent development.

RECOMMENDATIONS FOR FUTURE RESEARCH

This chapter contains limitations that may reduce the strength of the findings. As a result, additional research is needed to address the limitations of the study as well as to provide more data that will help higher education and student affairs professionals and university administrators in improving the quality of life for African American students on campus. For example, though the study utilized institutional data from a variety of postsecondary institutions, future research studies should also focus on single campuses. Thus institutional and student affairs researchers are encouraged to analyze differences in student involvement for African American students (as well as other underrepresented students) by class level to ensure that these students are taking full advantage of campus services and related programs. Another limitation of this study focused on the absence of statistical controls for important background variables and college experiences (Pascarella, 2001). Thus future research on this topic might consider the impact of gender, precollege academic ability, precollege student involvement, and/or college major on African American student involvement. Moreover, future research should focus on providing statistical information pertaining to the net effects of student involvement on African American students' educational outcomes. Also, future research, employing a multi-institutional sample, which explores the impact of college racial composition (i.e., attending a historically Black college or predominantly White college) on African American student involvement, would also add to our understanding of the effects of college on African American student involvement. Furthermore, future research should also analyze or test the effectiveness of the proposed conceptual model of African American student involvement to explain African American students' participation in student involvement and the quality of those college experiences.

References

Ancis, J. R., Sedlacek, W. E., & Mohr, J. J. (2000). Student perceptions of campus cultural climate by race. *Journal of Counseling & Development, 78*, 180–185.

Astin, A. W. (1984). Student involvement: A developmental theory for higher education. *Journal of College Student Personnel, 25*, 297–308.

Astin, A. W. (1985). Involvement: The cornerstone of excellence. *Change, 17*(4), 35–39.

Astin, A. W. (1991). *Assessment for excellence: The philosophy and practice of assessment and evaluation in higher education.* New York: Macmillan.

Astin, A. W. (1993). *What matters in college?: Four critical years revisited.* San Francisco: Jossey-Bass.

Bauer, K. W. (1995). Freshman to senior year gains reported on the College Student Experiences Questionnaire. *NASPA Journal, 32*, 130–137.

Baxter Magolda, M. B. (1992). Cocurricular influences on college students' intellectual development. *Journal of College Student Development, 33*, 203–213.

Cabrera, A. F., Nora, A., Terenzini, P. T., Pascarella, E. T., & Hagedorn, L. S. (1999). Campus racial climate and the adjustment of students to college: A comparison between White students and African-American students. *Journal of Higher Education, 70*, 134–160.

Chickering, A. W., & Reisser, L. (1993). *Education and identity* (2nd ed.). San Francisco: Jossey-Bass.

Cohen, J. (1988). *Statistical power analysis for the behavioral sciences* (2nd ed.). Hillsdale, NJ: Lawrence Earlbaum Associates.

Cooper, J. (1997). Marginality, mattering, and the African American student: Creating an inclusive college environment. *College Student Affairs Journal, 16*(2), 15–20.

Cuyjet, M. J. (1998). Recognizing and addressing marginality among African American college students. *College Student Affairs Journal, 18*, 64–71.

Decoster, D. A. (1989). [Review of the College Student Experiences Questionnaire]. In J. C. Conoley & J. J. Kramer (Eds.), *The tenth mental measurements yearbook* (pp. 197–199). Lincoln, NE: Buros Institute of Mental Measurements.

DeSousa, J. D., & King, P. M. (1992). Are White students really more involved in collegiate experiences than Black students? *Journal of College Student Development, 33*, 363–369.

DeSousa, J. D., & Kuh, G. D. (1996). Does institutional racial composition make a difference in hat Black students gain from college? *Journal of College Student Development, 37*, 257–267.

Feagin, J. R., Vera, H., & Imani, N. (1996). *The agony of education: Black students at White colleges and universities.* New York: Routledge.

Fleming, J. (1984). *Blacks in college: A comparative study of students' success in Black and White institutions.* San Francisco: Jossey Bass.

Flowers, L. A., & Pascarella, E. T. (2003). Cognitive effects of college: Differences between African American and Caucasian students. *Research in Higher Education, 44,* 21–49.

Hernandez, K., Hogan, S., Hathaway, C., & Lovell, C. D. (1999). Analysis of the literature on the impact of student involvement on student development and learning: More questions than answers? *NASPA Journal, 36,* 184–197.

Holmes, S. L., Ebbers, L. H., Robinson, D. C., & Mugenda, A. G. (2000–2001). Validating African American students at predominantly White institutions. *Journal of College Student Retention, 2,* 41–58.

Kuh, G. D. (1996). Guiding principles for creating seamless learning environments for undergraduates. *Journal of College Student Development, 37,* 135–148.

Kuh, G. D. (1999). How are we doing?: Tracking the quality of the undergraduate experience, 1960s to the present. *The Review of Higher Education, 22,* 99–119.

Kuh, G. D., & Hu, S. (2001). The effects of student-faculty interaction in the 1990s. *The Review of Higher Education, 24,* 309–332.

Kuh, G. D., Pace, C. R., & Vesper, N. (1997). The development of process indicators to estimate student gains associated with good practices in undergraduate education. *Research in Higher Education, 38,* 435–454.

Kuh, G. D., Schuh, J. H., Whitt, E. J., Andreas, R. E., Lyons, J. W., Strange, C. C., et al. (1991). *Involving colleges.* San Francisco: Jossey-Bass.

Kuh, G. D., Vesper, N., Connolly, M. R., & Pace, C. R. (1997). *College Student Experiences Questionnaire: Revised norms for the third edition.* Bloomington: Indiana University, Center for Postsecondary Research and Planning.

Littleton, R. A. (2002). Campus involvement among African American students at small predominantly White colleges. *College Student Affairs Journal, 21*(2), 53–67.

McKay, K. A., & Kuh, G. D. (1994). A comparison of student effort and educational gains of Caucasian and African-American students at predominantly White colleges and universities. *Journal of College Student Development, 35,* 217–223.

Mitchell, S., & Dell, D. (1992). The relationship between Black students' racial identity attitude and participation in campus organizations. *Journal of College Student Development, 33,* 39–43.

Moore, J., Lovell, C. D., McGann, T., & Wyrick, J. (1998). Why involvement matters: A review of research on student involvement in the collegiate setting. *College Student Affairs Journal, 17*(2), 4–17.

Nettles, M. T., Thoeny, A. R., & Gosman, E. J. (1986). Comparative and predictive analyses of Black and White students' college achievement and experiences. *Journal of Higher Education, 57,* 289–318.

Pace, C. R. (1984). *Measuring the quality of college student experiences: An account of the development and use of the College Student Experiences Questionnaire.* Los Angeles: University of California, Higher Education Research Institute, Graduate School of Education.

Pascarella, E. T. (1985). College environmental influences on learning and cognitive development: A critical review and synthesis. In J. C. Smart (Ed.), *Higher education: Handbook of theory and research* (Vol. 1, pp. 1–61). New York: Agathon Press.

Pascarella, E. T. (2001). Using student self-reported gains to estimate college impact: A cautionary tale. *Journal of College Student Development, 42*, 488–492.

Pascarella, E. T., & Terenzini, P. T. (1991). *How college affects students: Findings and insights from twenty years of research.* San Francisco: Jossey-Bass.

Pascarella, E. T., & Terenzini, P. T. (2005). How college affects students: a third track of research. San Francisco, CA: Jossey-Bass.

Rosnow, R. L., & Rosenthal, R. (1996). Computing contrasts, effect sizes, and counternulls on other people's published data: General procedures for research consumers. *Psychological Methods, 1*, 331–340.

Sampel, D. D., & Seymour, W. R. (1971). The academic success of Black students: A dilemma. *Journal of College Student Personnel, 12*, 243–247.

Schwitzer, A. M., Griffin, O. T., Ancis, J. R., & Thomas, C. R. (1999). Social adjustment experiences of African American college students. *Journal of Counseling & Development, 77*, 189–197.

Solórzano, D., Ceja, M., & Yosso, T. (2000). Critical race theory, racial microaggressions, and campus racial climate: The experiences of African American college students. *Journal of Negro Education, 69*, 60–73.

Sutton, E. M., & Kimbrough, W. M. (2001). Trends in Black student involvement. *NASPA Journal, 39*, 30–40.

Taylor, C. M., & Howard-Hamilton, M. F. (1995). Student involvement and racial identity attitudes among African American males. *Journal of College Student Development, 36*, 330–336.

Terenzini, P. T., Pascarella, E. T., & Blimling, G. S. (1996). Students' out-of-class experiences and their influence on learning and cognitive development: A literature review. *Journal of College Student Development, 37*, 149–162.

Terenzini, P. T., Springer, L., Pascarella, E. T., & Nora, A. (1995). Influences affecting the development of students' critical thinking skills. *Research in Higher Education, 36*, 23–39.

Terenzini, P. T., & Wright, T. M. (1987). Influences on students' academic growth during four years of college. *Research in Higher Education, 26*, 161–179.

Tinto, V. (1993). *Leaving college: Rethinking the causes and cures of student attrition* (2nd ed.). Chicago: University of Chicago Press.

Upcraft, M. L., & Schuh, J. H. (1996). *Assessment in student affairs: A guide for practitioners.* San Francisco: Jossey-Bass.

Watson, L. E., & Kuh, G. D. (1996). The influence of dominant race environments on student involvement, perceptions, and educational gains: A look at historically Black and predominantly White liberal arts institutions. *Journal of College Student Development, 37*, 415–424.

White, C. L. (1988). Ethnic identity and academic performance among Black and White college students: An interactionist approach. *Urban Education, 23*, 219–240.

Williams, M., & Winston, R. B., Jr. (1985). Participation in organized student activities and work: Differences in developmental task achievement of traditional-aged college students. *NASPA Journal, 22*(3), 52–57.

Wolfle, L. M. (1983). Effects of higher education on achievement for Blacks and Whites. *Research in Higher Education, 19*, 3–9.

Means, Standard Deviations, Mean Differences, and Effect Sizes of African American Students' Library Experiences in College

Library Experiences	Mean		Standard Deviation		Mean Difference	Effect Size
	Freshmen	Seniors	Freshmen	Seniors		
Used the library as a quiet place to read or study materials brought in	2.23	2.34	.89	.91	.11*	.12
Used the card catalogue or computer to find materials on a specific topic	2.48	2.74	.96	.91	.26*	.27
Asked the librarian for help finding material on a specific topic	2.19	2.32	.88	.83	.13*	.15
Read something in the reserve book room or reference section	1.90	2.10	.87	.89	.20*	.23
Used indexes (such as the Reader's Guide to Periodical Literature) to locate journal articles	1.91	2.21	.87	.91	.30*	.34
Developed a bibliography or set of references for use in a term paper or other report	2.29	2.59	.96	.93	.30*	.31
Found some interesting material to read just by browsing in the stacks	1.93	2.09	.91	.92	.16*	.17
Ran down leads, looked for further references that were cited in things read	1.75	1.98	.83	.86	.23*	.27
Returned to read a basic reference or document to which other authors had often referred	1.56	1.70	.76	.77	.14*	.18
Checked out books read (not textbooks) to read	1.94	2.14	.94	.96	.20*	.21

*$p < .001$

APPENDIX B

Means, Standard Deviations, Mean Differences, and Effect Sizes of African American Students' Experiences with Faculty in College

Experiences with Faculty	Mean		Standard Deviation		Mean Difference	Effect Size
	Freshmen	Seniors	Freshmen	Seniors		
Talked with a faculty member	2.71	3.07	.84	.81	.36*	.42
Asked instructor for information related to a course (grades, makeup work, assignments, etc.)	2.68	2.89	.85	.83	.21*	.25
Visited informally and briefly with an instructor after class	2.29	2.55	.84	.87	.26*	.30
Made an appointment to meet with a faculty member in his or her office	2.21	2.48	.86	.86	.27*	.31
Discussed ideas for a term paper or other class project with a faculty member	2.13	2.41	.88	.85	.28*	.32
Discussed career plans and ambitions with a faculty member	1.97	2.30	.87	.92	.33*	.37
Asked instructor for comments and criticism about work	2.08	2.23	.89	.90	.15*	.17
Had coffee, soda, or snacks with a faculty member	1.27	1.46	.61	.73	.19*	.29
Worked with a faculty member on a research project	1.23	1.40	.58	.77	.17*	.26
Discussed personal problems or concerns with a faculty member	1.48	1.64	.76	.82	.16*	.20

*$p < .001$

APPENDIX C

Means, Standard Deviations, Mean Differences, and Effect Sizes of African American Students' Course Learning Experiences in College

	Mean		Standard Deviation		Mean Difference	Effect Size
Course Learning Experiences	Freshmen	Seniors	Freshmen	Seniors		
Took detailed notes in class	3.39	3.47	.73	.69	.08*	.11
Participated in class discussions	2.91	3.05	.84	.81	.14*	.17
Underlined major points in the readings	3.01	3.23	.86	.81	.22*	.26
Tried to see how different facts and ideas fit together	2.75	3.04	.85	.79	.29*	.35
Thought about practical applications of the material	2.57	2.91	.86	.81	.34*	.40
Worked on a paper or project where ideas had to be integrated from various sources	2.70	3.06	.90	.83	.36*	.40
Summarized major points and information in readings or notes	2.79	2.99	.86	.85	.20*	.23
Tried to explain the materials to another student or friend	2.79	2.89	.84	.80	.10*	.12
Made outlines from class notes or readings	2.37	2.47	.99	.98	.10*	.10
Did additional readings on topics introduced and discussed in class	2.02	2.15	.89	.88	.13*	.15

*p < .001

APPENDIX D

Means, Standard Deviations, Mean Differences, and Effect Sizes of African American Students' Experiences with Art, Music, and Theater in College

Experiences with Art, Music, and Theater	Mean		Standard Deviation		Mean Difference	Effect Size
	Freshmen	Seniors	Freshmen	Seniors		
Talked about art (painting, sculpture, architecture, artists, etc.) with other students at the college	1.61	1.76	.81	.82	.15*	.18
Visited an art gallery or art exhibit on campus	1.43	1.62	.68	.73	.19*	.27
Read or discussed the opinions of art critics	1.26	1.36	.59	.64	.10*	.16
Participated in some art activity (painting, pottery, weaving, drawing, etc.)	1.31	1.41	.69	.72	.10*	.14
Talked about music (classical, popular, etc.) with other students at the college	2.35	2.34	1.07	.99	−.01	−.01
Attended a concert or other music events at the college	1.87	1.98	.95	.91	.11*	.12
Read or discussed the opinions of music critics	1.46	1.49	.78	.76	.03	.04
Participated in some music activity (orchestra, chorus, etc.)	1.47	1.45	.91	.86	−.02	−.02
Talked about the theater (plays, musicals, dance, etc.) with other students at the college	1.73	1.80	.88	.84	.07	.08
Attended a play, ballet, or other theater performance at the college	1.64	1.82	.85	.85	.18*	.21
Read or discussed the opinions of drama critics	1.30	1.34	.64	.65	.04	.06
Participated in or worked on some theatrical production (acted, danced, worked on scenery, etc.)	1.26	1.33	.67	.70	.07*	.10

*$p < .001$

APPENDIX E

Means, Standard Deviations, Mean Differences, and Effect Sizes of African American Students' Experiences in the Student Union in College

Experiences in the Student Union	Mean		Standard Deviation		Mean Difference	Effect Size
	Freshmen	Seniors	Freshmen	Seniors		
Had meals, snacks, etc. at the student union or student center	2.62	2.51	1.09	1.00	−.11*	−.10
Looked at the bulletin board for notices about campus events	2.81	2.75	.94	.92	−.06	−.06
Met friends at the student union or student center	2.58	2.52	1.08	1.04	−.06	−.06
Sat around in the union or center talking with other students about classes and other college activities	2.42	2.41	1.08	1.05	−.01	−.01
Used the lounge(s) to relax or study alone	2.11	2.06	1.06	1.01	−.05	−.05
Attended a film or other event at the union or other center in the residence hall	1.92	1.85	.98	.92	−.07	−.07
Attended social events in the student union or center	2.24	2.12	.99	.96	−.12*	−.12
Heard a speaker at the student union or center	1.87	1.88	.92	.88	.01	.01
Played games that were available in the student union or center (ping-pong, cards, pool, pinball, etc.)	1.92	1.74	1.00	.91	−.18*	−.18
Used the lounge(s) or meeting rooms to meet with a group of students for a discussion	1.83	1.98	.97	.97	.15*	.15

*$p < .001$

Means, Standard Deviations, Mean Differences, and Effect Sizes of African American Students'
Experiences with Athletic and Recreation Facilities in College

Experiences with Athletic and Recreation Facilities	Mean		Standard Deviation		Mean Difference	Effect Size
	Freshmen	Seniors	Freshmen	Seniors		
Set goals for performance in some skills	2.48	2.33	1.08	1.07	−.15*	.14
Followed a regular schedule of exercise or practice in some sport on campus	2.16	2.13	1.07	1.06	−.03	−.03
Used outdoor recreational spaces for casual and informal *individual* athletic activities	1.81	1.84	.98	.96	.03	.03
Used outdoor recreational spaces for casual and informal *group* sports	1.75	1.72	.96	.93	−.03	−.03
Used facilities in the gym for individual activities (exercise, swimming, etc.)	2.17	2.10	1.08	1.05	−.07	−.07
Used facilities in the gym for playing sports requiring more than one person	1.97	1.85	1.10	1.05	−.12*	−.11
Sought instruction to improve performance in some athletic activity	1.73	1.67	1.02	.96	−.06	−.06
Played on an intramural team	1.52	1.52	.95	.92	.00	.00
Kept a chart or record of progress in some skill or athletic activity	1.45	1.46	.86	.82	.01	.01
Was a spectator at college athletic events	2.40	2.35	1.13	1.09	−.05	−.04

*$p < .001$

APPENDIX G

Means, Standard Deviations, Mean Differences, and Effect Sizes of African American Students' Participation and Involvement in Clubs and Organizations College

Participation and Involvement in Clubs and Organizations	Mean		Standard Deviation		Mean Difference	Effect Size
	Freshmen	Seniors	Freshmen	Seniors		
Looked in the student newspaper for notices about campus events and student organizations	2.35	2.48	.99	.95	.13*	.13
Attended a program or an event put on by a student group	2.31	2.41	.97	.96	.10*	.10
Read or asked about a club, an organization, or a student government activity	2.22	2.31	.94	.91	.09*	.10
Attended a meeting of a club, an organization, or a student government group	2.09	2.35	1.05	1.09	.26*	.24
Voted in a student election	1.93	2.29	1.03	1.08	.36*	.34
Discussed policies and issues related to campus activities and student government	1.80	2.03	.89	.95	.23*	.25
Worked in some student organization or special project (publication, student government, social event, etc.)	1.68	2.07	.96	1.13	.39*	.38
Discussed reasons for the success or lack of success of student club meetings, activities, or events	1.74	2.07	.92	1.04	.33*	.34
Worked on a committee	1.57	2.01	.92	1.11	.44*	.43
Met with a faculty advisor or an administrator to discuss the activities of a student organization	1.44	1.80	.80	1.01	.36*	.40

*p < .001

Means, Standard Deviations, Mean Differences, and Effect Sizes of African American Students' Personal Experiences in College

Personal Experiences	Mean		Standard Deviation		Mean Difference	Effect Size
	Freshmen	Seniors	Freshmen	Seniors		
Told a friend why you reacted to another person the way you did	2.89	2.87	.95	.94	-.02	-.02
Discussed with other students why some groups get along smoothly and other groups do not	2.65	2.72	1.00	1.00	.07	.07
Sought out a friend to help with a personal problem	2.60	2.60	1.05	1.01	.00	.00
Elected a course that dealt with understanding personal and social behavior	1.97	2.25	.97	1.03	.28*	.28
Identified with a character in a book or movie and wondered what you might have done under similar circumstances	2.49	2.47	.98	.96	-.02	-.02
Read articles or books about personal adjustment and personality development	2.05	2.21	.95	.96	.16*	.17
Took a test to measure your abilities, interests, or attitudes	2.11	2.08	.92	.90	-.03	-.03
Asked a friend to tell you what he or she really thought about you	2.22	2.16	1.01	.98	-.06	-.06
Was in a group where each person, including yourself, talked about his or her personal problems	2.11	2.09	1.03	1.01	-.02	-.02
Talked with a counselor or other specialist about problems of a personal nature	1.51	1.51	.83	.83	.00	.00

*p < .001

Chapter 5

The Status of African American Faculty in the Academy

Where Do we Go from Here?

Barbara J. Johnson and Henrietta Pichon

Understandably, the time has come to address the educational pipeline from which African American faculty emerge (Cole & Barber, 2003; Turner & Myers, 2000). To date, little progress has been made in increasing the number of African American faculty in the academy. For example, from fall 1987 to fall 1998, African American faculty grew by only 1.9%, from 3% to 4.9%, respectively (National Center for Education Statistics [hereafter NCES], 1997, 2001). Perhaps one reason for the underrepresentation of African American faculty is the limited number of African Americans entering doctoral programs and subsequently electing to pursue a career in the professoriate (Austin, 2002; Cole & Barber, 2003; Turner & Myers, 2000). Additionally, barriers encountered in the promotion and tenure process may hinder the recruitment and retention of African American faculty (Austin, 2002; Turner & Myers, 2000). Moreover, salary disparities, isolation, stress, and racism are just a few of the obstacles that may preclude African Americans from advancing in the educational pipeline to faculty positions (Aguirre, 2000; Boice, 1992; Thomas, 2002; Turner & Myers, 2000). Furthermore, the amount of research relative to African American faculty remains limited (Johnson & Harvey, 2002).

The few studies that do exist tend to treat minority faculty members as one group, which often results in a situation of African American faculty being obscured. Consequently, this chapter refers to a number of studies regarding minority faculty as a whole, as the research studies focusing solely on African American faculty were sparse. This chapter will focus on gaining insight into the factors that impede the representation of African American faculty in the educational pipeline, including the experiences of African American graduate students and faculty at predominantly White institutions (PWIs) and historically Black colleges and universities (HBCUs). In addition, this chapter will provide a detailed analysis of the implications for policy, practice, and research.

REPRESENTATION IN THE ACADEMY

In considering the potential for African American faculty, doctoral program completion rates must be examined. As noted by the National Center for Educational Statistics (NCES, 2001), significant shifts have occurred in the number of doctoral degrees conferred by degree-granting institutions. In 1991, of the 39,294 degrees conferred, only 3.2% (1,248) were earned by African Americans. Ten years later, in 2001, of the 44,904 doctoral degrees conferred, 4.9% (2,207) of the recipients were African American, a 1.7% increase. Contrary to that, White students earned 65.8% of doctoral degrees in 1991 and 61.1% of the degrees in 2001. The biggest increase in doctoral degree completion, 2%, was seen in Asian/Pacific Islanders, while Hispanics increased by 1.5% and Native Americans saw little change, 0.01%.

According to the National Center for Educational Statistics (NCES, 2001), there were approximately 590,937 full-time instructional faculty in degree-granting institutions for fall 1999; 64% were males and 36% were females. Adding to that, 13.9% of all full-time faculty were minorities, while 82.8% were White. A closer examination of the minority faculty revealed that African Americans comprised only 4.9% of full-time instructional faculty in degree-granting institutions, and other minority groups were equally sparse: 2.8% were Hispanic, 5.8% were Asian, and 0.4% were Native American (another 3.3% were resident aliens, or ethnicity was unknown). In an article published in *The Journal of Blacks in Higher Education*, Cross and Slater (2000) offer grim projections. It is estimated that it would "take more than two centuries before Blacks achieve a level of parity in faculty positions compared to the Black percentage of the total U.S. population" (p. 23). Thus we have a long way to go to achieve full representation in the academic pipeline.

Prompted by *Adams v. Richardson* (1973), many public institutions began to see a growth in minority faculty at PWIs (Johnson & Scafide, 2002). When determining the distribution of faculty across institutional type, the National Center for Educational Statistics (2001) found that African American faculty were highly represented in 2-year public, private liberal arts, and public comprehensive institutions versus public and private doctoral or research institutions. Adding to that, African Americans were highly represented in the lower ranks of the academic hierarchy. For example, in 1999, 17% of African Americans held the position of full professor, while 25% were associate professors, 33% were assistant professors, and 25% were represented among instructors, lecturers, and others. On the contrary, White faculty during the same time ranked accordingly: 32% professor, 24% associate professor, 21% assistant professor, and 23% were represented among instructors, lecturers, and others. Also, Hispanic faculty ranked accordingly: 25% professor, 19% associate professor, 24% assistant professor, and

32% other. Asian faculty ranked: 26% professor, 26% associate professor, 31% assistant professor, and 17% other. Even more surprising is that African American females are more highly represented as assistant professors, instructors, and others than their male counterparts (NCES, 2002).

Lower-ranked positions and the barriers experienced in the pursuit of promotion and tenure often manifest themselves economically. Clearly, when persons are prevented from advancing through the pipeline, they are unable to take advantage of the many rewards of prosperity, including job security, home ownership, cultural activities, and family. The average salary for full-time faculty in fall 1998 was $56,850, with a male average of $61,680 and a female average of $48,370 (NCES, 2002). The salary disparity between genders is also found across ethnicities. White males earned the most, on average, across ethnicities, while Asian females earned the most of all women. For example, White males, on average, earned $61,950, while White females earned $48,200. In contrast, African American males and females earned $53,640 and $46,870, respectively. Hispanic males earned $66,350 and females earned $46,860, and Asian males and females earned $58,990 and $54,690, respectively. Perhaps the low average salaries of African American males and females coupled with the increasing emphasis on publications serve as deterrents to African Americans who obtain the doctorate but opt to pursue careers outside of academia (Turner & Myers, 2000).

In analyzing the NCES 1999 data, researchers noted that full-time faculty members not on a tenure track made less money than those in a tenure track position (NEA Update, 2001). As salary is often correlated to tenure status, it is important to understand who has tenure. According to the NCES (2002), 54% of White faculty had tenure and another 17% were on a tenure track. Tenure and tenure track positions for minorities look promising: 44% of African American faculty held tenure and 26% were on tenure track; 49% of Hispanics held tenure and another 22% were on tenure track; and 49% of Asian faculty held tenure and another 30% were on tenure track.

Additionally, salary concerns may also be commensurate with academic disciplines (NCES, 2002). Whites (24.3%) and Asians (41.5%), also the most highly paid, were highly represented in the natural sciences and engineering, while African Americans (26.3%) and Native Americans (27.6%) were highly represented in the social sciences and education. Adding to that, Hispanics (28.8%) were highly represented in the humanities. It should also be noted that females, Hispanics, and African Americans were disproportionately underrepresented in the natural sciences and engineering disciplines.

While the focus of this chapter is on African American faculty, we feel it is crucial to devote some discussion to graduate students within the pipeline. We assert that without a corresponding increase in the number of African American graduate students who elect to pursue a career in the professoriate, the percentage of African American faculty will remain at its current level. Thus a discussion of the environment that African American graduate students encounter may provide further insight into experiences of African Americans within the educational pipeline.

GRADUATE STUDENTS

During 2001, the Council of Graduate Schools (CGS) reported that African Americans represented 10% (98,307) of the total enrollment of graduate students (CGS, 2004). The NCES reported that in 2001, African Americans received 2,207 (4.9%) of the doctoral degrees. Of the 4.9% of doctorates awarded to African Americans, HBCUs conferred doctoral degrees to 222 (10.5%) (NCES, 2001). Frierson (1990) asserts that the enrollment and graduation of African American graduate students are directly correlated to African American faculty. Hence, one could speculate that if the number of African American faculty increased, then more African American graduate students would consider the professoriate. However, it is not that simple, African American graduate students may experience barriers that hinder their pursuit of a faculty position.

Pruitt and Isaac (1995) note that the environment that minority graduate students encounter may be more stressful and less supportive than reported by White graduate students. Perhaps the low percentage of minority faculty available to advise minority graduate students may manifest itself when students face resistance and rejection from non-minority faculty members with no interest or frame of reference relative to the subject matter (Pruitt & Isaac, 1995). In addition, because of the underrepresentation of minority faculty, minority graduate students may not have had the mentoring and support to prepare them for a career in academia (Blackwell, 1989). Even more troubling is that some graduate programs operate from the informal norm of allowing only those who resemble the faculty entrance to the academic profession (Weidman, Twale, & Stein, 2001). The low percentage of African Americans in graduate schools results in relatively few individuals available for faculty positions. Therefore, it would seem that an obvious solution would be to increase the supply by encouraging persons of color to attain doctoral degrees, especially in those fields where their numbers are the smallest (e.g., science, math, and engineering). Opponents of the educational pipeline approach maintain that a greater supply will not remove the other barriers within academia that hinder institutional and individual efforts at promoting growth in African American faculty (Turner & Myers, 2000). Because of this, institutions should focus not only on increasing the number of African American graduate students but on the quality of the African American students' experiences.

FACULTY IN ACADEMIA

Higher education institutions are generally concerned with structural diversity, which is the numerical representation of women and people of different racial and ethnic groups (Hurtado, Milem, Clayton-Pedersen, & Allen, 1998). Research (Hurtado et al., 1998) confirms that institutions desiring to improve the campus climate for diversity must first increase the structural diversity of the institution. Increasing the structural diversity provides a "critical mass" of individuals from diverse social and cultural backgrounds interacting across racial and ethnic and gender groups (Johnson & Scafide, 2002). However, improving structural diversity alone will not enhance the environment that faculty encounter, specifically African American faculty. Moreover, with the multiple programs aimed at increasing the number of minority Ph.D.s, how can the continual underrepresentation of African American faculty be explained? One plausible explanation lies within the climate of the academic workplace, specifically at PWIs.

PREDOMINANTLY WHITE INSTITUTIONS
AND THE PIPELINE

Research has found that African American faculty experience the same problems as all new faculty, but the problems they encounter are exacerbated because of their status as minorities (Aguirre, 2000; Boice, 1993a, 1993b; Johnsrud, 1993; Johnsrud & Des Jarlais, 1994; Menges & Exum, 1983; Johnsrud & Sadao, 1998; Turner & Myers, 2000; Turner, 2002). Exum, Menges, Watkins, and Berglund (1984) found that barriers to the advancement of minority faculty included lack of collegial support, confusion about expectations, and lack of knowledge of norms and expectations until too late in the promotion and tenure process. Some common barriers that African American faculty may experience in the academy include isolation, stress, and racism.

Isolation

A common complaint of new faculty is the sense of isolation as a result of their exclusion from informal networks within academia (Boice, 1992; Sorcinelli, 1992). However, minority faculty often describe their experiences as marginalizing, indicating they feel as if they are second-class members of the academy (Aguirre, 2000; Boice 1993a, 1993b; Tack & Patitu, 1992). Further exacerbating the sense of isolation is that new African American faculty may not have had substantial mentoring as graduate students (Blackwell, 1989). Moreover, Finkelstein's (1984) study revealed that African Americans are likely to have been trained in the least prestigious universities, which may result in further alienation by colleagues, particularly at a research-oriented university. Consequently, minority faculty who have not been adequately trained or mentored may be overwhelmed about expectations and experience even greater feelings of alienation (Tierney & Bensimon, 1996).

In some departments, senior faculty believe that they have fulfilled their obligation to diversify once they have hired one minority faculty member. This legacy of tokenism may lead to the perception that minority faculty were hired under special admission and are not deserving or capable of the position (Alexander-Snow & Johnson, 1999; Turner & Myers, 2000). Thus White faculty may not view minority faculty as legitimate participants in the academy (Aguirre, 2000), thereby further increasing stress and perhaps resulting in greater isolation of faculty of color (Alexander-Snow & Johnson, 1999).

Stress

All new faculty experience stress related to workloads, feelings of isolation, lack of collegiality, balance between work and family, and the tenure process (Boice, 1992; Menges, 1999; Sorcinelli, 1992). Although minority faculty encounter similar stresses, there are visible differences, especially relative to the workload. For example, minority faculty informally advise and mentor minority students in addition to the required advising load while also serving on numerous departmental and institutional committees that want minority representation— all roles that benefit the institution but go unrewarded in the promotion and tenure process (Aguirre, 2000; Turner & Myers, 2000). This major element of academic life, often referred to as "cultural taxation," works against minorities in the promotion and tenure process. Padilla (1994) defines cultural taxation as "the obligation to show good citizenship toward the institution by serving its needs for ethnic representation on committees, or to demonstrate knowledge and commitment to a cultural group, which may even bring accolades to the institution but which is not usually rewarded by the institution on whose behalf the service was performed" (p. 26).

Likewise, minority faculty perceived they had to prove themselves by working harder than anyone else and to cope without complaining (Aguirre, 2000; Boice 1992, 1993a, 1993b; Turner & Myers, 2000). Another factor related to workload that contributes to the stress level is that African American faculty members at PWIs are more likely than White faculty to value providing services to the community as an essential or important professional goal. This commitment to service could result in even more problems, particularly at institutions that do not value community service (Antonio, 2002; Astin, Antonio, Cress, & Astin, 1997; Brown, 1988).

Racism

African Americans have been socialized not to be overly sensitive by blaming problems on racism (Thomas, 2002). Many times minorities tend to rationalize what occurred or decide that their individual shortcomings are the problem (Thomas, 2002). Moreover, African Americans are constantly reminded of the "dominant culture in academe to which they are expected to become socialized" (Boice, 1992, p. 257). Research has found that African American faculty who conduct research on African Americans or social concerns reported that their research was devalued and trivialized (Aguirre, 2000; Exum, 1983; Turner & Myers, 2000). Minority faculty may also face criticism that their research is not published in the "right" journals, or that their research is not research but service and therefore not as valuable (Bronstein, 1993, cited in Luna & Cullen, 1995). Moreover, African American faculty may also feel pressured to focus on research interests deemed acceptable by their White colleagues, which may result in an intellectually and a professionally stifling academic environment because of the pressure to conform to mainstream research (Frierson, 1990). Thus faculty whose scholarship does not fall into the mainstream may encounter bias in the tenure process (Aguirre, 2000). Further, there is ample evidence that minority faculty are frequently treated unfairly in the promotion and tenure process (Aguirre, 2000; Menges & Exum, 1983; Turner & Myers, 2000).

HISTORICALLY BLACK COLLEGES AND UNIVERSITIES AND THE PIPELINE

We would be remiss if we did not discuss the role of HBCUs and their faculty in the educational pipeline. Because over half of full-time African American faculty (59%) are employed at HBCUs (NCES, 2004), it does not imply that there are not challenges at these institutions that can hinder the promotion and retention of African American faculty. Fields (1997) noted that there are perceptions among African American scholars that the promotion and tenure process at HBCUs may be more difficult than at PWIs. Furthermore, there are many factors that affect the pursuit of tenure at HBCUs. For example, faculty at HBCUs are often expected to teach heavy course loads (often two or four times that of faculty at many PWIs), engage in service activities, work with students, and publish, depending on the mission of the institution (Fields, 1997; Johnson, 2001; Johnson & Harvey, 2002).

Roebuck and Murty (1993) found African American faculty at HBCUs "adjusted well in a familiar milieu that met their personal, social, and career needs" (p. 203). Moreover, Johnson (2001) found that faculty at HBCUs learned institutional expectations and values relative to the promotion and tenure process through formal and informal methods. In contrast, Exum et al. (1984) found that African American faculty at PWIs were confused about expectations and norms. Although senior faculty informed junior faculty of what was necessary for promotion, they did not provide information on the daily tasks required of faculty (Johnson & Harvey, 2002).

Although faculty encounter challenges at HBCUs, African American faculty members prefer to teach at HBCUs to avoid the status ambiguities and racial conflict they may encounter at PWIs (Roebuck & Murty, 1993). Moreover, African American faculty in Roebuck and Murty's study viewed themselves as belonging to an "extended-family academic group," which resulted in feelings of belonging, psychological comfort, and success (p. 190). Their study also found that African American faculty at HBCUs did not perceive their work as a job but as a career. Billingsley (1982) found that one reason African American faculty remain at HBCUs is because of the large African American student population and the desire to educate African American students, as well as to build "strong Black faculties" to strengthen the educational pipeline.

With their long-standing emphasis on student contact, coupled with committed faculty, HBCUs are critical in the effort to increase the number of African American graduate students who subsequently pursue a career in the professoriate, as evidenced by Cole and Barber's (2003) study of the occupational choices of high-achieving minority students. This study provides evidence that faculty contact is crucial to increasing the presence of African Americans in the educational pipeline. Moreover, findings of this study revealed that high-achieving African American students at HBCUs were more likely to indicate that faculty encouraged them to consider academia as a career choice. Accordingly, faculty contact was reported as a key influence in the decision of African American students to pursue a career as a professor, with HBCUs having the highest level of faculty contact across all institutional types (Cole & Barber, 2003). Another testament of the influence of the faculty at HBCUs on students' decision to enroll and persist through graduate school is that three fourths of African American doctoral holders received their undergraduate degree at HBCUs (Foster, 2001; Roebuck & Murty, 1993).

How Does This Impact the Pipeline?

This overview of barriers that hinder African American faculty from promotion and retention in the academy impacts the pipeline in numerous ways. For example, African American undergraduate and graduate students may not have role models that nurture an interest in a career in the professoriate. Consequently, African American students may have to navigate the PWI in a haphazard manner. In addition, non-African American faculty and students are not exposed to individuals of other ethnic groups to further broaden and enhance their knowledge. Finally, African American faculty continue to lack the mentoring and critical mass vital to cultivating a campus climate that will actively promote and retain faculty, specifically African American faculty.

IMPLICATIONS

Even if the percentage of African American faculty increases, the climate they experience may limit their promotion and retention, particularly at PWIs. As noted by several scholars, adding diversity among faculty at any given institution has the potential to increase tension and divisiveness (Johnsrud & Sadao, 1998). To work in such an environment breeds feelings of isolation, stress, and racism. Through the adversity, African American faculty must continue to persist at all levels of the pipeline. However, this has proven to not be an easy task. The added stress, low-ranking status of many African American faculty, heavy workloads, and feelings of marginality contribute to the undesirability of the professoriate and subsequent retention of African American faculty (Thompson & Dey, 1998). Institutions must take steps to transform the psychological and behavioral climate if faculty diversity, and all that it encompasses, is to be achieved (Johnson & Scafide, 2002). Accordingly, some specific strategies can be employed to increase the chances of getting more African American faculty through the pipeline, thus begging the question, how can African American faculty get through the pipeline? A discussion of implications for policy, practice, and research follows, with a focus on increasing the representation of African American faculty and enhancing the climate that African American faculty encounter across all institutional types.

Implications for Policy

The academy is continuously under pressure regarding the type and amount of scholarship produced (Austin, 2002). By all accounts, the academy, collectively, defines what is "good." Thus professional associations and organizations need to recognize the contributions of all scholars. In *Scholarship Reconsidered: Priorities of the Professoriate*, Boyer (1990) took a bold step to address the challenges of current scholarship in meeting the needs of the students and/or preparing them for civic responsibility through the scholarship of discovery, integration, application, and teaching. In using Boyer's criteria for scholarship in connection with the American Association of University Professors (AAUP) tenure and promotion guidelines, institutions could establish a systematic method to include contributions of faculty relative to each institutional context.

To that end, Garza (1993), cited in Turner and Myers (2000), recommends that departments assess what constitutes rigorous scholarship for the purposes of tenure and promotion decisions. In times whereby research is weighted more heavily than service and teaching, the student has been forgotten in the shuffle. Attempts to offset these inequities are not always rewarded. Antonio (2002) found that faculty of color take a more holistic approach to teaching and are more likely than their White peers to view themselves as social change agents—all needed to develop civic-minded students. Thus these contributions are often not rewarded in the tenure and promotion process, and faculty of color are placed in a disadvantageous situation. The academy has to truly value African Americans' contributions to higher learning and to advocate for more nontraditional measures of research.

A nontraditional method for encouraging scholarship and preparation for the professoriate for African American scholars could be implemented by federal agencies, professional associations, and institutions. For example, this method could offer postdoctoral fellowships to recent African American doctoral graduates that allow for advanced training in research, often a requirement for landing a post at a research institution. Additionally, to facilitate accountability, accrediting agencies could establish benchmarks for faculty diversity for departments and institutions. Moreover, federal agencies could consider faculty diversity when awarding grants. Just as institutions that receive federal funds must comply with specific regulations in order to continue to receive funds, one of the criteria could include having a diverse faculty according to established benchmarks. Perhaps if associations, accrediting agencies, and federal agencies begin to hold institutions accountable for the lack of diversity, a concerted effort will be made to recruit and retain African American scholars.

Implications for Practice

Institutions of higher learning must make a concerted effort to recruit and retain African American faculty and faculty members of other marginalized groups. In doing so, institutions must be aware of the various challenges that face African American faculty (Johnson & Harvey, 2002; Thompson & Dey, 1998), recognize their own contribution to the marginalization of people (Jackson, 2004; Thompson & Dey, 1998), and understand the emotional and physical stressors experienced by marginalized groups (Thompson & Dey, 1998). As a means of addressing these issues, institutions must look at successful strategies to prepare, recruit, and retain African American faculty.

It has been suggested that faculty who are involved in mentoring relationships are more likely to further their professional and psychosocial development (Kram, 1986, cited in Luna & Cullen, 1995). In addition, a growing number of scholars (Butner, Burley, & Marbley, 2000; Frierson, 1990; Johnsrud & Sadao, 1998) encourage current African American faculty members to support one another and to create professional networks. Frierson (1990) suggests that African American senior faculty provide assistance to African American junior faculty as well as graduate and undergraduate students. Other African American faculty may be supportive in helping new faculty members become bicultural (Johnsrud & Sadao, 1998). Their ability to become bicultural includes being able to understand their own culture while maintaining a strong functional relationship with the majority culture.

Additionally, Butner, Burley, and Marbley (2000) go on to provide a how-to guide for coping with stress in the academy by suggesting the three Cs: collaboration, collegiality, and community. They suggest that African American faculty should collaborate with other faculty members. With regard to faculty responsibility, this will increase chances for presentations and article publications. Additionally, it will provide a system of support for the African American faculty, as well as lessen feelings of isolation associated with their minority status within the academic department. Additionally, African American faculty can be collegial by making meaningful connections with senior administration and faculty members within the department to discuss the role of faculty. These discussions should include the tenure and promotion processes, publications, and knowing when to say no. Not only will the faculty member become more familiar with the role of faculty within the department but will also build a sense of belonging within the department. Adding to that, African American faculty should become involved with the African American community surrounding the institution. This includes spirituality, cultural values that promote connectedness, and community projects. By becoming involved in the community, African American faculty may be able to create a sense of purpose and belonging outside of the academy that will validate their worth while navigating their way through the pipeline.

Graduate school preparation. Graduate school preparation programs for the professoriate are a form of anticipatory socialization process that occurs before the faculty member enters the academy (Johnson & Harvey, 2002). Since there is a significant percentage of African American faculty at HBCUs, this may be the best place to start a systematic effort to strengthen the pipeline of graduate students pursuing a career in the academic profession. Austin (2002) has developed several standards by which graduate schools should prepare students for the professoriate: advising, feedback, review of curricula, and opportunities for training, many of which are natural steps taking into consideration the changing student demographics, external constraints, technology, greater emphasis on student learning, and multiple ways of learning that have emerged.

Conversely, Austin (2002) recommends that more attention be paid to advising graduate students. Understandably, many graduate students are not often sure about their career aspirations, thus their advising session may be used as a tool to better help them assess and understand their strengths and areas that need improvement. To that end, advisors should have frank discussions with students regarding the changing role of the professor, departmental expectations, and the norms of the profession. Additionally, faculty should provide detailed feedback regarding achievement. One manner in which this can be accomplished is through self-reflection in the form of portfolios and journals. This method will allow students to see their accomplishments while they continue to meet other goals.

Furthermore, faculty should assess current curricula to determine if the existing programs are properly preparing students for the professoriate with regard to multicultural education, research and assessment, learning, technology, and institutional citizenship skills, as well as other facets related to the life of a professor. Lastly, graduate programs should provide students with training opportunities that mirror faculty responsibilities: teaching, service, and research. Thus institutions should develop mentoring programs for African American students interested in the academic profession across all institutional types.

Another means by which graduate students may be prepared for the professoriate is through academic departments and associations sponsoring interest sessions. Interest sessions for aspiring faculty at the undergraduate and graduate levels could inform students of the benefits of the profession, discuss how to negotiate the academy, and provide opportunities for networking and mentoring. To that end, academic associations need to conduct sessions that allow senior faculty to address rising scholars particularly African American scholars, about how to begin a career in academia.

Recruitment initiatives. Undoubtedly, anyone in the job market who has attended a conference or a professional meeting or has read excerpts from the *Chronicle* regarding the faculty search understands the ebb and flow of the search process. A person may send out countless curriculum vitae, a list of references, samples of work, and spend a considerable amount of time at conferences and annual meetings making connections and trying to get "in the know" in an attempt to land a faculty position. It is no wonder that African Americans get lost in the shuffle. Smith, Turner, Osei-Kofi, and Richards (2004) found that faculty of color were most likely to be hired when the job description contained information regarding ethnic or racial studies, or when the institution made a conscientious effort, "special hire," to diversify faculty by creating a position. Because it is not likely that science, technical, and business disciplines may not be able to add diversity indicators (ethnic studies), "special hires" are often identified in the traditional search and then are brought aboard for the unique perspective that they may add to the department. In their study, more than half of the African American faculty members were hired because of diversity indicators or "special hires." It also should be noted that over 65% of White faculty in their study entered the academy as a "special hire."

Socialization processes. Socialization into the academy refers to the process by which faculty members learn the norms, values, knowledge, and skills of the professoriate (Merton, as cited in Johnson & Harvey, 2002) that extend beyond the new faculty orientation. Socialization becomes important in the educational pipeline, because an unfavorable process could have a negative impact on promotion and tenure. Having a clear understanding of what is expected as a faculty member is the first step in the socialization process (Bellas & Toutkoushian, 1999; Johnson & Harvey, 2002). Bellas and Toutkoushian (1999) suggest that academic departments have to be very clear about promotion and tenure processes. Faculty should know the weight of various measures of research output and publications (e.g., book chapter, refereed journals, and co-authorship) within the first year of employment. The importance of getting African American faculty through the pipeline cannot be left to chance in the hope that a senior faculty member may or may not import essential information needed for the promotion and tenure process. Thus departments and institutions have to take the initiative by establishing a formal mentoring program that matches senior faculty members with new faculty members to "show them the ropes" while collaborating on papers, presentations, and research endeavors.

Additionally, departments and institutions should establish meaningful opportunities for faculty to discuss inequities within the academy and begin to develop solutions for addressing these issues. Moreover, institutions need to evaluate the campus climate and culture and proactively begin to cultivate an inclusive climate for students and faculty. This could be accomplished through roundtable discussions, workshops and seminars, an internally accessible Web site, and luncheons (Jackson, 2004). From these initiatives, department chairs can establish fair benchmarks for faculty to assess their plans, scholarship, and contribution to the department.

Support. Departments need to set aside funds to finance research initiatives, conference attendance, and instructional resources. Additionally, departments should reevaluate hiring, promotion, and tenure policies, with the goal of rewarding a wider variety of accomplishments and types of research, teaching, and service than traditionally recognized. Oftentimes a limited amount of time is provided for a faculty member to move from an assistant to an associate professor. If the faculty member has not performed accordingly, he or she will be asked to leave the department. However, the move from associate to full professor is less restrictive, and a faculty member could remain an associate professor indefinitely (as numbers connoted earlier in the chapter). Thus departments have to look beyond simply getting faculty past the first stage and also examine what resources are available to move faculty to senior faculty positions. Accordingly, Bellas and Toutkoushian (1999) suggest that departments should change the academic reward structure by broadening it to include less traditional measures of research, teaching, and service.

Implications for Future Research

As we prepare for the many challenges of getting African Americans through the educational pipeline, several questions remain unanswered, all of which may be addressed through future research. How do African American faculty at HBCUs and PWIs influence the postsecondary aspirations of African American undergraduate students? Why are African American graduate students not pursuing careers in the professoriate? How do graduates of HBCUs and PWIs perceive their graduate school experience, and, specifically, which factors influence their decision to persist or not? How will technology impact the educational pipeline? What will be the impact of the increasing number of part-time faculty hires on African American faculty in the pipeline? Which factors facilitate the successful promotion and tenure of African American faculty? Which policies and practices have institutions implemented to promote inclusive environments?

CONCLUSION

While we recognize that institutions should focus on increasing the structural diversity of the professoriate, any gain in the number of African American faculty will be short-lived if the institutional climate is not supportive. Likewise, if the graduate school environment does not espouse an ethos of inclusion, then we will continue to see African American students choose not to enter the professoriate. It is imperative that administrators and faculty at both HBCUs and PWIs design a systematic approach for strengthening the educational pipeline so that students are cultivated as undergraduates and graduates to consider careers in the professoriate. However, the strategies employed at HBCUs and PWIs may differ because of the student enrollment at these institutions.

Simultaneously, as institutions are focusing on increasing the structural diversity of the professoriate, an emphasis on providing a supportive climate may serve to increase the number of African American faculty who are promoted and retained at the institution. More importantly, African American faculty at PWIs and HBCUs have a significant role relative to whether African American students choose to enter the profession and their success within the academy. Where we go from here is not only the responsibility of White administrators at PWIs but also the responsibility of African American faculty at HBCUs and PWIs. It is imperative that administrators and faculty at PWIs and HBCUs work in tandem on systematic efforts to strengthen the educational pipeline at all levels in order to increase the representation of African American faculty in the pipeline.

REFERENCES

Adams v. Richardson, 351 F.2d 636 (D.C. Cir. 1972); 356 F.2d 92 (D.C. Cir. 1973); 480 F.2d 1159 (D.C. Cir. 1973).

Aguirre, A., Jr. (2000). *Women and minority faculty in the academic workplace: Recruitment, retention, and academic culture* (ASHE-ERIC Higher Education Report, Volume 27, Number 6). San Francisco: Jossey-Bass.

Alexander-Snow, M., & Johnson, B. J. (1999). Perspectives on faculty of color. In R. J. Menges & Associates (Eds.), *Faculty in new Jobs: A guide to settling in, becoming established, and building institutional support* (pp. 88–117). San Francisco: Jossey-Bass.

Antonio, A. L. (2002). Faculty of color reconsidered: Reassessing contributions to scholarship. *The Journal of Higher Education, 73*(5), 582–602.

Astin, H. S., Antonio, A. L., Cress, C. M., & Astin, A. W. (1997). *Race and ethnicity in the American professoriate, 1995–96*. Los Angeles: Higher Education Research Institute, UCLA.

Austin, A. L. (2002). Creating a bridge to the future: Preparing new faculty to face changing expectations in a shifting context. *The Review of Higher Education, 26*(2), 119–144.

Bellas, M., & Toutkoushian, R. (1999). Faculty time allocations and research productivity: Gender, race, and family effects. *The Review of Higher Education, 22*(4), 367–390.

Billingsley, A. (1982). Building strong faculties in Black colleges. *Journal of Negro Education, 51,* 4–15.

Blackwell, J. E. (1989). Mentoring: An action strategy for increasing minority faculty. *Academe, 75,* 8–14.

Boice, R. (1992). *The new faculty member: Supporting and fostering professional development*. San Francisco: Jossey-Bass.

Boice, R. (1993a). Early turning points in professorial careers of women and minorities. In R. J. Menges & M. D. Svinicki (Series Eds.), & J. Gainen & R. Boice (Vol. Eds.), *New directions for teaching and learning: Vol. 53. Building a diverse faculty* (pp. 71–80). San Francisco: Jossey-Bass.

Boice, R. (1993b). New faculty involvement for women and minorities. *Research in Higher Education, 34*(3), 291–241.

Boyer, E. (1990). *Scholarship reconsidered: Priorities of the professoriate*. Princeton, NJ: Carnegie Foundation for the Advancement of Teaching.

Brown, S. V. (1988). *Increasing minority faculty: An elusive goal*. Princeton, NJ: Educational Testing Service.

Butner, B., Burley, H., & Marbley, A. (2000). Coping with the unexpected: Black faculty at predominantly White institutions. *Journal of Black Studies, 30*(3), 453–462.

Cole, S., & Barber, E. (2003). *Increasing faculty diversity: The occupational choices of high-achieving minority students*. Cambridge, MA: Harvard University Press.

Council of Graduate Schools. (2004). *Organization and Administration of Graduate Education*. Washington, DC: Author.

Cross, T., & Slater, R. B. (Eds.). (2000). African Americans in faculty posts: Still tapping on the glass and hoping to get in. *The Journal of Blacks in Higher Education, 28*, 22–23.

Exum, W. H. (1983). Climbing the crystal stairs: Values, affirmative action, and minority faculty. *Social Problems, 30*, 383–399.

Exum, W. H., Menges, R. J., Watkins, B., & Berglund, P. (1984). Making it at the top: Women and minority faculty in the academic labor market. *American Behavioral Scientist, 27*, 301–324.

Fields, C. D. (1997). Tenure at HBCUs. *Black Issues in Higher Education, 14*(17), 30.

Finkelstein, M. J. (1984). *The American academic profession: A synthesis of social inquiry since World War II*. Columbus: Ohio State University Press.

Foster, L. (2001). The not-so-invisible professors: White faculty at the Black college. *Urban Education, 36*(5), 611–629.

Frierson, H., Jr. (1990). The situation of Black educational researchers: Continuation of a crisis. *Educational Researcher, 19*, 12–17.

Hurtado, S., Milem, J. F., Clayton-Pedersen, A. R., & Allen, W. R. (1998). Enhancing campus climates for racial/ethnic diversity: Educational policy and practice. *The Review of Higher Education, 21*(3), 279–302.

Jackson, J. (2004). The story is not in the numbers: Academic socialization and diversifying the faculty. *NWSA Journal, 16*(1), 172–185.

Johnson, B. J. (2001). Faculty socialization: Lessons learned from urban Black colleges. *Urban Education, 36*(5), 630–647.

Johnson, B. J., & Harvey, W. (2002). The socialization of Black college faculty: Implications for policy and practice. *The Review of Higher Education, 25*(3), 297–314.

Johnson, B. J., & Scafide, K. (2002). Faculty diversity. In *Encyclopedia of Education* (2nd ed., Vol. 3, pp. 775–779). New York: Macmillan Reference.

Johnsrud, L. K. (1993, Spring). Women and minority faculty experiences: Defining and responding to diverse realities. *New Directions for Teaching and Learning, 53*, 3–16.

Johnsrud, L. K., & Des Jarlais, C. D. (1994). Barriers to tenure for women and minorities. *The Review of Higher Education, 17*, 335–353.

Johnsrud, L. K., & Sadao, K. C. (1998). The common experience of "otherness": Ethnic and racial minority faculty. *Review of Higher Education, 21*(4), 315–342.

Luna, G., & Cullen, D. L. (1995). *Empowering the faculty: Mentoring redirected and renewed* (ASHE-ERIC Higher Education Report, 3). Washington, DC: George Washington University, Graduate School of Education and Human Development.

Menges, R. J. (Ed.). (1999). *Faculty in new jobs: A guide to settling in, becoming established, and building institutional support*. San Francisco: Jossey-Bass.

Menges, R. J., & Exum, W. H. (1983). Barriers to the progress of women and minority faculty. *Journal of Higher Education, 54*, 123–143.

National Center for Education Statistics. (1997). *Instructional faculty and staff in higher education institutions: Fall 1987 to Fall 1992.* U.S. Department of Education. Washington, DC: Author.

National Center for Education Statistics. (2001). *Background characteristics, work activities, and compensation of faculty and instructional staff in postsecondary institutions: Fall 1998.* U.S. Department of Education. Washington, DC: Author.

National Center for Education Statistics. (2002). *Gender and racial/ethnic differences in salary and other characteristics of postsecondary faculty: Fall 1998.* U.S. Department of Education. Washington, DC: Author.

National Center for Education Statistics. (2004). *Historically Black colleges and universities, 1976 to 2001.* U.S. Department of Education. Washington, DC: Author.

NEA Update. (2001). Tenure. *National Education Association Higher Education Research Center, 7*(3).

Padilla, A. M. (1994). Ethnic minority scholars, research, and mentoring: Current and future issues. *Educational Researcher, 23*(4), 24–27.

Pruitt, A., & Isaac, P. D. (1995). Discrimination in recruitment, admission and retention of minority graduate students. *The Journal of Negro Education, 54*(4), 526–536.

Roebuck, J. B., & Murty, K. S. (1993). *Historically Black colleges and universities: Their place in American higher education.* Westport, CT: Praeger.

Smith, D., Turner, C., Osei-Kofi, N., & Richards, S. (2004). Interrupting the usual: Successful strategies for hiring diverse faculty. *The Journal of Higher Education, 75*(2), 133–160.

Sorcinelli, M. D. (1992). New and junior faculty stress: Research and responses. In M. D. Sorcinelli & A. E. Austin (Eds.), *Developing new and junior faculty* (pp. 27–37). San Francisco: Jossey-Bass.

Tack, M. W., & Patitu, C. L. (1992). *Faculty job satisfaction: Women and minorities in the peril* (ASHE-ERIC Higher Education Report No. 4). Washington, DC: George Washington University, School of Education and Human Development.

Thomas, J. M. (2002). *The experiences of international faculty on U.S. campuses: Understanding issues of socialization.* Unpublished doctoral dissertation, University of New Orleans, Louisiana.

Thompson, C., & Dey, E. (1998). Pushed to the margins: Sources of stress for African American college and university faculty. *The Journal of Higher Education, 69*(3), 324–345.

Tierney, W. G., & Bensimon, E. M. (1996). *Promotion and tenure: Community and socialization in academe.* Albany: State University of New York Press.

Turner, C. S. V. T. (2002). Women of color in academe. *The Journal of Higher Education, 73*(1), 74–93.

Turner, C. S. V. T., & Myers, Jr., S. L. (2000). *Faculty of color in academe: Bittersweet success.* Needham Heights, MA: Allyn and Bacon.

Weidman, J. C., Twale, D. J., & Stein, E. L. (2001). *Socialization of graduate and professional students in higher education. A perilous passage?* ASHE-ERIC Higher Education Report, Vol. 28(3). San Francisco: Jossey-Bass.

Chapter 6

A National Progress Report of African Americans in the Administrative Workforce in Higher Education

Jerlando F. L. Jackson and Brandon D. Daniels

A defining feature of the past two decades in the United States is the increased racial and ethnic diversity. This significant shift in racial and ethnic demographics, in turn, has changed the composition of the U.S. workforce. Contemporary discourse on the American workforce is hard pressed to not include a single agenda item focused on these pronounced shifts. As a result of this change in the tone and focus on racial and ethnic diversity, it has in fact become the chief characteristic of the American workforce. In short, there has been a proliferation of non-Whites entering the labor force. For example, from 1990 to 2000, the U.S. population increased by 33 million people. Over 280 million people were counted in 2000, and of that number, census data show that the total population was comprised of 75.1% Whites and 12.3% African Americans, with the remainder consisting of Asian Americans and Native Americans (U. S. Census Bureau, 2001). Further, as of July 2002, the number of people who claimed African American as their racial identity grew to 38.3 million (U. S. Census Bureau, 2003). The African American population is growing more rapidly than the total population and will grow 38.6% by 2008, compared to 11.4% for the White population (Humphreys, 2003).

While the reality of the demographic shifts of the workforce is apparent, America's ability to adequately address these shifts is questionable. According to Waters (1992), the issue of workforce diversity presents the United States with four concerns. First, a culturally diverse workforce will bring with it different values, assumptions, and expectations. Second, there is a critical need, on behalf of organizations, to understand how to manage a diverse workforce. Third, there is a need to develop appropriate methods to capture the benefits of diversity. Fourth, organizations will have to confront the difficult and delicate issues not previously addressed in the past. While it is critical for the various

115

sectors (e.g., business and education) in the United States to address these and many other concerns, clearly the American workforce struggles with its best asset—racial and ethnic diversity.

Just as the American workforce struggles with fully utilizing ethnically and racially diverse talents, so does the higher education workforce. In many ways, the aforementioned concerns may be more heightened in higher education because of the prerequisites (i.e., advanced degree training) needed to enter specific areas of the workforce. The primary purpose of this chapter is to provide a progress report of African Americans in the higher education administrative workforce using national-level data. This chapter is divided into four sections. The first section provides a review of previous research on African Americans in college and university administration. The second section describes the national employment landscape for African Americans in the higher education administrative workforce. The third section describes an empirically based model that institutions could use to help recruit and retain African American administrators. The final section includes implications for research, policy, and practice.

HISTORICAL CONTEXT FOR THE PARTICIPATION OF AFRICAN AMERICANS IN THE HIGHER EDUCATION ADMINISTRATIVE WORKFORCE

One observation evident from performing a computer-assisted search for research on African Americans in the higher education administrative workforce is that this body of research is small, but growing (Crase, 1994). A significant portion of this research was focused on the experiences of African American administrators at predominantly White institutions (PWIs). The higher education administrative workforce has for some time been highly populated by White males; therefore, African Americans and other diverse groups have had an extremely difficult time becoming integral participants on college and university administrative staffs. Nonetheless, for decades, African Americans garnered more success securing administrative positions connected to diversity and multiculturalism but continued to be grossly underrepresented when it came to positions central to the operation of the institution (e.g., budget and finance) or institutional mission (e.g., research) (Benjiman, 1997).

Prior to the civil rights movement there were virtually no African Americans in the administrative workforce at PWIs. Historically Black colleges and universities (HBCUs) were the only real opportunities that African Americans had to become administrators (Wilson, 1989). As a result of African American students' demands, civil rights legislation, affirmative action regulations, and increased social consciousness, many PWIs attempted to increase the representation of African Americans in the administrative workforce (Jones, 1977). To meet the previously cited institutional demands for increased diversity in the administrative workforce during the 1960s, many of these African Americans were appointed to develop special recruitment programs, administer Black Studies programs, and serve as special consultants for minority relations. Most of these African American administrators had little or no preparation for their jobs and were either taken from the faculty ranks or given positions where they had to be trained on the job (Cunningham, 1992).

The most visible of these positions headed what was often referred to as Educational Opportunities Programs or EOP (Jones, 1972). Jones purported that too often African American administrators were given responsibility for the affirmative action program, Black or ethnic studies, or African American student services. At the time, individuals in these positions were described as primarily males who were new to their jobs and often had little to no power or resources (Kitano & Miller, 1970). James Bush (1977) professed that many PWIs felt that they had met their social responsibility once they hired a minority administrator. Many of these institutions were even accused of enacting lower standards to increase the number of African American administrators at their institution (Bridges, 1996).

Cunningham (1992) stated that African Americans had a unique dilemma in White academia—too many people expect too many things from them. Calvert Hayes Smith (1980) reported that African American administrators were given responsibility, but they were not given power and authority in the formal administrative structure commensurate with that responsibility. Moreover, these administrators found themselves isolated from their White counterparts. Therefore, they found their roles and positions ill defined, with a lack of authority, and they questioned the rational for their recruitment (Watson, 2001). Further, Cunningham (1992) suggests that regardless of the job description or title, the major function of these African American administrators was to troubleshoot with African American students and the African American community. Smith (1980) more profoundly stated in his book that because African American administrators were initially hired to pacify the African American community and/or to demonstrate that the hiring institution is an "equal opportunity employer," neither of which is legitimate, the leadership that they could provide based on their knowledge of given issues was neither accepted nor respected by those with influence.

Lindsay (1994) expounded on this belief by stating that those African American administrators who were able to obtain administrative positions at these PWIs were often seen as high achievers, but also seen as the "token" or "solo" African American administrator (Lindsay, 1994). These "solo" African American administrators were often perceived as representatives of their racial group or as "symbols" rather than as individuals by the majority group. Although these individuals earned these positions, they worked under high pressure and were subject to grand expectations and extreme evaluations (Fernandez, 1981). Often these individuals were encouraged to behave in ways stereotypical for their group. These distorted behaviors were generally used to justify the exploitation of and discrimination against them (Fontaine & Greenlee, 1993).

Another intriguing line of inquiry on African Americans in the higher education administrative workforce covered job-based competency. This can be divided into two areas: (1) the role that African Americans' ethnicity and competence play in being hired as administrators; and (2) African Americans' perceptions of their competence as they see it and as they perceive it to be seen by others, including their peers. An undergirding aspect of this aforementioned research purports that when African American administrators were hired in their positions, they were expected to be more competent, more experienced, and more qualified than their peers—even for the same position. Bush (1977) stated that in the perceived relationship between African American administrators and their White counterparts, African Americans felt equal to their peers but did not think that the same viewpoint was reciprocated. Moreover, Bush concluded that this increased pressure for African American administrators to be more competent also increased the level of stress experienced working at PWIs. In these positions, African Americans were expected to be more self-reliant, and their behavior was under constant scrutiny by their White counterparts. In conjunction, at PWIs there was little empathy, because there was no awareness of what it meant to be African American. Although there was not an extensive literature base on African American administrators in the higher education administrative workforce, historical literature provided the authors with a solid foundation for the development of this chapter.

THE NATIONAL EMPLOYMENT LANDSCAPE FOR AFRICAN AMERICANS IN THE HIGHER EDUCATION ADMINISTRATIVE WORKFORCE

In this section, descriptive national-level data highlight the status of African Americans in administrative roles at colleges and universities. These national-level data highlight differences between African Americans and their counterparts on various demographic and related characteristics (e.g., employment status and gender). Discussion of the higher education administrative workforce included both academic leaders and student affairs practitioners. Data for this section were computed using two national data sets[1]: (1) the National Study of Postsecondary Faculty (NSOPF: 99) and (2) the National Association for Student Personnel Administrators (NASPA) Salary Survey, 1999.

Academic Leaders

On balance, African Americans' time spent on various activities was quite similar to all races and ethnicities, except in two cases (see Table 6.1). First, African Americans spent significantly less time dedicated to research activities (4.0%) compared to all racial and ethnic groups (11.3%). Second, on average, African Americans participated in administrative activities more than the other groups. Therefore, in comparison to other postsecondary faculty, African Americans were more often engaged in administrative activities, and less so in research activities. The discussion of underparticipation in research activities will be left for another inquiry; however, this section examines African American participation in both academic leadership and student affairs administration.

The average age of academic leaders was 51.7 compared to 50.7 for African Americans (see Table 6.2). In all age categories, African Americans had a higher percent average, except for the age category of 55–64 compared to the other groups. The percentage disparity at 65 years and older may represent the initial wave of African American administrators hired in response to community and campus demands for administrative diversity. In conjunction, the representation in the under-35 age category through the 45–54 age category may typify a new commitment to administrative diversity. Nonetheless, the average age distribution suggests that overall growth should occur for African Americans in the higher education administrative workforce over generations.

The gender gap in academic leadership positions was pronounced among all groups, 63.1 to 36.9, in favor of males (see Table 6.3). When examining the gender gap for African Americans, it was reversed. In fact, African American women outnumbered African American men in academic leadership positions

TABLE 6.1
Percentage Distribution of Full-Time Instructional Faculty and Staff
by Time Spent on Various Activities, and by Race/Ethnicity: Fall 1998

	Principal Activity			
Race/Ethnicity	Teaching Activities	Research Activities	Administration Activities	Other[1] Activities
All Races/Ethnicities	64.5	11.3	12.8	11.4
Black/African American, Non-Hispanic	67.5	4.0	16.1	12.3

[1]Includes clinical service, on sabbatical from this institution, technical activities, other institutional activities such as library services, community public service, subsidized performer, and artist-in-residence.

Data Source: U.S. Department of Education, National Center for Education Statistics, 1999 National Study of Postsecondary Faculty: 1999 (NSOPF: 99)

Note: Percentages may not sum to 100 due to rounding.

TABLE 6.2
Average Age and Percentage Distribution of Full-Time Academic Leaders
by Race/Ethnicity: Fall 1998

			Percentage in Each Category				
Race/Ethnicity	Average Age	Under 35	35–44	45–55	54–64	65–70	71 or older
All Races/ Ethnicities	51.7	5.5	14.6	39.5	33.9	4.7	1.8
Black/African American, Non-Hispanic	50.7	6.7	16.3	48.3	18.3	8.0	2.5

Data Source: U.S. Department of Education, National Center for Education Statistics, 1999
National Study of Postsecondary Faculty: 1999 (NSOPF: 99)

Note: Percentages may not sum to 100 due to rounding.

by 5.6%. More specifically, African American men held 47.2% of the academic leadership positions, whereas African American women held 52.8%. Of all the ethnic and racial groups, African Americans were the only group where the gender gap was reversed—in favor of females. When examining the highest degree attained, African Americans held slightly fewer doctorate degrees (54.3%) than the other groups combined (55.3%), but African Americans modestly held more master's/first professional degree (43.6%) in comparison to their counterparts (37.7%). Lastly, fewer African Americans in academic leadership positions simply had a bachelor's degree or less compared to the other groups. There are at least two ways to look at this finding: (1) African Americans in academic leadership positions, on the whole, had attained higher credentials (97.9% to 93%); or (2) Other groups were more successful in obtaining academic leadership positions with a bachelor's degree or less.

TABLE 6.3
Percentage of Distribution of Full-Time Academic Leaders by Gender and
Highest Educational Credential Attained and by Race/Ethnicity: Fall 1998

	Gender		Highest Credential Attained		
Race/Ethnicity	Male	Female	Doctorate Degree	Master's/First Professional Degree	Bachelor's Degree or Less
All Races/Ethnicities	63.1	36.9	55.3	37.7	7.0
Black/African American, Non-Hispanic	47.2	52.8	54.3	43.6	2.1

Data Source: U.S. Department of Education, National Center for Education Statistics, 1999
National Study of Postsecondary Faculty: 1999 (NSOPF: 99)

Note: Percentages may not sum to 100 due to rounding.

TABLE 6.4

Percentage Distribution of Full-Time Academic Leaders
by Carnegie Classification and by Race/Ethnicity: Fall 1998

	Carnegie Classification			
Race/Ethnicity	Research Institutions	Doctoral Institutions	Comprehensive Institutions	Liberal Arts Institutions
All Races/Ethnicities	39.8	15.7	28.4	16.2
Black/African American, Non-Hispanic	30.2	9.3	29.5	30.9

Data Source: U.S. Department of Education, National Center for Education Statistics, 1999
National Study of Postsecondary Faculty: 1999 (NSOPF: 99)

Note: Percentages may not sum to 100 due to rounding.

An examination of the employment status of academic leadership positions by Carnegie Classification showed, for the most part, that African Americans were located at institutions with less emphasis on research (see Table 6.4). African Americans at research institutions represented 30.2%, while their counterparts held 39.8% of these positions. Likewise, African Americans held 9.3% of the academic leadership positions compared to 15.7% for all groups. In contrast, African Americans had a higher representation at comprehensive institutions (29.5%) compared to their counterparts (28.4%). The same was true for liberal arts institutions, with African Americans holding 30.9% in comparison to 16.2% for their counterparts.

While the Carnegie Classification provides one perspective on the kinds of institutions where academic leaders were employed, institutional control and type provided additional perspectives (see Table 6.5). As it relates to institution control, African Americans had a higher representation at public institutions, and a lower representation at private institutions. More specifically, African Americans represented 61.2% at public institutions, while all other races and ethnicities represented 66.2%. In addition, African Americans held 38.8% of

TABLE 6.5

Percentage of Distribution of Full-Time Academic Leaders
by Institutional Control and Institutional Type and by Race/Ethnicity: Fall 1998

	Institutional Control		Institutional Type	
Race/Ethnicity	Public	Private	4-Year	2-Year
All Races/Ethnicities	66.2	33.8	86.3	13.7
Black/African American, Non-Hispanic	61.2	38.8	80.9	19.1

Data Source: U.S. Department of Education, National Center for Education Statistics, 1999
National Study of Postsecondary Faculty: 1999 (NSOPF: 99)

Note: Percentages may not sum to 100 due to rounding.

the academic leadership positions at private institutions, and their counterparts held 33.8%. As for institutional type (4-year vs. 2-year), while African Americans were largely concentrated at 4-year institutions, African Americans were overrepresented at 2-year institutions and underrepresented at 4-year institutions in comparison to the other groups. African Americans held 80.9% of academic leadership positions at 4-year institutions compared to 86.3% for their counterparts, and they held 19.1% at 2-year institutions compared to 13.7% for their counterparts.

The distribution of academic leaders by program area demonstrated that African Americans were equally represented in the agriculture/home economics field compared to the other groups (see Table 6.6), while in business they were underrepresented (1.8%) compared to the other groups (5.6%). However, in education, African Americans were significantly overrepresented (27.3%) compared to the other groups (12.9%). African Americans were underrepresented in both the engineering (4.2% to 4.0%) and fine arts fields (4.7% to 1.1%). In contrast, African Americans were overrepresented in the health sciences. Both the fields of humanities (14.5% to 11.9%) and natural sciences (13.8% to 5.6%) showed underrepresentation for African Americans. Nonetheless, in social sciences, African Americans were overrepresented (14.6%) compared to the other groups (11.4%). Lastly, African Americans were underrepresented (16.4%) in the "other fields" in comparison to the other groups (17.9%). For the most part, African Americans were largely concentrated in program areas deemed "caring fields" (i.e., home economics, education, health sciences, and social sciences).

An analysis of employment by region revealed that African Americans had a higher percentage distribution than their counterparts in three regions (i.e., New England, Mideast, and Southeast). The largest concentration of African American academic leaders was located in the Southeast region (43.9%). The second largest population was in the Mideast region (16.0%). The Great Lakes was the third largest population, with 13.8%. With 12.4%, the Far West was the fourth largest region. The fifth largest region was the Southwest (5.6%), followed by New England (5.5%). The two regions with the smallest African American representation were the Plains (1.7%) and Rocky Mountains (1.0%).

The distribution of academic leaders by rank showed that African Americans more than likely were associate professors, assistant professors, instructors, or other ranks compared to the other groups by percentage distribution (see Table 6.7), whereas, the other races and ethnicities, by percentage distribution, were more likely to be full professors. For example, 18.9% of African American academic leaders were full professors compared to 36.8%. Approximately 26.8% of African American academic leaders were associate professors compared to 19.7%. Likewise, 16.0% of African American academic leaders were assistant professors compared to 7.8%. As for academic leaders who were instructors, 14.4% were African Americans, and 13.4% were from the other racial

TABLE 6.6
Percentage Distribution of Full-Time Academic Leaders, by Race/Ethnicity, and by Program Area and Region: Fall 1998

	Race/Ethnicity	
	All Races/Ethnicities	Black/African, Non-Hispanic
Agriculture/Home Economics	1.8	1.8
Business	5.6	1.8
Education	12.9	27.3
Engineering	4.2	4.0
Fine Arts	4.7	1.1
Health Sciences	13.1	15.6
Humanities	14.5	11.9
Natural Sciences	13.8	5.6
Social Sciences	11.4	14.6
All Other Fields	17.9	16.4

	Race/Ethnicity	
	All Races/Ethnicities	Black/African Non-Hispanic
New England	5.3	5.5
Mideast	13.1	16.0
Great Lakes	16.8	13.8
Plains	9.3	1.7
Southeast	26.2	43
Southwest	9.9	5.6
Rocky Mountains	5.7	1.0
Far West	13.9	12.4

Data Source: U.S. Department of Education, National Center for Education Statistics, 1999
National Study of Postsecondary Faculty: 1999 (NSOPF: 99)

Note: Percentages may not sum to 100 due to rounding

TABLE 6.7

Percentage Distribution of Full-Time Academic Leaders by Academic Rank
and by Race/Ethnicity: Fall 1998

	Academic Rank				
Race/Ethnicity	Full Professor	Associate Professor	Assistant Professor	Instructor or Lecturer	Other Ranks/ Not Applicable
All Races/Ethnicities	36.8	19.7	7.8	13.4	22.3
Black/African American, Non-Hispanic	18.9	26.8	16.0	14.4	23.9

Data Source: U.S. Department of Education, National Center for Education Statistics, 1999
National Study of Postsecondary Faculty: 1999 (NSOPF: 99)

Note: Percentages may not sum to 100 due to rounding.

and ethnic groups. Lastly, 23.9% of academic leaders with "other rank" were
African Americans, and all other races and ethnicities were 22.3%.

A key aspect of the selection process for academic leaders is their performance as faculty. Two indicators used for evaluation are publications and presentations (see Table 6.8). An evaluation of the average number of career
publications and presentations revealed lower numbers in general and significantly lower numbers in specific categories for African Americans. The "coin of
the realm" in academe is refereed publications. African Americans had 10.4 refereed career publications compared to 24.4. Nonrefereed publications were not
much different with African Americans, at 11.9, and other groups at 18.5. As
for total career books, monographs, and reports, African Americans had 7.0
compared to 9.8. Lastly, African Americans had 49.4 career presentations and
exhibits compared to 62.8.

TABLE 6.8

Average Number of Publications and Presentations in Career for Academic Leaders
by Race/Ethnicity: Fall 1998

	Publications and Presentations			
Race/Ethnicity	Refereed Publications	Nonrefereed Publications	Books, Monographs, and Reports	Presentations and Exhibits
All Races/Ethnicities	24.4	18.5	9.8	62.8
Black/African American, Non-Hispanic	10.4	11.9	7.0	49.4

Data Source: U.S. Department of Education, National Center for Education Statistics, 1999
National Study of Postsecondary Faculty: 1999 (NSOPF: 99)

Note: Percentages may not sum to 100 due to rounding.

TABLE 6.9

Average Income of Full-Time Academic Leaders by Source of Income
and Race/Ethnicity: Fall 1998

	Source of Income				
Race/Ethnicity	*Total Earned Income*	*Basic Salary from Institution*	*Other Income from Institution*	*Outside Counsulting Income*	*Other Outside Income*
All Races/Ethnicities	71,617.8	67,680.2	9,560.5	7,840.1	7,127.4
Black/African American, Non-Hispanic	60,698.7	58,465.9	6,817.0	3,972.3	low n

Data Source: U.S. Department of Education, National Center for Education Statistics, 1999
National Study of Postsecondary Faculty: 1999 (NSOPF: 99)

Note: Percentages may not sum to 100 due to rounding.

Average income for academic leaders was examined for differences by source. For the most part, African Americans had lower incomes in all five source areas (see Table 6.9). The average total income for academic leaders shows that all races and ethnicities earned $71,617.80 compared to African Americans, with $60,698.7. The "basic salary from institution" category shows $67,680.2 for all races and ethnicities compared to $58,465.9 for African Americans. The category "other income from institution" shows $6,817.0 for African Americans compared to $9,560.5 for the other groups. In the "outside consulting" category, African American earned, on average, $3,972.3, while the other groups earned $7,840.1. Lastly, all races and ethnicities earned $7,127.4 from "other outside income," while the number of African Americans who reported data was too low to compute.

Student Affairs Administrators

When examining the gender of all races and ethnicities for student affairs administrators, it was almost balanced between males and females (50.8% to 49.2%) (see Table 6.10). However, when exploring gender for African American student affairs administrators, the gender gap emerged. For instance, African American males constituted 44.5% of student affairs administrators, whereas African American females comprised 54.5%. As for the highest degree attained, African Americans had a slightly higher percentage distribution of doctorate degrees (31.1%) compared to the other races and ethnicities combined (26.8%). Likewise, African Americans modestly had a higher percentage distribution of master's/first professional degree (63.6%) in comparison to their

TABLE 6.10

Percentage Distribution of Full-Time Student Affairs Administrators
by Gender and Highest Educational Credential Attained and by Race/Ethnicity: Fall 1998

	Gender		Highest Credential Attained		
Race/Ethnicity	Male	Female	Doctorate Degree	Master's/First Professional Degree	Bachelor's Degree or Less
All Races/Ethnicities	50.8	49.2	26.8	53.5	19.7
Black/African American, Non-Hispanic	44.5	54.5	31.1	63.6	15.2

Data Source: National Association for Student Personnel Administrators (NASPA) Salary Survey, 1999

Note: Percentages may not sum to 100 due to rounding.

counterparts (53.5%). Lastly, a smaller percentage distribution of African Americans in student affairs administrative positions simply had a bachelor's degree or less (15.2%) compared to the other races and ethnicities (19.7%).

The distribution of student affairs administrators by institutional type and control provided a needed perspective on the kinds of institutions at which these administrators were employed (see Table 6.11). When considering institutional type (2-year institution, 4-year college, and university),[2] African Americans were overrepresented at 2-year institutions, underrepresented at 4-year colleges, and overrepresented at universities, by percentage distribution, in comparison to the other groups. African Americans held 11.7% of student affairs administrative positions at 2-year institutions compared to 7.7%, and they held 26.7% at 4-year colleges compared to 37.4%. Lastly, African Americans held 61.6% of the student affairs administrative positions at universities compared to 54.9%. As it relates to institution control, African Americans had

TABLE 6.11

Percentage of Distribution of Full-Time Student Affairs Administrators,
by Institutional Type and Institutional Control and by Race/Ethnicity: Fall 1998

	Institutional Type			Institutional Control	
Race/Ethnicity	2-Year Institution	4-Year College	University	Public	Private
All Races/Ethnicities	7.7	37.4	54.9	62.1	37.9
Black/African American, Non-Hispanic	11.7	26.7	61.6	71.4	28.6

Data Source: National Association for Student Personnel Administrators (NASPA) Salary Survey, 1999

Note: Percentages may not sum to 100 due to rounding.

a higher representation at public institutions and a lower representation at private institutions in relation to their counterparts. More specifically, African Americans represented 71.4%, while all other races and ethnicities represented 62.1%. In addition, African Americans held 28.6% of the student affairs administrative positions at private institutions, and their counterparts held 37.9%.

African American student affairs administrators employed at institutions with less than 1,000 students represented 4.3% of the sample (see Table 6.12). Approximately 18% of African Americans worked at institutions with between 1,000 and 2,499 students. Institutions with between 2,500 and 4,999 students employed 16.4% of the African Americans holding student affairs positions. Eleven percent of African Americans worked at institutions with between 5,000 and 9,999 students. Institutions with between 10,000 and 19,999 students employed 24.1% of African American student affairs administrators. Fourteen percent of African Americans in student affairs worked at institutions that had between 20,000 and 30,000 students. Lastly, 12% were employed at institutions with over 30,000 students. The largest percentage of African Americans in student affairs positions was employed at institutions that enrolled between 10,000 and 19,999 students. The group of institutions that employed the next largest percentage of African Americans enrolled between 1,000 and 2,499 students. An analysis of income for student affairs administrators revealed results in opposition to their academic leadership counterparts. On average, African Americans in student affairs positions earned more than other groups combined. For example, African Americans earned, on average, $64,061.6, while the other groups earned $59,665.

The region that employed the largest percentage of African American student affairs administrators was Region III (see Table 6.13). Region IV-East employed the second largest percentage, with 20.7%. Approximately 16.3% of the African American sample was employed in Region II. Region IV-West had 13.9% of the African American sample. Seven and a half percent of the African American sample worked in Region VI. African Americans in Region I constituted 6.4% of the sample. The region that employed the lowest percentage of African Americans was Region V (see Appendix for region map).

The analysis of diversity by position showed that senior student affairs officers had the largest percentage of African Americans holding this single position (see Table 6.13). However, the majority (65.1%) of African Americans were located in positions lower than the dean of students. Collectively, 27.3% of these African Americans worked in the senior student affairs office (i.e., SSAO, Associate SSAO, and Assistant SSAO). Within the dean of students' office, the assistant dean of students comprised 11% of the African American sample, followed by the dean of students' position (7.5%), and 5.5% comprised the associate dean of students. Approximately, 48.6% of African Americans sampled held director-level positions. Of the director's positions, the top three positions for African Americans were counseling, union, and housing. The position that employed the lowest percentage of African Americans was director of registration.

TABLE 6.12

Percentage Distribution of Full-Time Student Affairs Administrators
by Institutional Size and Average Income by Race/Ethnicity: Fall 1998

	Percentage in Each Category							Average Income
Race/Ethnicity	Under 1,000	1,000– 2,499	2,500– 4,999	5,000– 9,999	10,000– 19,999	20,000– 30,000	Over 31,000	Total Earned Income
All Races/Ethnicities	6.4	22.3	17.0	18.5	20.4	8.9	6.6	59,665.0
Black/African American, Non-Hispanic	4.3	18.0	16.4	11.0	24.1	14.0	12.0	64,061.6

Data Source: National Association for Student Personnel Administrators (NASPA) Salary Survey, 1999

Note: Percentages may not sum to 100 due to rounding.

TABLE 6.13

Percentage Distribution of Full-Time Student Affairs Administrators, by Race/Ethnicity, and by Region and Position: Fall 1998

	Race/Ethnicity			Race/Ethnicity	
	All Races/Ethnicities	Black/African, Non-Hispanic		All Races/Ethnicities	Black/African Non-Hispanic
Region I	8.9	6.4	SSAO	11.4	14.0
Region II	16.0	16.3	Associate SSAO	4.0	7.1
Region III	24.8	32.0	Assistant SSAO	4.4	6.2
Region IV-E	21.6	20.7	Dean of Students	4.4	7.5
Region IV-W	15.6	13.9	Associate Dean of Students	3.6	5.5
Region V	6.9	3.0	Assistant Dean of Students	4.1	11.0
Region VI	6.2	7.5	Director of the Counseling Center	9.4	9.1
			Director of Financial Aid	7.1	4.5
			Director of Career Counseling	9.2	5.8
			Director of the Health Center	8.3	4.9
			Director of the Student Union	6.7	7.5
			Director of the Security	6.5	4.9
			Director of Admissions	6.8	4.5
			Director of Registration	5.3	0.6
			Director of Housing	8.9	6.8

Data Source: National Association for Student Personnel Administrators (NASPA) Salary Survey, 1999

Note: Percentages may not sum to 100 due to rounding.

A Proposed Solution: The ERA Model

Institutional commitment to diversity still remains a concern for many colleges and universities (Cabrera, Nora, Terenzini, Pascarella, & Hagedorn, 1999; Holmes, Ebbers, Robinson, & Mugenda, 2000). Media reporters who cover higher and postsecondary education have flagged access, retention, and advancement for African Americans in the administrative workforce at predominantly White institutions (PWIs) as major areas of focus (Bennefield, 1999; Black Issues in Higher Education, 1999). The higher and postsecondary education literature is saturated with recommendations for retaining African American students and faculty, but there is little empirical or practice-based knowledge pertaining to the retention of African American administrators (Jackson & Flowers, 2003). One of the biggest challenges for institutions, as it relates to engaging, retaining, and advancing (ERA) African American administrators, is to use past research to build a conceptual framework for policy implementation. Based on previous research by the first author (i.e., Jackson, 2001, 2002, 2003, 2004a, 2004b; Jackson & Flowers, 2003; Jackson & Contreras, in press), the ERA model was developed and subsequently revised. What follows is a description of the model. Two basic concepts serve as anchors for this model: (1) Institutions must establish relationships with the surrounding people of color community, and (2) Institutions must commit to the principles of diversity and affirmative action (see Figure 6.1).

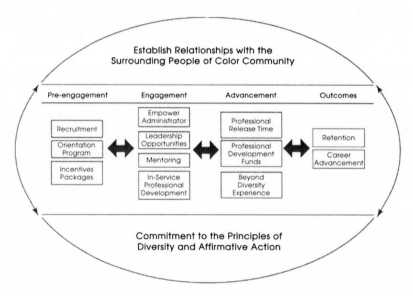

Figure 6.1 The Engagement, Retention, and Advancement Model for African Americans in the Higher Education Administrative Workforce

The first phase of this model is the pre-engagement phase, which constitutes the first set of activities between the institution and the potential candidate before he or she arrives on campus. This is a critical phase, because it sets the tone for interactions in the remaining phases of the model. This phase is composed of three components. The first component is recruitment—the main focus of this component is to use recruitment as a retention tool. Institutions that have well-thought-out and published procedures for recruitment and hiring are more likely to send a positive message to potential employees. The second component is the establishment of an orientation program. The orientation should include a community aspect, which provides an introduction to community leadership and network systems, and a campus aspect, which introduces the administrator to the students, faculty, and staff of the institutions. The last component of this phase is to offer a competitive incentives package. It is thought that the professional relationship with the African American administrator is shaped during the negotiation process. This component is important, because too often administrators can be lured away by other institutions willing to offer a better benefits package.

The next phase of the model is the engagement phase, which occurs when the administrator assumes his or her responsibility on campus, becomes engaged with the campus community, and begins to better understand his or her assigned responsibilities and role on campus. The first step is empowering the administrator. This entails providing the African American administrator with the power and authority to give direction and leadership to his or her operating unit. The next component is leadership opportunities. These opportunities help groom the African American administrator for job advancement within the institution and help him or her engage in a full range of leadership opportunities. Mentoring is the third component within this phase. It is important that institutions develop mentoring programs that focus on career and academic development for African American administrators. These programs provide a critical aspect for professional development. It is also important to make sure that these administrators are paired with seasoned administrators for guidance. The last component of the engagement phase is in-service professional development, which is quite helpful because it supplements skills the African American administrator brought to the job. It is important that these training sessions be aligned with the position that the African American administrator holds.

The next phase of the ERA model is advancement. This is an important phase because it relates to providing growth for African American administrators and ultimately promotes retention. The first component of the phase provides two forms of professional release time for the African American administrator. The first form is release time to pursue research and professional activities. The second is monthly release time to allow interested administrators sufficient time to connect with the African American student population. The next component is providing professional development funds to ensure that the African American administrator is able to participate in key opportunities. The last component is to provide work-related experience beyond the scope of diversity. These opportunities can be used to help the African American administrator move beyond diversity experiences and gain a better understanding of the whole campus.

The last phase of the model is outcomes. The outcomes for this model are retention and career advancement for African American administrators at PWIs. The retention part of this phase refers to equally maintaining African American administrators in their position in comparison to their White counterparts. Career advancement refers to the promotion within or outside of the home institution, with the ultimate goal of retention in the field of administration. These two components play an important role in seeking to improve the status of African American participation in the higher education administrative workforce.

The main purpose of this model is to address issues that were important in creating an environment conducive for African American administrators in the workplace, based on empirical research of professional development and growth factors such as aspects for engagement, retention, and advancement. The model was based on the premise that the more positive linkages between the components, the more likely an African American administrator will stay and grow as an administrator. Another purpose of this model is to produce useful information to help individual institutions committed to diversifying their administrative workforce to do so.

CONCLUSION

In sum, this chapter was written to serve as a resource for researchers, policy makers, and practitioners interested in diversifying the higher education administrative workforce. This document is timely in that institutions will continue to grapple with the inescapable growth of racial and ethnic diversity on their campuses. Inasmuch as higher education continues to be viewed as a "public good" for all citizens, institutions will have to learn how to adequately absorb change in the form of racial and ethnic diversity, just as they did for gender and social economic status in past decades. Accordingly, institutions will have to advance their thinking about diversity goals beyond the student population, which in this context is a transit population, to opening new doors of opportunity that lead directly to key decision-making positions. Original data reported in this chapter do provide important lessons as institutions continue to march toward achieving diversity in the higher education administrative workforce.

First, African American faculty tended to be less involved in research activities and more involved in administrative activities on their individual campuses. This finding is also supported by data that demonstrate that African American academic leaders had fewer publications and presentations than their counterparts. Likewise, African American faculty got involved in primary administrative duties much earlier in their careers compared to other groups, as evidenced by the average rank at which they assumed their administrative duties. Second, for both African American academic leaders and student affairs administrators, the gender gap was reversed in comparison to the at-large administrative workforce. On average, African American women held more administrative positions compared to African American men. Third, African Americans in both administrative sectors had attained higher credentials, by percentage distribution, than their counterparts.

Fourth, African Americans in the administrative workforce were uniformly employed at similar types of institutions in both sectors. For example, African Americans in both sectors were overrepresented at 2-year institutions and underrepresented at 4-year institutions. Simultaneously, the majority of African Americans were employed at public as opposed to private institutions. Fifth, faculty that assumed administrative duties largely came from the "caring professions" such as education and health sciences, and less so from the hard or natural sciences. Sixth, for the most part, the largest concentration of African Americans in the administrative workforce was employed in the Southeastern region of the United States. Seventh, African Americans tended to earn, on average, less money than their counterparts in academic leadership positions and more money than their counterparts in student affairs administration. Lastly, African Americans were more likely to be employed in lower-level administration positions as opposed to upper-level positions.

IMPLICATIONS

Implications for this chapter focus on important outcomes aimed at diversifying the higher education administrative workforce with regard to African Americans. Accordingly, these outcomes are intended to prepare practitioners for lives as administrative professionals, to foster thoughtful inquires for researchers, and to provide sound knowledge for policy makers. The changing administrative workforce demographics call for

- articulation of and focus on comprehensive recruitment and retention practices that are widely needed to build a highly competitive, racially diverse workforce;
- a new intentionality about addressing "silent" discrimination that has been muted by the fear of confronting the reality of workplace conditions for people of color;
- involvement of majority groups in the "authentic appreciation" of the "value-added" aspects of cultural differences;
- transparent assessment and evaluation procedures during the hiring process that emphasize the benefits of racial and ethnic diversity rather than the perceived challenges of managing diverse talents; and

- connection of desired outcomes to policy development and daily practice procedures to ensure that achieving administrative diversity becomes an essential aspect of the institutional culture.

What do these outcomes imply for researchers, policy makers, and practitioners? Ponder the following implications:

1. *Create a research policy and practice dialogue about achieving diversity in the administrative workforce.* More empirical research is needed to explore the complex challenges on both the individual and institutional levels of achieving administrative workforce diversity. This dialogue should move beyond an academic discussion and spark a broader policy dialogue about the need to marshal and foster diverse talents in key decision-making roles. Most importantly, systematic efforts must be made to ensure that practitioners are well versed on how to implement the resulting research and policy.

2. *Identify institutional goals.* Clearly, in most cases, institutions will begin with numerical benchmarks. However, these institutions must also move beyond simple typologies based on quantitative dimensions to include the delineation of the kinds and levels of interaction based on qualitative dimensions. If institutional participants are to be held accountable for developing work conditions suitable for promoting administrative diversity, then a clear set of quantitative and qualitative goals must be articulated. These discussions should not only include researchers for the development of appropriate institutional goals but also policy makers, campus leaders, faculty, staff, and students.

3. *Rethink the selection procedures.* Another consideration is to acknowledge the need to substantially retool the selection procedures of the hiring process for administrative positions. While faculty-related work has been long deemed appropriate measures to select key administrative positions (e.g., presidents), a clear connection between faculty-related work and perceived performance in administration must be articulated. For example, publications and presentations may provide appropriate measures for faculty performance but may not be adequate to assess administrative potential. Data contained within this chapter show that if this remains a key criteria, African Americans will continue to lag behind their counterparts in securing these administrative positions.

NOTES

1. The NSOPF: 99 used complex sampling and applied appropriate weights to equal the total population of postsecondary faculty—956,616. The NASPA Salary Survey (1999) included a random sample of 419 institutions that was deemed representative of the member institutions of the NASPA.

2. The NASPA database did not contain variables aligned with Carnegie's Institutional Classification but did provide a modified classification system: (1) 2-year institution; (2) 4-year college; and (3) 4-year university.

References

Benjiman, L. (1997). *Black women in the academy: Promises and perils.* Gainesville: University of Florida Press.

Bennefield, R. M. (1999). Trench warriors: On the front lines. *Black Issues in Higher Education, 16,* 69–71.

Black Issues in Higher Education. (1999).Vital signs. *Black Issues in Higher Education, 25,* 85–93.

Bridges, C. R. (1996). The characteristics of career achievement perceived by African American college administrators. *Journal of Black Studies, 26*(6), 748–767.

Bush, J. A. (1977). The minority administrator: Implications for social work education. *Journal of Education for Social Work, 13*(1), 15–22.

Cabrera, A. F., Nora, A., Terenzini, P. T., Pascarella, E. T., & Hagedorn, L. S. (1999). Campus racial climate and adjustment of students to college. *The Journal of College Student Development, 35,* 98–102.

Crase, D. (1994). The minority connection: African Americans in administrative/ leadership positions. *Physical Educator, 51*(1), 15–20.

Cunningham, J. J. (February 1992). *Black administrators as managers in higher education.* Paper presented at the National Conference of the Research of Minority Professors, Houston, TX.

Davis, J. D. (Ed.). (1994). *Coloring the halls of ivy: Leadership and diversity in the academy.* Bolton, MA: Anker.

Fernandez, J. P. (1981). Racism *and sexism in corporate life: Changing values in American business:* Lexington, MA: Lexington Books.

Fontaine, D. C., & Greenlee, S. P. (1993). Employment factors of African Americans. *The Western Journal of Black Studies, 39,* 41–54.

Holmes, S. L., Ebbers, L. H., Robinson, D. C., & Mugenda , A. G. (2000). Validating African American students at predominately White institutions. *Journal of College Student Retention: Research, Theory, & Practice, 2,* 41–58.

Humphreys, J. M. (2003). The multicultural economy 2003: America's minority buying power. *Georgia Business and Economic Conditions, 63*(2), 3.

Jackson, J. F. L. (2001). A new test for diversity: Retaining African American administrators at predominately White institutions. In L. Jones (Ed.), *Retaining African Americans in higher education: Challenging paradigms for retaining Black students, faculty, and administrators* (pp. 93–109). Sterling, VA: Stylus.

Jackson, J. F. L. (2002). Retention of African American administrators at predominantly White institutions: Using professional growth factors to inform the discussion. *College and University, 78*(2), 11–16.

Jackson, J. F. L. (2003). Engaging, retaining, and advancing African Americans in student affairs administration: An analysis of employment status. *NASAP Journal*, *6*(1), 9–24.

Jackson, J. F. L. (2004a). Engaging, retaining, and advancing African Americans to executive-level positions: A descriptive and trend analysis of academic administrators in higher and postsecondary education. *Journal of Negro Education*, *73*(1), 4–20.

Jackson, J. F. L. (2004b). An emerging engagement, retention, and advancement model for African American administrators at predominantly White institutions: The results of two delphi studies. In D. Cleveland (Ed.), *A long way to go: Conversations about race by African American faculty and graduate students in higher education* (pp. 211–222). New York: Peter Lang.

Jackson, J. F. L., & Contreras, C. (in press). Applying an engagement, retention, and advancement model for administrators of color in higher education. In C. Lewis & V. B. Bush (Eds.), *African Americans in higher education organizations: Using cultural capital to shape the future*.

Jackson, J. F. L., & Flowers, L. A. (2003). Retaining African American student affairs administrators: Voices from the field. *College Student Affairs Journal*, *22*(2), 125–136.

Jones, P. E. (1972). *Proposal for education professional development act: Short term training institute for minority administrators*. Iowa City: University of Iowa Press.

Jones, P. E. (March 1977). *The changing profile of Black administrators in predominately White colleges and universities*. Paper presented at the Second Annual Conference on Blacks in Higher Education, Washington, DC.

Kitano, H., & Miller, D. (1970). *An assessment of educational opportunity programs in California higher education*. Sacramento: California Coordinating Council for Higher Education.

Lindsay, B. (1994). African American women and Brown: A lingering twilight or emerging dawn. *Journal of Negro Education*, *63*(3), 430–442.

Smith, C. H. (1980). The peculiar status of Black educational administrators—The university setting. *Journal of Black Studies*, *10*(3), 323–334.

U.S. Census Bureau. (2001). All across the U.S.A.: Population distribution and composition, 2000. Retrieved June 7, 2004, from http://www.census.gov/population/pop-profile/2000/chap02.pdf

U.S. Census Bureau. (2003). Young, diverse, urban: Hispanic population reaches all-time high of 38.8 million, new Census Bureau estimates show. Last updated June 19, 2003. Retrieved June 7, 2004, from http://www.census.gov/Press-Release/www/releases/archives/ hispanic_origin_population/001130.html

Waters, H. (1992). Race, culture and interpersonal conflict. *International Journal of Intercultural Relations*, *16*, 437–454.

Watson, L. W. (2001). In their voices: A glimpse of African American women administrators in higher education. *NASPA Journal*, *(4)*1, 7–16.

Wilson, R. (1989). Women of color in academic administration: Trends, progress, and barriers. *Sex Roles*, *21*(1–2), 85–97.

APPENDIX

NASPA Regions

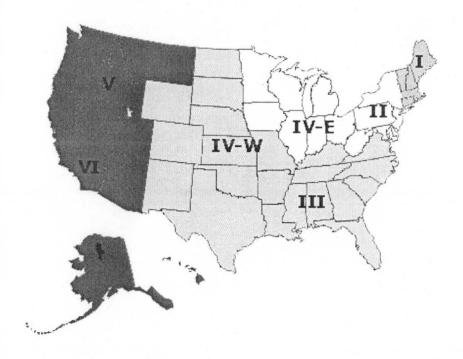

Part III

Social Influences

Chapter 7

Securing the Ties That Bind

Community Involvement and the Educational Success of African American Children and Youth

Mavis G. Sanders and Tamitha F. Campbell

Community involvement has played a prominent role in the education of African Americans. This involvement has taken a variety of forms and has been essential to African Americans' educational progress and attainment. For example, religious and civic community leaders were central in the struggle for legal access to schools and school desegregation. Throughout the late nineteenth and early twentieth centuries, religious and philanthropic associations established private schools when African Americans were barred from common schools (Durham, 2003). African American communities supported under-resourced schools in the Jim Crow South (Walker, 1996). Their commitment allowed these schools to function despite overwhelming disadvantages. Community newspapers from as early as the initial decades of the 1900s describe the active involvement and exchange that existed between African American schools and their local communities. Local churches, for example, hosted school clubs, and community members attended and celebrated school events and activities (Phelps-Stokes, 1929). In the late 1960s, African American communities in large urban centers sought greater control over the education of Black students to slow the tide of failure that had come to characterize the schooling process in these institutions (Hess, 1999). Community involvement, in a variety of forms, including after-school programs, mentoring and tutoring activities, and fund-raising efforts, has continued into the twenty-first century.

The historic and contemporary support and involvement of individuals, agencies, and institutions in their local and extended communities significantly contributed to the educational progress of African American students, who currently graduate from high school and enter postsecondary institutions at a

141

higher rate than any other historical period (Infoplease, 2004). However, more progress is needed. Educational statistics show that African Americans have yet to achieve the goal of educational equity that they have long sought.[1] For example, the current proportion of African American students receiving special education services (15%) is higher than the proportion of White (11%), Hispanic (11%), and Asian/Pacific Islander (6%) students. Furthermore, in 1999, 18% of African American students compared to 9% of European American students had repeated at least one grade. Grade retention is a key predictor of high school dropout, which is linked to higher unemployment and lower earning potential. In 2000, 16% of African Americans between the ages of 18 and 24 had not completed high school, compared to 8% of European American young adults. While African American student enrollment in postsecondary institutions increased from 19% of 18-to-24-year-old young adults in 1980 to 31% in 2000, the completion rate of African American students at these institutions still lags behind that of their European American counterparts. Additionally, African Americans enrolled in postsecondary institutions are underrepresented in the fields of science, mathematics, and technology.

In this chapter, we argue that continued community involvement is essential if greater numbers of African American children and youth are to thrive in the educational system. We further argue that this involvement should be structured to support African American students' academic efforts in *and* out of school. The chapter is organized into four sections. First, we briefly discuss research that shows the benefits of community involvement for African American children and youth. Second, we describe how schools can support and enhance African American students' educational opportunities and experiences through school-based programs of community partnerships. We describe potential community partners and activities that can be implemented to meet key goals for students' learning. We also provide examples of effective school-community partnerships that have been implemented by schools serving African American students.

Third, we discuss why community agencies, institutions, and volunteers also must support the school success of African American students through activities that extend beyond school hours and walls. We draw on current educational literature to describe the importance of these organizations for students' learning, school engagement, and overall well-being, as well as factors that influence organizational effectiveness. To further illustrate their significance, we provide four examples of community-based activities that complement and expand the school experience of African American children and youth. Fourth, we discuss challenges that school and community leaders and educational policy makers must address in order to improve and enrich educational opportunities and outcomes for African American students in the twenty-first century.

AFRICAN AMERICAN STUDENT SUCCESS:
WHAT ROLE DOES THE VILLAGE REALLY PLAY?

> Like the other forms of capital . . . [social capital] is a resource that can be employed to aid in producing something—in this case, the development of youth. Social capital consists of the relations between persons of the sort that exist in the community. (Coleman, 1987, p. 8)

Many factors influence the educational success and persistence of African American children and youth. Among these are appropriately resourced and funded schools, capable and visionary principals, and well-trained and well-supported teachers, all buttressed by well-designed and well-implemented educational policies (Sanders, 2000). The literature described next further suggests that in addition to these critical factors, community involvement and support also play a significant role in the school success of African American students.

Community involvement, defined as "the actions that organizations and individuals . . . take to promote student development" (Nettles, 1991b, p. 380), is increasingly viewed as an effective means to provide students with resources and opportunities that support academic achievement and educational attainment. While all students are said to benefit from such involvement, African American students stand to benefit more due to their disproportionate representation in high-risk schools and communities (Lippman, Burns, & McArthur, 1996). According to Nettles (1991a):

> Far too many African American students have great needs for support and services, yet resources in the schools and government agencies are shrinking. Long neglected in educational research, the formal and informal roles of community entities are being recognized as important in efforts to improve the academic outcomes of African American children and youth. (pp. 143–144)

Recent empirical research supports Nettles's assertion. For example, a study of 827 African American adolescents found that students' involvement in community-based organizations, such as the Black church, indirectly influenced academic achievement through its positive and significant influence on their academic self-concept (Sanders, 1998). A subset of these students was interviewed to enhance the interpretation of the survey data. Focal students reported that church provided them with opportunities to engage in a number of activities that required school-related skills, such as public speaking and reading and analyzing texts, in a supportive, nurturing environment. The social capital garnered through the relationships between these youth and caring, supportive adults provided them with the motivation and conception of self necessary for academic success.

Other studies have generated similar findings. McPartland and Nettles (1991) evaluated Project Raise, a community-based program in Baltimore, Maryland, that provided academic support services to young African American adolescents in low-performing schools. These services included tutoring, mentoring, and attendance monitoring. Seven institutions—two churches, a college, a university, two businesses, and a fraternity—sponsored the project that was funded by two local foundations. After 2 years, the authors reported that students participating in Project Raise achieved better attendance and English grades than non-Raise students in the same grade.

Fashola and Cooper (1999) studied community-based after-school programs serving predominantly African American students. They found that several of these programs, including the Howard Street Tutoring Program, in Chicago, had measurable effects on students' achievement. They also found that the most effective programs linked to the school-day curriculum, trained its volunteer tutors, and provided opportunities for one-to-one tutoring. This study further underscored the role that community-based organizations can play in improving educational outcomes for African American students.

Evaluations of other after-school programs have generated similar findings. For example, Gardner and colleagues (2001) found that an after-school program implemented through a partnership between a local African American church, a public school, and Ohio State University's College of Education had significant effects on the reading and mathematics achievement of 10 African American males who participated in the program. The students were enrolled in grades 3–5, were at least 1 year below grade level (as measured by Ohio's state proficiency tests), and were experiencing social-behavioral problems before entering the program. Eight males from the church and five pre-service teachers volunteered for the program. They were trained by university faculty to provide social and academic support to participants using peer-mediated strategies. The program was housed at the church, offered 5 days a week, and began directly after school at 3:30 P.M.

An analysis of pre-test and post-test results showed that all students improved their reading scores on the Slosson Oral Reading Test and their accuracy and fluency rates on multiplication facts—both targeted academic skills. Gardner and colleagues (2001) concluded:

> [T]he Mount Olivet after-school program provides a unique opportunity for all invested members (i.e., urban schools, parents, at-risk students, university teacher preparation programs, community resources) to be involved in a positive solution that addresses the problems of poor test scores among urban students. (pp. 22–23)

School and community-based mentoring programs also have shown positive effects on the school-related behaviors of African American students. Lee and Cramond (1999), for example, evaluated a national community-based mentoring program on the educational and professional aspirations of 130 African American students. The results showed that students who persisted in the program for at least 1 year had significantly higher aspirations than students who were on the program's waiting list. Mentors also can influence African American students' successful transition to and completion of postsecondary institutions. In a qualitative study examining 21 African American college students and their mentors, Freeman (1999) found that the mentors, some who were university affiliated and others who were community based, provided extended learning opportunities, nurturing, and/or personal support that positively influenced students' social adjustment and academic success.

The preceding studies support and extend Nettles's (1991b) comprehensive review of community involvement and economically disadvantaged students conducted over a decade ago. Nettles examined research on 13 community-based initiatives. These programs provided social support and resources, instructional assistance, or a combination of the two for primarily African American and other students of color. Nettles concluded that although effects differed based on program focus and quality of implementation, the programs showed an overall pattern of positive effects. These effects were strongest for programs with an instructional or a support focus compared to those with mixed foci. According to Nettles (1991b),

> It is clear that the programs can have positive effects on school-related behaviors and achievement as well as on attitudes and risk-taking behavior. . . . [T]he consistency of positive outcomes for attendance, pregnancy status and contraceptive behavior, and persistence in school suggests that community programs may be potentially useful interventions. (p. 397)

Thus while more empirical research is needed, a growing body of data has documented the importance and impact of community involvement on African American students' achievement and school success. We now discuss how this involvement can be mobilized through school-based community partnerships.

COMMUNITY INVOLVEMENT IN SCHOOLS SERVING AFRICAN AMERICAN CHILDREN AND YOUTH

> Schools, too often below par by any measure, are experienced as hostile and demeaning environments where neither inner-city youth nor their interests are taken seriously. (McLaughlin, Irby, & Langman, 1994, p. 76)

In 2000, African American children and youth comprised approximately 17% of all students in K–12 public schools (for this and the following statistics, see Hoffman, Llagas, & Snyder, 2003). Most African American students attended public schools where students of color represented the majority of the student body. Thirty-seven percent of African American students were enrolled in schools where students of color accounted for 90% or more of the student population. The majority of African American public school students lived either in a large city (32%) or in the urban fringe of a large city (24%). In 2 of the 10 largest U.S. public school districts (Chicago, 52%, Philadelphia, 65%), African Americans constituted more than 50% of the student population.

The urban schools that are attended by a majority of African American students were found to have larger enrollments and higher concentrations of poverty, on average, than suburban or rural schools at both the elementary and secondary levels.[2] Teachers in these schools also were found to have fewer resources available to them. These schools were less likely to have gifted and talented programs, and were more likely to have behavior problems, particularly in the areas of student absenteeism, classroom discipline, and school safety. Thus these schools stand to benefit a great deal from the support and resources that can be mobilized through well-planned and well-organized community partnership programs.

SCHOOL-BASED COMMUNITY PARTNERSHIPS

School-community partnerships can be defined as the connections between schools and community individuals, organizations, and businesses that are forged to directly or indirectly promote students' social, emotional, physical, and intellectual development. Community within this definition of school-community partnerships is not constrained by the geographic boundaries of neighborhoods but refers more to the "social interactions that can occur within or transcend local boundaries" (Nettles, 1991b, p. 380).

Schools can link with a variety of community partners, the most common partners are large corporations and small businesses. Other community partners include universities and educational institutions; government and military agencies; health care organizations; faith-based organizations; national service and volunteer organizations; senior citizen organizations; cultural and recreational institutions; media organizations; sports franchises and associ-ations; other groups such as fraternities and sororities; and community volunteers who can provide resources and social support to youth and schools (see Table 7.1).

TABLE 7.1
Potential Partners for School-Community Collaboration

Types of Community Partners	For Example...
Businesses/Corporations	Local businesses, national corporations and franchises
Universities and Educational Institutions	Colleges, universities, high schools, and other educational institutions
Health Care Organizations	Hospitals, health care centers, mental health facilities, health departments, health foundations and associations
Government and Military Agencies	Fire departments, police departments, chamber of commerce, city council, other local and state government agencies and departments
National Service and Volunteer Organizations	Rotary Club, Lions Club, Kiwanis Club, VISTA, Concerned Black Men, Inc., Shriners, Boy and Girl Scouts, YWCA, United Way, Americorp, Urban League
Faith Organizations	Churches, mosques, synagogues, other religious organizations and charities
Senior Citizens Organizations	Nursing homes, senior volunteer and service organizations
Cultural and Recreational Institutions	Zoos, museums, libraries, recreational centers
Media Organizations	Local newspapers, radio stations, cable networks, etc.
Sports Franchises and Associations	Minor and major league sports teams, NBA, NCAA, etc.
Other Community Organizations	Fraternities, sororities, foundations, neighborhood associations, political, alumni, and local service organizations
Community Individuals	Individual volunteers from the surrounding school community

Source: Adapted from Sanders (2001).

Partnership activities also may have multiple foci. Activities may be student centered, family centered, school centered, or community centered. Student-centered activities include those that provide direct services or goods to students, for example, mentoring and tutoring programs, contextual learning and job-shadowing opportunities, and the provision of student awards, incentives, and scholarships. Family-centered activities are those that have parents or entire families as their primary focus. This category includes activities such as parenting workshops, GED and other adult education classes, parent/family incentives and awards, family counseling, and family fun and learning nights. School-centered activities are those that benefit the school as a whole, such as beautification projects or the donation of school equipment and materials, or activities that benefit the faculty, such as staff development and classroom assistance. Community-centered activities have as their primary focus the community and its citizens, for example, charitable outreach, art and science exhibits, and community revitalization and beautification projects (Sanders, 2001).

The kinds of community partnerships that schools implement also can vary in complexity. If viewed on a continuum, simple partnerships on the far left end are characterized by short-term exchanges of goods or services (see Figure 7.1). Such partnerships require very little coordination, planning, or cultural and structural shifts in school functioning, thus they are relatively easy to implement, especially for schools that lack the leadership, resources, or experience needed for more complex models of school-community partnerships. When well implemented, their impact is likely to be positive, albeit limited.

Community partnership activities increase in complexity and duration as one moves along the continuum. Activities located in the middle of the continuum might include a partnership between a school and a local library to provide parent workshops on supporting children's literacy development at a variety of community sites. On the far right end of the continuum, activities are long term and characterized by bi- or multi-directional exchange, high levels of interaction, and extensive planning and coordination (see Figure 7.1). For example, community resources and supports can be integrated with educational services in the form of full-service community schools. Several variations of community schools exist. These include school-based health clinics, facilities that provide health counseling, education, and services in school buildings operated by outside health agencies; school-based youth centers, centers that provide after-school, recreational, mentoring, employment, and other needed services to students in extended day programs; and family resource centers, facilities located in schools where parents can receive support and services such

FIGURE 7.1   Community Partnerships: Range of Complexity

Simple Partnerships	*Complex Partnerships*
Short term	Long term
Unidirectional exchange	Bi- or multi-directional exchange
Low level of interaction	High level of interaction
Limited planning	Extensive planning and coordination
(e.g., incentives for awards programs, donation of school materials/supplies	(e.g., full-service community schools, professional development schools)

as employment assistance, immigration information, food, clothing, counseling, and early child care (Dryfoos, 1998a).

As noted earlier, such partnerships require a great deal of planning and co-ordination of resources, space, time, and funding. Dryfoos (1998b) further sug-gests that in addition to extensive principal leadership and support, a full-time coordinator is also required in order to organize and sustain such programs. While these complex partnerships can yield significant benefits (Amato, 1996; Newman, 1995), they are difficult to implement, especially for schools with high needs and low resources.

Community partnerships, therefore, whether with businesses or health agen-cies, whether focused on students or families, or whether simple or complex, are viable means of improving educational opportunities and outcomes for students. Recognizing the importance of multiple sources of support for students' learning, several school reform initiatives include a community involvement or outreach component (Comer, 1993). One such program that can be organized as a whole-school reform model, or as a component of whole-school reform, is the School, Family, and Community Partnership Program of the National Network of Part-nership Schools (NNPS).[3] This program guides schools in using Epstein's frame-work of six types of involvement and a team approach to develop comprehensive partnerships with students' families and community-based organizations and vol-unteers to achieve important goals for students' learning and school success (Sanders & Epstein, 2000b). The following examples of school-community part-nership activities are drawn from school members of the NNPS.

EXAMPLES OF SCHOOL-COMMUNITY PARTNERSHIP ACTIVITIES

Many schools throughout the United States have successfully overcome common obstacles, such as lack of time, resources, and faculty involvement, to design and implement community partnerships to create safer, better resourced, and more supportive learning environments for students. Urban schools serving primarily African American students often have significantly more obstacles to overcome, including high student and staff mobility and limited resources, in order to es-tablish effective community partnerships (Sanders & Epstein, 2001a). Yet some urban schools have been able to do so. These schools have been able to imple-ment partnership activities to achieve important goals for students and learning. Partnership activities include mentoring and tutoring programs, community pa-trol squads to ensure that students are safe walking to and from school (Sanders, 1996), reading incentive programs (Jansorn & Salinas, 2002), and job shadowing and internship programs for high school students (Sanders & Lewis, 2005).

Next we describe an elementary school that was the focus of a case study on community involvement (see Sanders & Harvey, 2002). The school worked collaboratively with 10 community partners to implement a variety of student-centered activities. We highlight six that were student-focused collaborative efforts to provide a practical example of how high-needs schools can partner with multiple community agencies and volunteers, in simple and moderately complex ways, in order to enhance students' learning opportunities and school experiences. The partnership activities were designed and implemented using a team composed of school faculty and staff and parent and community representatives. A team approach ensures that multiple perspectives are included in key decision making, reduces teacher overload and burnout, and helps schools create systematic and sustainable partnership programs (Sanders & Epstein, 2000a).

The School

The focal school is one of 183 public schools serving 103,000 students in a city of approximately 600,000 residents. It is situated in a residential and commercial section of the city and has an enrollment of approximately 360 students in grades K–5. The entire student population is African American. In 1999, about 10% of the students received special education services, and 79% received free or reduced-price meals.

The Community Partners

During the 1998–99 school year, the focal school had 10 documented community partners. Six of these partners and their involvement activities are briefly described next.

- *A Community Empowerment Initiative and a Local Church*: These organizations implemented an after-school program with academic, cultural, and behavioral objectives for students. Students were assisted with homework, attended field trips, and engaged in recreational and cultural activities. The program began at 2:30 P.M. and ended at 5:15 P.M., Monday through Friday. The after-school program had a predesigned parent/community involvement component, which included a 4-hour per month volunteer requirement. Parents could volunteer or have representatives such as older siblings, grandparents, and other family members volunteer for them. The program was offered free to its participants.

- *A Local Church*: The church has an outreach committee that provided school supplies to students in need and also provided refreshments for school parties, including Valentine's Day and Christmas parties. Members of the outreach committee also worked as volunteers in the student cafeteria.
- *A Health Care Facility*: The facility provided health information to staff, students, and parents through workshops and classroom presentations. Topics included cholesterol management, HIV prevention and treatment, attention deficit disorder, parenting skills, diabetes management, and CPR certification. The organization provided refreshments for school events, such as family fun and learning nights, father and son banquets, and the annual school picnic. The organization also sponsored a student academic recognition program, which honored academically successful students at quarterly awards-breakfasts.
- *A Health Care Agency*: The agency had a community outreach initiative, Partnership in Education Program, that included about 42 volunteers who worked with three schools. Seven volunteers from this agency supported the focal school in a variety of ways. They acted as tutors for students with academic problems. They also held book drives for the school. During the 1998–99 school year, the agency donated 600 books to the school as well as several computers that are used in its computer center.
- *A Suburban Elementary School*: The PTA at this elementary school donated books to the focal school's library. The partner school also shared with the focal school a book credit that allowed the school to purchase new books from Scholastic Press. The school formally adopted the focal school during the 1999–2000 school year.
- *A Non-Profit Foundation*: The foundation sponsored the Hundred Book Challenge program. As a participant of the program, the school was provided with rotating classroom libraries with books, color-coded by level. Teachers assessed students' reading levels and assigned them colors. Students selected books coded with these colors and read, in class, 30 minutes each day. Students also were encouraged to take books home and read to their parents. Every book that the student read was recorded, and after a certain number were read, students received incentives such as pens and pencils. Students who read 100 books or more were recognized at the school's quarterly awards breakfasts.

As a result of these partnerships, the school had computers that students regularly used, classrooms and a library full of books, an incentive program for honor-roll students, an after-school program, financial support for partnership activities and events, and relationships with community businesses, organizations, and individuals that brought the school and its community partners a great deal of satisfaction. These partnerships supported the school's efforts to provide a challenging and nurturing learning environment for its students. This kind of support is important for school improvement, especially for urban schools that are increasingly asked to improve students' academic and behavioral outcomes, often without the necessary increases in material and human resources.

Unfortunately, the focal school is the exception, not the rule (Davies, 2002). Schools that serve large percentages of African American students are less likely than schools serving more affluent students to create such partnerships. This fact emerges from national statistics on parental and community involvement in schools (NCES, 1998, 2001). Furthermore, even when schools reach out to community partners, the practices they implement may not fully meet the needs of *all* students, especially those in socioeconomically distressed neighborhoods (Heath & McLaughlin, 1996) or with special learning needs (Gardner, et al., 2001). Schools also may be hampered in the activities and support they can provide by federal or local regulations and requirements. Consequently, community involvement in the education of African American children and youth should not be limited to school-based activities. Community agencies, organizations, and volunteers also have a vital role to play beyond school walls.

African American Students and Community Involvement beyond School Walls

> The [youth organization] is an opportunity to become something. The people here, they'll help you become what you wanna become. They trust me. It makes me feel good. People here care, and I can *become something*. (McLaughlin, Irby, & Langman, 1994, p. 76, emphasis in original).

Clark (2002) found that how students use their out-of-school time had a significant influence on their academic success as measured by standardized test scores. Students who spend more time engaged in out-of-school learning activities guided by adults with high standards for achievement are more likely to be academically successful than students who spend more unstructured out-of-school time. McLaughlin et al. (1994) also discussed the importance of adult-supervised out-of-school activities for student success. They stated:

> For adolescents who are in school, some 40% of their waking hours are uncommitted. When school doors shut behind them in the early after-

noon, these young people are often claimed by the streets. . . . Youth who find their way from the streets to the few effective youth organizations in their neighborhoods encounter different environments that transform their discretionary hours into resources and opportunities for growth and hope. (p. 76)

The authors referred to these community-based organizations as "urban sanctuaries," which were diverse in the activities they offered, their funding sources, and their local and national affiliations, foci, goals, and strategies. However, these sanctuaries shared a common belief that youth in the community were "a resource to be developed, not a problem to be managed (McLaughlin et al., 1994, p. 76)"; high expectations for participants' behavior and performance; challenging and meaningful activities; and leadership by effective, talented, and committed adults, whom the authors referred to as "wizards."

While all caring and capable adults can provide needed support for African American students' learning and success, research suggests that caring and capable African American adults have an especially important role to play. For example, Zirkel (2003), in a longitudinal study of 80 12–14 year-olds, found that students who reported having at least one race- and gender-matched role model at the beginning of the study performed better academically up to 2 years later, reported more achievement-oriented goals, enjoyed achievement-relevant activities to a greater degree, thought more about their futures, and looked up to adults rather than peers more often than did students without a race- and gender-matched role model. These results were stronger for youth of color than for European American adolescents.

Based on an analysis of student questionnaire and diary data, as well as on parent interviews, Zirkel (2003) concluded that race- and gender-matched role models helped youth of color develop a deeper sense of their place and value in the larger society than mentors who did not share these characteristics. Race- and gender-matched role models also helped African American adolescents and other youth of color to begin to understand the social resources that they could draw upon to achieve their personal and professional goals. African American adults also can guide African American students' positive racial identity development, which has been directly linked to student academic achievement (see Nieto, 1998, pp. 289–291; Taylor, et al., 1994).

Thus community-based agencies, organizations, and programs, in addition to supporting schools that serve African American students, also have a vital role to play in supporting these students when they are out of school. Although no national database of community organizations that serve African American youth during non-school hours exists, studies and reports suggest that many such initiatives operate in the United States. Some of these organizations are large in scope; others are small. While in no way exhaustive, the four examples that follow illustrate the important contributions that these organizations make to the African American students they serve. Working from the premise that many schools serving African American students, while perhaps well intentioned, are indeed struggling to meet the developmental needs of their children and youth, these community organizations strengthen the educational pipeline for participating students. Furthermore, recognizing that systemic and bureaucratic infrastructures may limit the ability of school-based leaders to provide the types of educational supports and opportunities that African American students need in order to realize their full personal and academic potential, these community organizations provide a variety of services and activities that schools cannot.

Howard University's Upward Bound Program

The original Upward Bound pilot programs were established in the summer of 1965 on 17 college campuses in the United States. The Office of Economic Opportunity (OEO) created the program during President Johnson's "War on Poverty." It was an experimental program to help students of color and low-income White students attain a college education. The original pilot programs provided academic tutoring and cultural enrichment activities to 2,061 students, 1,500 of whom were recent high school graduates. Of the original participants, 80% were admitted to college in the fall of 1965, and 69% of freshmen who entered in 1965 remained and graduated.

Howard University's Upward Bound (HUB) program was established on this historical Black college campus in 1965 as one of the original pilot sites. The HUB provides a social and an academic pre-college experience in a collegiate setting. It serves 130 students annually who are: (1) U.S. citizens or resident aliens; (2) low income; (3) first-generation college bound; (4) enrolled at a targeted junior or senior high school; (5) enrolled in at least the ninth grade; and (6) in need of academic support.

The HUB has four major goals. These are to improve students' academic skills, assist students with the selection of college majors and careers, guide students' personal, social, and cultural development, and assist students with the educational planning required to achieve personal and professional goals. The program provides a range of student services, including academic, personal, and career counseling; instructional classes in English, mathematics, foreign language, science, and computer applications; assistance with college admissions and financial aid applications; college tours; and cultural and recreational excursions (Howard University, 2004).

The program director attributes the success and longevity of the HUB to several features, including consistent employees, effective professional development, alumni involvement, and, importantly, strong interpersonal relationships. He stated, "From ninth grade on, we consider these students our family. They know that we are here for them" (J. E. Bell, personal communication, March 25, 2004). During the program's nearly 40 years, it has served more than 5,000 African American youth in Washington, DC.

The Urban League's Black Scholars Early Recognition Program

The National Urban League was founded in 1910 to provide social services to African Americans and to guard their civil rights. The league is a non-profit, non-partisan, community-based organization. It has 100 affiliates in major cities in the United States, including Rochester, New York. The Rochester Urban League has several educational programs to support African American students. One such program is the Black Scholars and Early Recognition program.

In 1980, the Rochester Urban League created the Black Scholars program to recognize the outstanding academic achievement of graduating Black high school students. To participate in the program, a student in the twelfth grade must have a six-semester, unweighted GPA from the ninth, tenth, and eleventh grades of 3.0 or better. In 1985, the Urban League of Rochester introduced the Early Recognition program to cultivate students at an early age so that they could participate in the Black Scholars program. To be recognized early for this program, a student in the tenth grade must have a two-semester GPA of 2.5 or better, and a student in the eleventh grade must have a four-semester cumulative unweighted GPA from ninth and tenth grades of 2.5 or better.

When recognized in the tenths and eleventh grades, students have the opportunity to attend seminars on the college application process, financial aid, coping and survival skills for seniors, and other details to assist in navigating the college experience. Students who are accepted as Black Scholars in the twelfth grade can apply for select scholarships for African American students and admittance into the Black Scholars Mentor program, which pairs the high school student with a local and respected professional for the purpose of guidance and networking. The Urban League and the community celebrate the successes of these students in a culminating ceremony in which all honorees receive plaques, awards, scholarships, and dinner with family, friends, and community leaders (National Urban League, 2004).

Through the program, the Urban League unites community organizations, businesses, and the Rochester Public School System around advancing African American student achievement. In the fall, each high school in the Rochester City School District recommends students for the Early Recognition program. Each spring, high schools recommend students to be named as Black Scholars. Also, local churches, fraternities and sororities, the Manhattan Golf Club, Kodak, Chase Manhattan Bank, and local colleges and universities provide scholarships specifically for the Black Scholars program, using the Urban League as their focal contact (A. Rouse, personal communication, March 26, 2004). This integrated support for youth is systematic, reliable, and well organized.

CDF Summer Freedom Schools

The Children's Defense Fund (CDF) has been a strong advocate for poor children and children of color since its founding by Marian Wright Edelman in 1973. This non-profit organization, which grew out of the civil rights movement of the 1960s, is multifaceted and addresses many needs of children that may impede academic growth, including gang and gun violence, teen pregnancy, immunizations and health care, and fair and equal educational access and opportunities. With an understanding that the community and parents are critical partners in a child's educational future, the CDF has launched educational campaigns to highlight strategies that help children overcome obstacles to their social, emotional, cultural, physical, and educational development and well-being. Among these initiatives is the CDF Summer Freedom Schools (Children's Defense Fund, 2004). According to its director, the purpose of this community-based summer program is to cultivate social, cultural, and historical awareness among students ages 5–18 (J. Middleton-Hairston, personal communication, March 25, 2004). Community organizations that would like to begin Freedom Schools must apply to the CDF; once accepted, they receive training and support.

Freedom Schools are free to participants and seek to extend learning opportunities through the summer months, especially for students who might otherwise not receive such services. Carefully selected and trained college student interns teach at the schools, which typically run for 6 consecutive weeks. One of the most successful Freedom School sites is in Kansas City, where Freedom Schools are housed in seven churches in Missouri and Kansas. The curriculum is centered on reading, writing, self-esteem, and critical thinking. However, recognizing that students are motivated to make educational gains through different catalysts, the Freedom Schools also offer social and cultural activities and learning opportunities. In addition, Freedom Schools work with participants' families to guide and support their active involvement and advocacy for their children during the regular school year. In the summer of 2003, more than 700 Kansas City students attended Freedom Schools, and all enrollment slots for the 2004 summer program had been filled by March 2003 (Kauffman Foundation, 2004).

Four Corner Sharp Program

In addition to initiatives supported by large national organizations such as the Urban League, smaller, local, community-based initiatives also provide valuable services to African American students, such as the Four Corner Sharp Program in Montgomery County, Maryland, which offers academic support, counseling, and mentoring to students suspended from school. This federally funded program houses students who are suspended for 3 or more days in a nearby church facility. For students to participate in the program, parents must attend an orientation meeting, sign a consent form, and provide transportation to and from the location. When parents cannot attend the required orientation, the program director comes to the school to meet with the parent, student, and administrator or visits the student's home.

Once students are accepted into the program, the director travels to each school to collect academic assignments, data on students' referral/suspension history, and lunch. This is the director's full-time job. He is committed and dependable, a true community "wizard." One of the bonuses of his program is that he submits a progress report on students' behavior and performance while in his program. Another bonus is that he serves as a mentor, counseling students regarding patterns of, and alternative choices to, misbehavior. More programs of this nature are needed to help urban schools that struggle with student behavioral problems and high suspension rates. Unfortunately, like many other such initiatives, this worthwhile program constantly faces funding challenges.

CONCLUSION

Community involvement is one factor shown to influence African American students' successful navigation of the educational pipeline. Such involvement can occur through school-based programs of partnership or through community-based initiatives during non-school hours. Either approach requires educational and community leaders and policy makers to address key challenges to ensure effective practice. These are considered next.

Moving School Leaders toward More Effective Community Partnerships

Theoretically, school, family, and community partnerships are a way to fashion a web of school-based support for all students, especially those at greatest risk for academic failure. For example, schools can recruit and train classroom tutors to provide the support and assistance necessary for all students to master challenging curriculum. Schools also might create apprenticeships or service learning projects so that students are helped to see the relevance of school persistence and possibly paid a wage for their work efforts. The list of desirable partnership activities is a long one, but unfortunately many schools do not take advantage of what community partners can offer.

If meaningful school-community partnerships are to move from their limited reality to their theoretical potential, educators must be prepared to rethink and transform the way they educate students. Students must be viewed holistically, and educators, especially school principals (Sanders & Harvey, 2002), must understand their role as not only transmitting information and managing school buildings and budgets but also facilitating the development of close ties among students and caring, responsible adults. Merz and Furman (1997) used the German term *geimeinshaft* to describe this approach to educational change and reform. Geimeinshaft reform efforts emphasize the importance of nurturing relationships and interpersonal connections for the academic success and well-being of children and youth.

This transformation in schooling will require leadership from progressive educators at all levels—state, district, and school. Progressive principals in K–12 schools must model for their faculty and staff a genuine openness to community involvement and actively communicate with individuals in the community about possible areas of collaboration. Progressive teachers in K–12 schools must work to open their classrooms to family and community members. Progressive faculty in higher education must draw on current research and successful practices to bring the need for meaningful partnerships with students' families and communities to the forefront of their courses for pre-service and in-service teachers and administrators. While much progress has been made over the last 3 decades (Epstein, 2002; Henderson & Mapp, 2003), more remains to be done to institutionalize partnerships as educational best practice.

Moving Community Leaders toward More Effective Community-Based Partnerships

The community also must embrace its rightful role and responsibility in offering social services and educational and cultural enrichment as extensions to the school day and year to address community ills and needs that negatively affect academic achievement. Through such engagement, community organizations express their high expectations for African American children's school success, and, equally important, their commitment to assisting students in meeting these expectations. These messages can be communicated and social and cultural values transmitted through mentoring, tutoring, and artistic, athletic, service, and leadership activities, not for the few but for the many.

When discussing community contributions to the school outcomes of African American students, Nettles (1991a) argued that often community programs are more effective for some subgroups of participants and not for others. She further stated the following:

Moreover the voluntary nature of community programs (students are typically free to participate at will) and the practice of eliminating students who failed to participate regularly tended to result in participant groups that may have been motivated to overcome adversity (and were therefore less at risk than students with lesser motivation). (p. 143)

It is unclear if the underrepresentation of high-risk youth and reduced program effectiveness for these youth are due to recruitment practices, activities offered, requirements and incentives for participation, other factors, or a combination of factors. However, it is an area that community organizations must consider in the design and implementation of community-based initiatives. Questions of outreach and retention are especially important if the community is to serve African American children and youth who are at greatest risk for school failure and dropout.

Community-based organizations that serve African American youth also would benefit from greater interorganizational information exchange and coordination. As stated previously, there is currently no national database of community-based organizations serving African American children and youth. As a result, useful information about funding, recruitment and retention of participants and staff, evaluation strategies and sources for technical support, and best practices is not shared among the leaders of these initiatives. Consequently, many organizations, such as the Four Corner Sharp Program, struggle alone to find ways to sustain their initiatives over time. Moreover, parents and schools in search of community organizations that can support and broaden students' learning experiences are without a central resource to identify such programs. The information sharing made possible by a national database would assist community-based organizations in refining, focusing, and delivering their services to African American youth.

Moving Educational Policy toward Greater Support of School-Community Partnerships

Heath & McLaughlin, in 1987, wrote that each institution, the home, school, and community,

has a unique and necessary contribution to make to the development of academically successful, motivated, healthy, and effective children. Their combined contributions form the heart of a child resource policy. (p. 580)

Since the publication of this statement, federal policies, including recent reauthorizations of the Elementary and Secondary Education Act (ESEA) and the Individuals with Disabilities Education Act (IDEA), have been amended to reflect a growing awareness of the importance of family and community involvement in the education of children and youth. Such policies have been constructed to encourage states, districts, and schools to develop strategies and programs for meaningful school, family, and community partnerships.

While the greater emphasis has been on family involvement, schools also are encouraged to link with businesses and community-based organizations to provide children and youth with services that support academic progress. For example, based on Epstein's framework for family involvement (Epstein, 2002), Title I of No Child Left Behind (NCLB) requires that in addition to linking with families, schools also develop community partnerships to support students' learning (U.S. Department of Education, 2004a). In addition, the 21st Century Community Learning Centers initiative, part of Title IV of NCLB, encourages urban and rural schools to connect with community organizations to support students' academic and social success (U.S. Department of Education, 2004b).

Although such policies and programs exist, their interpretation and development at the state, district, and local levels determine their impact on educational practice and student outcomes (Osher & Quinn, 2003). States and districts differ in the support they provide to school leaders to identify and link with community organizations and resources. They also differ in the extent to which they reduce bureaucratic barriers to the fluid exchange of resources between schools and community-based organizations (Dryfoos, 1998a).

Future federal policy must, thus, provide greater incentives to states and districts to devise strategies that encourage meaningful school-community collaboration. Such incentives may include more funding to support staff in district offices of family and community involvement, or to hire district- and/or school-level personnel whose sole responsibility is to help schools identify, coordinate, and evaluate school-community partnerships. While Dryfoos (1998a) noted the important school-community linkages that have resulted from the 21st Century Community Learning Centers initiative, she further observed the following:

> The big gap in funding is for the infrastructure that pulls all these activities together. An administrator must be available to identify resources, write proposals, monitor program activities, supervise the staff, and make sure the pieces work as a comprehensive, integrated package. (p. 41)

Furthermore, federal policy in education should be combined with policies and funding to encourage community-based agencies to reach out to schools. Albeit difficult, this coordinated policy approach is necessary if school-community partnerships are to ensure the safety net that we propose for African American children and youth.

Community involvement, then, both in *and* out of schools, can support African American students' successful navigation through elementary, secondary, and postsecondary institutions. It cannot supplant the importance of consistently excellent teaching in well-resourced and safe schools. However, the ties that result from such involvement can help bind African American children and youth to brighter and more productive futures.

NOTES

1. The statistics that follow are taken from Hoffman, Llagas, and Snyder (2003). See References for full citation.

2. The following statistics are taken from Lippman, Burns, and McArthur (1996). See References for full citation.

3. For more information, visit http://www.partnershipschools.org.

REFERENCES

Amato, P. R. (1996). Explaining the intergenerational transmission of divorce. *Journal of Marriage and the Family, 58*, 628–640.

Children's Defense Fund. (2004). *Freedom schools: "I can and must make a difference!"* Retrieved March 8, 2004, http://www.childrensdefense.org/freedomschools/default.asp

Clark, R. (2002). Ten hypotheses about what predicts student achievement for African American students and all other students: What the research shows. In W. R. Allen, M. B. Spencer, & C. O'Conner (Eds.), *African-American education: Race, community, inequality, and achievement: A tribute to Edgar G. Epps.* Oxford, UK: Elsevier Science.

Coleman, J. (1987). Social capital and the development of youth. *Momentum, 18*, 6–8.

Comer, J. (1993). *School power: Implications of an intervention project.* New York: Free Press.

Davies, D. (January 2002). The 10th school revisited: Are school/family/community partnerships on the reform agenda now? *Phi Delta Kappan*, 388–392.

Dryfoos, J. (1998a). The rise of the full-service community school. *The High School Magazine, 6*(2), 38–42.

Dryfoos, J. (1998b). *Safe passage: Making it through adolescence in a risky society. What parents, schools, and communities can do.* New York: Oxford University Press.

Durham, J. (2003). The other side of the story: The world of African American academies in the South after the Civil War. *The Negro Educational Review, 54*(1–2): 3–16.

Epstein, J. (2002). *School, family, and community partnerships: Preparing educators and improving schools.* Boulder, CO: Westview Press.

Fashola, O., & Cooper, R. (1999). Developing the academic talents of African American students during the non-school hours: Four exemplary programs. *The Journal of Negro Education, 68*(2), 130–137.

Freeman, K. (1999). No services needed?: The case for mentoring high-achieving African American students. *Peabody Journal of Education, 74*(2), 15–26.

Gardner, III, Cartledge, G., Seidl, B., Woolsey, M., Schley, G., & Utley, C. (2001). Mt. Olivet after-school program: Peer-mediated interventions for at-risk students. *Remedial and Special Education, 22*(1), 22–23.

Harlem Children's Zone Project. (2004). *Harlem children's zone.* Retrieved March 26, 2004, http://www.hcz.org/hczproject/hcz-pl.htm

Heath, S. B., & McLaughlin, M. W. (1987). A child resource policy: Moving beyond dependence on school and family, *Phi Delta Kappan, 68,* 576–580.

Heath, S., & McLaughlin, M. (1996). The best of both worlds: Connecting schools and community youth organizations for all-day, all-year learning. In J. Cibulka and W. Kritek (Eds.), *Coordination among schools, families, and communities: Prospects for educational reform* (pp. 50–69). Albany: State University of New York Press.

Henderson, A., & Mapp, K. (2003). *A new wave of evidence: The impact of school, family, and community connections on student achievement.* Austin, TX: Southwest Educational Development Laboratory.

Hess, Jr., G. (1999). Community participation or control? From New York to Chicago. *Theory into Practice, 38*(4), 217–24.

Hoffman, K., Llagas, C., & Snyder, T. (2003). *Status and trends in the education of Blacks.* Washington, DC: National Center for Education Statistics.

Howard University. (2004). *Upward Bound.* Retrieved on March 1, 2004, http://www.howard.edu/schooleducation/Programs/TRIO-02.htm

Infoplease. (2004). *African Americans by the numbers: From the U.S. Census Bureau.* Retrieved February 3, 2004, http://www.infoplease.com/spot/bhmcensus1.html

Jansorn, N., & Salinas, K. (2002). *Promising partnership practices 2002: The 5th annual collection from members of the National Network of Partnership Schools.* Baltimore, MD: Center on School, Family, and Community Partnerships, Johns Hopkins University Press.

Kaufman Foundation. (2004a). *Freedom schools expand to serve 1,000 children this summer.* Retrieved March 24, 2004, http://www.emkf.org/pages/361.cfm

Kauffman Foundation (2004b). *Kauffman thought book.* Kansas City, MO: Author.

Lee, J., & Cramond, B. (1999). The positive effects of mentoring economically disadvantaged students. *Professional School Counseling, 2*(3), 172–178.

Lippman, L., Burns, S., & McArthur, E. (1996). *Urban schools: The challenge of location and poverty.* Washington, DC: National Center for Education Statistics.

McLaughlin, M., Irby, M., & Langman, J. (1994). Urban sanctuaries: Neighborhood organizations that keep hope alive. *Phi Delta Kappan, 76.*

McPartland, J., & Nettles, S. (1991). Using community adults as advocates or mentors for at-risk middle school students: A two-year evaluation of Project Raise. *American Journal of Education, 99*, 568–586.

Merz, C., & Furman, G. (1997). *Community and schools: Promise and paradox.* New York: Teachers College Press.

National Center for Educational Statistics (NCES). (1998). *Parent involvement in children's education: Efforts by public elementary schools.* Washington, DC: Author.

National Center for Educational Statistics (NCES). (2001). *The condition of education, 2001.* Washington, DC: Author.

National Urban League. (2004). *The State of Black America 2004: The complexity of Black progress.* New York: Author.

Nettles, S. (1991a). Community contributions to school outcomes of African American students. *Education and Urban Society, 24* (1), 132–147.

Nettles, S. (1991b). Community involvement and disadvantaged students: A review. *Review of Educational Research, 61*(3): 379–406.

Newman, L. (April 1995). *School-agency-community partnerships: What is the early impact on student school performance?* Paper presented at the annual meeting of the American Educational Research Association, San Francisco, CA. (ERIC Document Reproduction Service No. ED385950)

Nieto, S. (1998). *Affirming diversity: The sociopolitical context of multicultural education,* 3rd edition. New York: Longman.

Osher, D., & Quinn, M. (2003). Policies matter: For students, for teachers, and for better outcomes. *Preventing School Failure, 47*(2), 52–58.

Phelps-Stokes, H. (1929). *Excerpt on education from the Phelps-Stokes papers.* Retrieved January 23, 2004, http://www.cti.itc.virginia.edu/~aas405a/phelps.html

Sanders, M. G. (1996). School-family-community partnerships focused on school safety. *Journal of Negro Education, 65*(3), 369–374.

Sanders, M. G. (1998). The effects of school, family, and community support on the academic achievement of African American adolescents. *Urban Education, 33*(3), 385–409.

Sanders, M. G. (Ed.). (2000). *Schooling students placed at risk: Research, policy, and practice in the education of poor and minority adolescents.* Mahwah, NJ: Lawrence Erlbaum.

Sanders, M. G. (2001). A study of the role of "community" in comprehensive school, family and community partnership programs. *The Elementary School Journal, 102*(1),19–34.

Sanders, M. G., & Epstein, J. L. (2000a). Building school, family, and community partnerships in secondary schools. In M. G. Sanders (Ed.), *Schooling students placed at risk: Research, policy, and practice in the education of poor and minority adolescents* (pp. 339–362). Mahwah, NJ: Lawrence Erlbaum.

Sanders, M. G., & Epstein, J. L. (2000b). The National Network of Partnership Schools: How research influences educational practice. *Journal of Education for Students Placed at Risk, 5*(1–2), 61–76.

Sanders, M. G., & Harvey, A. (2002). Beyond the school walls: A case study of principal leadership for school-community collaboration. *Teachers College Record, 104*(7), 1345–1368.

Sanders, M., & Lewis, K. (2005). Building bridges toward excellence: Community involvement in high schools. *High School Journal, 88*(3), 1–9.

Taylor, R., Casten, R., Hickinger, S., Roberts, D., & Fulmore, C. (1994). Explaining the school performance of African American adolescents. *Journal of Research on Adolescents 4*, 21–44.

U.S. Department of Education. (2004a). Elementary and secondary education. Retrieved June 2, 2004, http://www.ed.gov/policy/elsec/leg/esea02/pg2.html#sec1118

U.S. Department of Education. (2004b). 21st Century Community Learning Centers. Retrieved June 2, 2004, http://www.ed.gov/programs/21stcclc/index.html

Walker, V. (1996). *Their highest potential: An African American school community in the segregated South*. Chapel Hill: University of North Carolina Press.

Zirkel, S. (2003). Is there a place for me? Role models and academic identity among White students and students of color. *Teachers College Record, 104*(2), 35.

Chapter 8

How African American Families Can Facilitate the Academic Achievement of Their Children

Implications for Family-Based Interventions

Jelani Mandara and Carolyn B. Murray

The current academic underachievement of African American children is a deplorable consequence of centuries of systematic discrimination in all areas relevant to academic success (Cress-Welsing, 1990; Murray & Jackson, 1997; Woodson, 1990). However, regardless of the causes of the current situation, parents still have the greatest power and responsibility to facilitate the academic achievement of their children. That does not mean that other social systems do not impact African American achievement, but that the impact of those other systems can be moderated by family strengths (Kumpfer & Alvarado, 2003). Unfortunately, most African American parents have been conditioned to think that the educational system has the primary power and responsibility for their children's achievement. This is not only an erroneous assumption about the role of the educational system but, given the problems of the public schools that most African American children attend (Lankford, Loeb, & Wyckoff, 2002; Murray & Jackson, 1997), this assumption can be deleterious to their academic success.

For African American parents to take primary responsibility for their children's academic achievement, there are several areas of child development that they must attempt to modify or control via their socialization practices. They must facilitate: (1) achievement-oriented expectations and goals; (2) academic behavioral habits; (3) academic self-confidence; (4) general psychological health; (5) self-control; (6) feelings of personal power or agency; and (7) critical thinking skills in their children. Furthermore, they must create a physical space conducive to achievement and actively inhibit the impact of anti-achievement factors such as underachieving peers, destructive media influences, and systematic discrimination in the school system (e.g., low teacher expectations, tracking, and nonacademic curricula).

The purpose of this chapter is to highlight a comprehensive set of factors within the home and school system that African American parents must confront to influence these areas of child development. This chapter is organized around the following areas: (1) general socialization; (2) differential socialization based on gender; (3) racial socialization; (4) direct academic socialization; and (5) problems in the public school system of which parents must be aware. This chapter is not written for African American parents per se, but for those interested in creating comprehensive and culturally relevant family-based interventions with African American families.

General Socialization and Discipline

General socialization is composed of parental demandingness and parental responsiveness. Parenting styles, or the dispositional patterns of behaviors parents use to socialize their children, involve the classification of parents based on some combination of these dimensions (Mandara, 2003). A long tradition of theoretical and empirical research consistently finds four prototypical parenting styles: authoritative, authoritarian, permissive, and neglectful (Baumrind, 1991; Mandara, 2003). What is critical to understand for the development of effective family-based interventions with African Americans is that the definitions and effectiveness of parenting styles are culturally specific (Mandara & Murray, 2002). The optimal parenting style for European Americans is not necessarily optimal for African Americans, because cultural beliefs, societal norms, expectations, and treatment are different. For instance, the same behaviors that society considers explorations or "kids being kids" for European American children are more likely to be considered juvenile delinquency for African American children. In a like manner, middle-class European American parents can safely assume that teachers will have high expectations of success for their children, while African American parents of all socioeconomic statuses have to assume the exact opposite (Murray & Jackson, 1997). These different circumstances require different parenting strategies. Furthermore, there are different cultural goals for and expectations of children that impact the effectiveness of different parenting strategies (Mandara, 2004).

In general, to facilitate the important traits of self-control, agency, and psychological health in children, family-based academic achievement interventions should be designed to promote authoritative parenting for all groups (Baumrind, 1996). However, African American authoritativeness is qualitatively different than European American authoritativeness. The form of authoritativeness most associated with high academic achievement for African

Americans is relatively higher on demandingness and parental control and relatively lower in their acquiescence to child demands than the optimal European American parenting style (see Mandara, 2004, for a review). However, it is clearly not enough for interventions to stress to African American parents the need to be high in demandingness and responsiveness. Parents also need a more detailed understanding of the specific strategies they should employ. A brief discussion of aspects of each major dimension follows.

Demandingness

It is imperative that African American parents maintain behavioral control over their children from the time their children are toddlers until they are mature enough to make well-informed and rational decisions for themselves. Maintaining firm control during the younger ages and gradually allowing children more freedom as their self-control increases is the best way to develop these skills. This does not mean that parents should be oppressive and restrictive of every move their children make (Mandara & Murray, 2002). However, they must have a set of clearly defined and consistent rules and expectations for appropriate behavior (Baumrind, 1996). It also must be made clear to African American parents that the main way of promoting appropriate behaviors is not only to punish unwanted behavior but to reward children for appropriate behaviors (Netzel & Eber, 2003). This has historically been an underutilized socialization strategy of African American parents, but it is critical to reinforce those behaviors parents want and expect from their children.

Similarly, general communication is an effective strategy for increasing behavioral compliance (Jaccard, Dodge, & Dittus, 2003; Smetana, Crean, Daddis, 2002). African American parents must move away from the traditional, "Do it because I said so" explanations. Children will respond best and begin to develop better critical thinking skills when they are given rational reasons for specific rules and expectations (McDowell, Parke, & Wang, 2003). We believe that clarifying that each rule is ultimately for the child's best interest, and not because the parents are trying to be malicious, will reduce the rebellion problems many parents encounter with their adolescents.

Another very important goal of African American parents, particularly those who live in often chaotic and disorganized communities, is to facilitate order, structure, and consistency in their homes (Johnson, Cowan, & Cowan, 1999; Smith et al., 2001). Parents should strive to maintain consistent bedtimes, even for adolescents, consistent mealtimes, preferably with as many family members together as possible, and a moderate level of clearly defined and equitable chores. This type of structure will develop the important traits of time management skills and self-control.

Although the recent trend in discipline interventions is to focus on rewarding positive behaviors (Netzel & Eber, 2003), as it should be, these interventions often ignore the fact that punishing unwanted behavior is still an important dimension of parenting (Mandara, 2004). Parents not only have to set rules, order, and structure, they must also reinforce those rules when children disobey. For African American parents, ordinary spanking, not child abuse, especially in the context of a generally authoritative home, is an effective way to develop and maintain the parental control necessary to facilitate the desired traits of self-control and emotional stability (Deater-Deckard, Dodge, Bates, & Pettit, 1996). As with firm control in general, African American children raised around other African Americans perceive spanking to be an appropriate form of discipline for misbehavior (Gunnoe & Mariner, 1997; Mandara, 2004). Although well intentioned, the ethnocentric biases of many who create family-based interventions with African Americans make it difficult for them to accept that fact about spanking. Instead of avoiding the issue, family-based interventions need to more clearly define and explain the appropriate use, times, and ages to spank children.

For instance, interventions should teach parents to: (1) only spank on the child's buttocks; (2) only spank between the ages of about 18 months to 10 at the oldest; (3) only spank a child when it is clear to the child why he or she is getting a spanking, preferably at the moment of blatant disobedience; (4) use other forms of discipline such as time-out and taking away possessions first; and (5) not spank a child more than five or six times a year, and much less as children get older, unless there is a dysfunctional parent, child, and/or parent-child relationship. In general, the fear of being spanked will usually serve as an adequate means of maintaining control and discipline. Once a child develops the self-control and cognitive skills necessary to reflect on the causes and consequences of her or his behavior, spanking will no longer be needed or effective.

Responsiveness

Although consistent, firm, yet not oppressive discipline should be a critical dimension of any intervention with African American families, a focus on responsiveness should be just as critical (Baumrind, 1996). As discussed earlier, the need for positive reinforcement is also a critical concern for family-based interventions. All children respond best to learning environments when they are given continued and sincere praise for their accomplishments and appropriate behavior (Henderlong & Lepper, 2002). In light of the negative images and other destructive feedback to which African American children are exposed, praise and other forms of positive reinforcement may be especially critical to them (Ward, 2004).

Another related aspect of responsiveness that interventions must stress is emotional warmth and communication between parents and their children. All children require reassurance that they are loved, respected, and hold a special place in someone's heart (Mandara & Murray, 2002). Many African American children are reared with several siblings or other children, often with one parent who is burdened with work and other time constraints. Thus the "lap time" every child requires becomes limited (Cress-Welsing, 1990). However, individual parents or caretakers should dedicate regular times with individual children where they do something enjoyable for the child (e.g., walk to the park) and allow the child to talk about himself or herself and his or her wishes and needs. This does not mean that parents have to be at the beck and call of their children, but they must be responsive to their children's needs for love, encouragement, and respect. These are critical for the development of general psychological health and agency (Mandara & Murray, 2002). The children who are defensive, loud, and act out in order to be seen are children who did not receive enough lap time (Cress-Welsing, 1990).

Traditionally, many African American parents' discipline has been overly restrictive of their children's movements. This is probably an artifact of society's insistence that African Americans know their place, and thus it was more of a survival mechanism than anything else. However, interventions should teach African American parents the necessity of allowing children the freedom to explore and feel as if they have control over their environment (Mattanah, 2001). This does not mean that parents should not maintain firm control. Finding the balance between firm parental control and allowing the child personal freedom is one of the most delicate aspects of raising children. Interventions have to teach parents how to establish age-appropriate boundaries while allowing children the freedom to explore and control their environment within those boundaries.

GENDERED SOCIALIZATION

Another critical issue to understand when dealing with African American families is the interaction of parenting styles with family structure and gender. Over 60% of African American children are raised in single mother-headed homes (Fields, 2003), and thus one must discuss their development within this context (Mandara & Murray, 2000). European American and other American racial groups' parents have historically tended to have lower educational goals and expectations of their daughters relative to their sons. However, several authors have argued that this may be just the opposite in mother-headed African American families, because the old adage in African American communities, that

"Black mothers love their sons and raise their daughters," is true (Mandara & Murray, 2000; McLoyd, 1990). In practical terms, this implies that the average African American mother tends to expect more, rely on more, and generally control and guide her daughters more than her sons. In addition, the average African American father is just the opposite, because he tends to push his boys to achieve, is physically rougher, more demanding, controlling, and guiding of his sons than with his daughters and more than mothers (Mandara & Murray, 2000). Therefore, for African American boys, one consequence of growing up predominately with a single mother is that they are raised without the traditional rough-and-tumble fatherly socialization.

These socialization strategies are critical to the development of traits important for academic achievement. For instance, even after Social Economic Status (SES) is controlled, single-parent African American boys tend to have lower academic achievement (Teachman, Day, Paasch, Carver, & Call, 1998), self-esteem, self-control, agency (Mandara & Murray, 2000), perceptions of their masculinity (Mandara, Murray, & Joyner, 2004), and higher delinquency and drug use (Anderson, 2002) compared to African American boys who grew up living with both parents. Because single-parent girls still get the "raising" (i.e., tough love) from their mothers, they usually do not suffer from the same low levels of achievement, self-confidence, and self-control as their brothers (Mandara & Murray, 2000). However, because they miss the "love" (i.e., coddling) of their fathers, they tend to seek out this nurturance from other males. Thus they tend to be more sexually precocious, active, and more likely to be teen mothers compared to father-present girls (Ellis, et al., 2003). Therefore, those who create family-based interventions with African Americans have to make parents aware of this probably subconscious tendency to differentially socialize their boys and girls. Both girls and boys require discipline and responsiveness.

The problem for single-parent boys is that they also require the more physically demanding rough-and-tumble play that they may miss when their fathers are absent. We cannot expect mothers to wrestle or play football with their boys the way fathers do. However, the more physically demanding environment that fathers facilitate is important for males' physical and psychosocial development (Mandara, et al., 2004). Furthermore, African American mothers' tendency to protect their boys from the many societal obstacles they face (e.g., gang violence, police brutality) may inadvertently make them physically and mentally weak and dependent, which will ultimately facilitate low self-confidence and low achievement orientations. Therefore, interventions must stress the importance of getting all children, but especially father-absent boys, involved in physically and psychologically demanding activities and around older responsible males. In addition, interventions have to stress the importance of boys being involved with men who have the disciplinary authority a father would (especially their real fathers, uncles, and grandfathers). That does not mean that single mothers cannot do a good job of raising boys; it simply means that what we can reasonably expect them to do often falls short of what boys need, and if those who create interventions are serious about helping this group, then they will have to deal with that fact.

RACIAL SOCIALIZATION

The psychological health and self-confidence of children are largely dependent on how they view others of their salient social groups (e.g., family, gender, and race). Therefore, racial minority parents have the important task of instilling a positive racial identity in their children (Caughy, O'Campo, Randolph, & Nickerson, 1992; Murray & Mandara, 2002). This can be an especially difficult task for parents of African descent, because they have to continually combat the negative racial stereotypes from the mass media (Ward, 2004), educational system (Murray & Jackson, 1997), and Western religious mythology (Cress-Welsing, 1990) if they expect their children to have positive feelings and constructive thoughts about their race and about themselves as members of that race. The difficulty for those who wish to create family-based interventions arises from the fact that many African American parents do not believe in discussing racial issues with their children, and many others use ineffective or even counterproductive strategies when they do (Murray & Mandara, 2002). However, racial socialization must be a critical component of any comprehensive intervention with African American families (Coard, Wallace, Stevenson, & Brotman, 2004).

Researchers have identified four types of racial socialization messages that African American parents use to varying degrees (see Mandara, 2004, for a recent review). Each type of message has been related to academic achievement and/or psychological health (Caughy, et al., 1992; Murray & Mandara, 2002). The form of racial socialization that is positively associated with high academic achievement and psychological health stresses positive feelings toward and knowledge of one's history and race, as well as the ability of a child to achieve and control her or his destiny in spite of racism (Mandara, 2004). African American parents who do not stress racial pride and heritage, or teach their children that they have the power to achieve in spite of barriers, tend to have children who suffer from low academic achievement and/or low self-esteem and other psychological problems (Caughy, et al., 1992; Murray & Mandara, 2002). Therefore, it is critical that African American parents include in their family routines behaviors that will transmit certain racial messages and prevent others.

First and foremost, African American parents have to monitor the negative images and stereotypes with which their children will be bombarded. This will be best accomplished by limiting exposure to negative images. The racist and sexist religious mythology to which African American children are exposed will ultimately make them feel and think that they are inferior to Whites and will make girls feel that they are inferior to males. As long as African American children are subjected to such mythology, they will continue to suffer the psychological and behavioral consequences of such beliefs (Cress-Welsing, 1990).

Unsupervised television is undoubtedly another destructive force in the lives of African American children (Ward, 2004), and the demeaning and sexist songs proliferating on the radio are equally problematic (Johnson, Jackson, & Gatto, 1995). Therefore, the combination of TV and radio in music videos represents the most psychologically debilitating form of media to date. Recent experiments have shown that African American adolescents randomly exposed to view "gansta rap" videos were much more likely to endorse general violence and aggression (Johnson, et al., 1995) and violence toward women (Johnson, Adams, Ashburn, & Reed, 1995; Johnson, et al., 1995) and relate to materialism and drug dealers than those assigned to a no-violence video or no video control group. Furthermore, those assigned to the gansta rap video expressed less confidence that a young African American male character in a study vignette would achieve his academic goals (Johnson et al., 1995). Unfortunately, African American children watch 3 to 6 hours of television every day, with most of it unsupervised and much of it sexist music videos on BET or MTV (Ward, 2004). This is clearly an issue about interventions to which African American parents must be alerted.

Not only do parents have to limit exposure to destructive images, they also have to constantly discuss and dispel the myths. Parents need to openly discuss with their children the reality of racism and other "isms" and why certain characterizations are destructive and may only apply to a small percentage of African Americans. The constant portrayal of African Americans as underachievers and the glorification of European Americans in television, radio, school, and religious mythology help promote beliefs in children that African Americans are not and cannot be highly successful in school (Murray & Mandara, 2002). Thus many African American children begin to dis-identify with school because they want to identify with what they have been taught African Americans are (i.e., underachievers), while others dis-identify with African Americans because they want to identify with academic achievers. It is imperative that African American parents make it clear to their children that there is no inherent dichotomy between achieving academically and embracing their culture. They can, and should, do both.

The other racial socialization task of parents is to instill a sense of pride in their children. The best way to help parents do this is by having them continually discuss African and African American history and accomplishments, especially as they relate to achieving. Furthermore, African American parents can expose their children to positive images by taking them to cultural events that let children view African Americans engaged in productive activities such as in marketplaces, museums, and community bookstores. Exposing African American children to positive Black art, toys, books, and cultural events such as Kwanzaa is another way of instilling pride and confidence (Caughy, et al., 1992). It also is important that parents realize that instilling racial pride does not mean denigrating others. The African American parents with the most underachieving children tend to teach their children to have a disdain for Whites (Marshall, 1995; Murray & Mandara, 2002). Therefore, the focus of African American parents' racial socialization should not be on anti-White messages but on positive Black messages and images.

DIRECT ACADEMIC SOCIALIZATION

Clearly, a central focus of any family-based academic achievement intervention should be to enhance the direct academic socialization that children receive on a daily basis. Interventions must teach parents the skills and necessity of being actively involved in their children's schoolwork, monitoring their time, play, and friends, having high expectations of academic achievement, and creating a physical space conducive to learning. Because of significant time and financial constraints, the direct academic socialization of children often gets pushed down the priority list for many African American parents. However, parents have to understand that it is one of the most important duties they have as parents in America.

Parental involvement in school activities and homework greatly influences the academic achievement of African American children, especially in the early years (Marcon, 1999). However, many African American parents, who were themselves undereducated as children, are not aware of how important it is to the academic achievement of their children, or exactly what involvement entails. Furthermore, many parents do not begin to work with their children until problems in school begin (Halle, Kurtz-Costes, & Mahoney, 1997). However, parents have to understand the necessity of supplementing and reinforcing the material that their children are given in school with extra learning material, before their children begin to struggle. This is especially important during the summer, when African American children tend to fall behind their European American classmates (Schacter, 2003).

To direct the involvement of parents, helpful interventions would include providing parents with guidance in developing a realistic summer curriculum for their children (Schacter, 2003). A useful resource for parents would be a hierarchically arranged list of skills that their children need to attain during a specified period of time, curricular materials such as workbooks and other resources, and simple measures for evaluating their children's progress toward each milestone. Such resources would give parents direction as to where to focus their energy and the ability to monitor the progress of their children.

In addition, many are unaware of the nature and degree of involvement that is most conducive to achievement (Halle, et al., 1997). Prospective interventions have to explicate exactly how to do homework with a younger child, without actually doing the work for the child, and how to monitor and evaluate the homework of an adolescent. Furthermore, it is important that parents learn to allocate a specific time each day for working on homework and academic skills with their children. This is not only good for achievement and developing learning skills, but the children's time management skills and self-control will be greatly enhanced by a structured schedule. Therefore, parental time management workshops would be a useful endeavor for family-based interventions.

Involvement also includes the strict monitoring of schoolwork and communication with children and teachers about the parents' goals and expectations for their children's academic success (McWayne, et al., 2004). Parents must talk to their children on a daily basis about their day at school, future assignments, and performances on past assignments. They need to understand their children's academic strengths and weaknesses. This will be further helped by frequently contacting their children's teachers. The relationships that African American parents establish with their children's teachers are critical for a variety of reasons (discussed in more detail in the next section) but underestimated in importance. African American parents have to let teachers know that they have high expectations of success for their children, and that they will work with their children to meet these expectations. It is critical for African American parents to make it clear to their children's teachers that they are partners in their children's achievement. Helpful interventions would include training parents how to effectively communicate with their children's teachers.

One of the most important skills that interventions can teach parents is how to foster learning situations in everyday life (Nasir, 2002). In general, the home environment needs to be constructed in such a way that it is cognitively stimulating. Having plenty of books, other reading materials, and cognitively stimulating toys and games around the home is critical to this endeavor. In a recent study we conducted using national longitudinal data, the amount of newspapers and magazines around African American mothers' homes when they were children accounted for a large amount of variance in not only their cognitive development but even in their children's cognitive development, even after SES and family functioning were controlled. Being poor is a very weak excuse for not having an intellectually stimulating environment. Many charities give away used children's books and toys, or sell them for minimal charges. This is an example of why parents must learn to prioritize their time and use of resources in such a way that their children's academic success is at the top of the list.

Playing intellectually stimulating games with their children such as Scrabble, chess, and dominoes is also a convenient way to reinforce and further develop their children's math, reading, and critical thinking skills (Nasir, 2002).

Children usually associate games with fun and recreation, so they are usually very receptive to them. Furthermore, African American parents need to learn how to discuss challenging and complex issues with their children such as politics, history, and culture. The point is to make their children comfortable thinking about complex issues. They must learn to replace radio, television, and video game time with reading and intellectually challenging activities.

Along those same lines, African American parents have to learn the importance of out of the home stimulation. Frequent trips to museums, zoos, and libraries are wonderful yet underutilized ways of developing learning skills. Even long drives or train rides help stimulate children's thinking and curiosity. Unfortunately, many inner-city African American children rarely get to see anything of the world other than their immediate environment. Helpful interventions would include organized frequent field trips to cognitively stimulating places.

PROBLEMS IN THE PUBLIC SCHOOL SYSTEM

The school is an essential agent for knowledge acquisition, socialization, and acceptance in society (Pianta, 1999). What we learn in school influences our perception of ourselves and others, as well as our values and behaviors. However, the problems in the public school system are multidimensional and complex. One of the most destructive and least understood problems is based on teachers' expectations of African American children (Ferguson, 1998). Known as the conditioned failure model, Murray and Jackson (1997) propose that because teachers hold low expectations for African American children, African American children may be rewarded for failure and punished for success by their teachers. What is produced is a "vicious cycle" that results in a general mitigation of student aspirations and achievement behavior, culminating in poor scholastic performance. How this process operates, and what parents can do to assuage the consequences, will be discussed in this section.

Teacher Expectations

Just as human beings do generally, the way teachers think about other persons, store and integrate information about them, and later use this information to draw inferences about them or make social judgments is derived from societal stereotypes of groups (Jackson, 2002). These social cognitions lead to teachers' expectations of students' abilities and behaviors. Expectations lead to self-fulfilling prophecies, which refer to situations in which one person's expectations about a second person lead the second person to act in ways that confirm the first person's original expectations (Rosenthal, 2002). According to the conditioned failure model, teachers' low and negative expectations concerning the intellectual ability of African American students may lead them to make attributions to ability for academic failure, but not for academic success (Jackson, 2002). Thus consciously, but to a greater extent unconsciously, teachers come to the classroom having internalized beliefs about African American children that manifest in children receiving treatment consistent with those beliefs (Alexander, et al., 1987).

These lowered expectations significantly impact children's views of what others think of them. For instance, African American children as young as age 5 tell their parents, "My teacher doesn't like me." When asked by the parent, "Why do you think that?'" the child cannot articulate how he or she knows. Most parents then ignore the child's distress, thinking that since the child cannot give them a concrete example, the child must be mistaken, or in need of attention. Children know that they are being treated differently, even if they cannot tell you what is being done to them. Many argue that young children are much better at decoding nonverbal and verbal communication than adults (Widen & Russell, 2004). On the other hand, they cannot always express what they feel in concrete language. As adults, we can say, "You used a different tone of voice with me than you did with her. You (the teacher) gave him cues to the answer, and you were abrupt with me, cutting me off before I finished."

Furthermore, although children develop other aspects of their self-concepts from interacting with their families (Mandara & Murray, 2002), their academic self-concepts are shaped in large part by their experiences at school (Campbell, Pungello, Miller-Johnson, 2002). In the early elementary years, it is more important to the child that he or she is liked than that he or she is smart. Thus a child will play the "clown" if his or her classmates will like him or her or "dumb" if that is what pleases the teacher. Therefore, the teacher's lowered expectations and biased behavior lead to a variety of self-fulfilling behaviors that greatly impacts the child's self-perceptions and her or his own expectations of success (Murray & Jackson, 1997). Children who succumb to these expectations reduce their anxiety in the short run by making the teacher like them more but ensure substandard performance in the long run. This seems to be particularly true for African American children, since teachers have been found to be more influential to their achievement than they are to White children's achievement (Ferguson, 1998).

To help get African American children out of this cycle of failure, it is imperative that interventions unashamedly address to African American parents the potential bias their children will face from their teachers. To reduce the effects of teachers' expectations, parents have to learn how to take a more active role in developing the academic self-concepts of their children and not let this be primarily the domain of teachers. This is yet another reason direct academic socialization at home is so critical. Parents have to be the ones to set the standards that their children strive to achieve.

Furthermore, parents have to be advocates for their children by constantly, yet nondefensively, informing their children's teachers about their high expectations and standards for success. Parents must also talk to other parents and school administrators and make sure their child is in the classroom with the teachers who have been shown to have the most success with African American students. Not all teachers are as biased as the average. In general, parents should look for those teachers who are known to be strict disciplinarians and who have high standards for all of their students.

Tracking

Based on teacher judgments, African American children as early as kindergarten are disproportionately relegated to low ability tracks, while European American middle-class children are more likely to be placed on the average to upper tracks (Oakes, 1985). Tracking is the grouping of children supposedly by "intellectual ability" to expose them to the appropriate curriculum. Although over 30 years ago the Supreme Court ruled that tracking was illegal at the elementary school level, most still track. However, tracking has not been found beneficial to children on the low or high ability tracks (Kershaw, 1992; Oakes, 1985). More importantly, few children change tracks once placed, especially those on the low ability track (Kershaw, 1992).

A major reason for the lack of flexibility between tracks is that the curriculum varies from one track to another. For instance, in kindergarten or first grade, while high ability tracked children are reading stories and learning abstract concepts, children on the average track are only learning by rote sight words, and children on the slow track are printing the letter "A" repetitiously. At the end of the school year, all of the children are administered the same achievement test, and of course high track students tend to score better than average track ones, who score better than those on the slow track. Thus the curriculum acts as a ceiling to a child's upward mobility and fulfills the teacher's initial expectation.

Too many parents do not know that their children are being tracked, because elementary schools no longer track by classrooms (Oaks, 1985). Instead, students of the same grade level are placed in the same room (Kershaw, 1992). However, when it is time to read or do math, they are separated into "ability" groups and put at different tables. Again, children know, but young children cannot articulate what is happening to them. They are victims who internalize the labels the teacher assigns to them. They assume that they are sitting at the slow ability table because they are not as smart as the children sitting at the high ability table. Teachers do not have to say that they are dumb. Whether their group is called the "red birds," "fire trucks," or whatever, children know that they have been placed in groups based on how smart they are judged to be by their teachers. Most children accept the label that significant others, especially teachers, put on them. This eventually brings their self-concept in line with the label, and they eventually act accordingly.

In order for parents to get their children out of the social-caste-affirming institution of tracking, interventions must include teaching parents that they do not have to stand for their children being tracked into low ability groups (Oaks, 1985). They also must clarify to African American parents that rigorous or challenging instruction is important for all students, at all grade and ability levels. Parents should set the goal of having their children continually challenged. Furthermore, parents who have children in low ability groups should insist on interventions such as tutoring to help bring their children up to the level of those in the high ability tracks. These extracurricular activities will motivate children to excel and reduce the grip teachers often have on their academic self-concepts. Once children have gained acceptable levels of competence and skills, parents must make sure teachers do not place their children back into the lower tracks. Parents must be taught how to make teachers and other educational authorities accountable.

Teacher Sentiment and Evaluations

One of the most insidious consequences of teacher expectations is the biased sentiment teachers have about students. Most evidence from social psychology studies suggests that humans prefer information consistent with expectations about social categories (Jones, 1972; Rosenthal, 2002). For instance, in Rosenthal and Jacobson's (1968) classic study, students who were expected to improve intellectually were liked more by teachers than those who were not expected to improve. The more the children who were not expected to improve actually did improve, the more unfavorably their teacher rated them. This was especially true for children in the low ability classrooms that had an overrepresentation of Mexican Americans. According to Jones (1972), "Teachers, like many of us, prefer a stable and predictable environment. If their expectations are continually confirmed then traditional or prior judgments will not have to be checked and they will be free to think about other things. When their expectations are not confirmed, they are obliged to recheck their judgment process or otherwise explain the disconfirmation. This is not convenient" (p. 139). Given these biases, teachers tend to have more positive feelings toward low-achieving African American students than high-achieving ones. The reverse is true for European American students (Murray & Jackson, 1997).

The tendency of some teachers to confirm their expectations also impacts their evaluations of students' work. In an achievement-related context, sympathy may be elicited when another's failure is perceived as caused by low ability (consider the emotional response to a retarded child who experiences academic difficulty). In contrast, anger is often a dominant emotion when another's failure is attributed to lack of effort (think of the teacher's reaction to the bright student who does not complete assignments). In the classroom this plays out in various ways. For instance, teachers may tell an African American boy that he is doing very well, while they may scold a European American girl for doing the same quality work. Furthermore, when setting achievement goals, teachers may tell the African American child that they want to see him get at least 6 out of 10 correct answers on the spelling test, while they may tell the European American child that they want to see her get all 10 answers correct. Massey and colleagues (1975) found that African American students who were given the least amount of work in school believed that they were trying extremely hard because of teacher feedback. According to the authors, African American children were allowed to delude themselves because of the teacher's distorted system of evaluation.

Both teacher-expressed sentiment and grades reinforce students' past performance and greatly influence students' attributions of success and failure. In general, attributing achievement and failure to effort is more likely to increase children's self-esteem when they achieve, because they feel like they earned it, and it makes them work harder when they do not achieve, because they feel like they can achieve. For instance, lower math scores have been associated with attributing failure to lack of ability and attributing success to external factors (Bempechat, Graham, & Jimenez, 1999). However, African American students whose teachers expect them to perform poorly are likely to receive different treatment than those students who are expected to do well. Consequently, by the third grade, many African American children have been conditioned to attribute their success to external causes such as luck or easy exams and to attribute their failure to internal stable causes such as innate ability.

Those who have failed begin to think that they are not smart, and thus they will always fail (Campbell, et al., 2002). On the other hand, some students are uncertain about their academic ability, often because they are arbitrarily rewarded by the teacher. Such students would be motivated to obtain equivocal or biased information from the environment about their self-worth by employing self-handicapping strategies (Murray & Jackson, 1997). Many successful African American students are made to feel ambivalent about their performance due to a perceived real rejection by teachers. Thus for the African American child, internalizing a teacher's negative expectations results in a dysfunctional attribution-affect pattern, which culminates in the last stage of the conditioned failure model, underachievement.

A primary goal of interventions should be to make parents aware of the process by which their children are being conditioned to fail (Franklin, Franklin, & Draper, 2002; Murray & Jackson, 1997). Although some parents may be aware of the problems of low teacher expectations and even tracking, few will be aware of some teachers' dysfunctional and distorted sentiments and evaluations. Therefore, it is extremely important that parents monitor their children's performance and grades. Parents must be sensitive to discrepancies in performance and teacher sentiment and feedback. This is another reason it is imperative for parents to work with their children at home. Parents need to know the abilities and capabilities of their children when evaluating their grades and progress in class and teacher feedback (Franklin, et al., 2002). Whenever there is a mismatch between child performance and feedback, or capabilities and teacher expectations, parents must bring this to the teacher's attention. If the problem persists, then parents must inform school administrators and ask that the teacher be trained, or have their child transferred to another class.

Interventions should also include teaching parents how to monitor their children's developing attributions of success and failure. Although it is better to attribute failure to lack of effort, African American parents of underachievers are in a quandary, because much of their children's failure is in fact due to systemic problems at the school, beyond children's control (Alexander, Entwisle, & Thompson, 1987; Lankford, et al., 2002). It is appropriate for parents to teach their children from approximately third grade on about teachers' often biased expectations and other forms of overt and covert racism in American society. However, African American parents must make great efforts to ensure that their children's knowledge of these obstacles does not make them develop an external locus of control and feelings of powerlessness. African American children must be raised to know that they can manifest their will on their environment. This can be best accomplished by following the suggestions throughout this chapter and by letting children know that they have the ability and power to be academically successful, despite the obstacles they will face in America.

Conclusion

It is clear that African American children are not performing up to their capabilities in America's public schools. It was argued that regardless of the causes of the problems, parents have the primary responsibility for the academic achievement of their children. The goal of this chapter, then, was to highlight several important socialization strategies with which family-based interventions must be concerned when trying to facilitate the academic achievement of African American children. Interventions must include helping parents develop the knowledge, skills, and capabilities to carry out these important parenting tasks. The finding that African American children perform best and are more psychologically healthy when their parents are strict disciplinarians, as well as warm, loving, and respectful of their children, was also discussed. Therefore, those who create well-intentioned interventions have to realize that parental strictness and firm control are adaptive for African Americans, especially in the context of a warm and loving parent-child relationship. The permissive parenting style that is in vogue and stressed by most current parenting interventions is detrimental to European American youth (Baumrind, 1996) as well as African American youth (Mandara & Murray, 2002). Unlike what is pushed by many therapists and drug companies, firm yet loving discipline will eliminate the need for drugging children so they can behave in school.

It also was argued that the traditional fatherly socialization that stresses firm discipline, rough-and-tumble play, and pressure to achieve is missing for many African American children. We no longer have the luxury of pretending that this is not a problem for millions of African American children. The true intentions of therapy, policy, and family-based interventions will be revealed by the importance they place on the father absence problem in African American families. In this chapter, strategies for mitigating the impacts of growing up without the day-to-day presence of a father or father figure were discussed.

Many strategies for the racial socialization and direct academic socialization of African American children also were discussed. African American children perform best in school when their parents actively attempt to instill racial pride and increase their children's sense of power to overcome barriers. African American parents also need to be actively involved in the day-to-day learning activities of their children. Among many other suggestions, we argued that reducing external sources of interference from the mass media is critical for both proactive racial socialization and academic socialization. One of the biggest myths about African American parents is that they do not have the time or financial capacity to create a more culturally affirming or learning conducive home environment for their children. This, however, is a consequence of the low expectations that society has of African Americans and is a primary reason that most interventions with African American families are ineffective.

Finally, we discussed the conditioned failure model, which articulates the process by which low and negative teacher expectations impact African American academic achievement. The model argues that irrespective of whether a given teacher's expectation is positive or negative, a teacher tends to like students who meet his or her expectations. To the extent that positive sentiments manifest in rewards, it can be seen that African American students are often rewarded for failure and punished for success. Hence, the inequity, which often occurs in the educational environment, may have less to do with tangibles such as books, buildings, or equipment than with intangibles such as the differential distribution of teacher reinforcements and emotions. Such a reinforcement distribution adversely affects the motivational base of African American students. Thus due to processes over which they have little control, they are conditioned to fail. We discussed many strategies that parents can employ to remove their children from the vicious cycle of conditioned failure.

We conclude this chapter with a few recommendations for local, state, and federal policy makers to facilitate parents' quests to increase the academic achievement of their children. First and foremost, policy has to be directed at funding comprehensive and culturally specific parenting and family functioning interventions (Kumpfer & Alvarado, 2003). Unlike those interventions that are currently funded, policy makers should make sure that future interventions are comprehensive enough to cover the areas of parenting discussed in this chapter, and that they are based on a model of cultural specificity. Although interventions will probably be most accepted and effective when facilitators are of the same ethnic group and/or use the language of the people for whom the intervention is intended, this is of secondary importance to the success of interventions. Culturally specific and thus relevant interventions are those that teach the specific behavioral patterns of cultural groups associated with the best outcomes for members of those groups. This chapter addressed many such parenting strategies for African Americans.

Policy makers also must create a family policy that is serious about keeping African American parents in long-term, loving, and stable marriages (Mandara & Murray, 2000). Larger tax breaks and other financial incentives for married couples with children under age 18 or in college and free or greatly subsidized marital therapy before and during marriage would be very helpful. More funding for research into the causes of marital problems also is needed. Those policy makers, social scientists, and practitioners who balk at such policy measures have ignored the empirical evidence (Mandara & Murray, 2000). Furthermore, they have apparently never tried to raise children alone with the average African American mother's income, let alone be raised with only one, usually overworked and stressed, parent. As we discussed earlier in this chapter, in conjunction with these efforts, policy also should be directed toward exposing single-parent African American children and adolescents to older, responsible males who have the disciplinary authority of their real fathers. The time of reacting to the Moynihan Report (Moynihan, 1965) has long come and gone.

Finally, given the problems in public schools, African American children's need for firm discipline and emotional warmth, and the need for proactive racial socialization strategies, we believe that independent, African-centered schools are by far the best option for African American children at this time. The success of children attending the Marcus Garvey School in Los Angeles and other independent schools is a shining example of what can be achieved when African American children receive firm discipline, sincere praise and love, and high expectations and are immersed in a culturally affirming curriculum (Rivers & Rivers, 2002).

REFERENCES

Alexander, K. L., Entwisle, D. R., & Thompson, M. S. (1987). School performance, status relations, and the structure of sentiment: Bringing the teacher back in. *American Sociological Review, 52*, 665–682.

Anderson, A. L. (2002). Individual and contextual influences on delinquency: The role of the single-parent family. *Journal of Criminal Justice, 30*, 575–587.

Bankston, C. L., & Caldas, S. J. (1998). Family structure, schoolmates, and racial inequalities in school achievement. *Journal of Marriage & the Family, 60*, 715–723.

Baumrind, D. (1991). The influence of parenting style on adolescent competence and substance use. *Journal of Early Adolescence, 11*, 56–95.

Baumrind, D. (1996). The discipline controversy revisited. *Family Relations: Journal of Applied Family & Child Studies, 45*, 405–414.

Bempechat, J., Graham, S. E., & Jimenez, N. V. (1999). The socialization of achievement in poor and minority students: A comparative study. *Journal of Cross-Cultural Psychology, 30*, 139–158.

Campbell, F. A., Pungello, E. P., & Miller-Johnson, S. (2002). The development of perceived scholastic competence and global self-worth in African American adolescents from low-income families: The roles of family factors, early educational intervention, and academic experience. *Journal of Adolescent Research, 17*, 277–302.

Caughy, M. O., O'Campo, P. J., Randolph, S. M., & Nickerson, K. (1992). The influence of racial socialization practices on the cognitive and behavioral competence of African American preschoolers. *Child Development, 73*, 1611–1625.

Coard, S. I., Wallace, S. A., Stevenson Jr., H. C., & Brotman, L. M. (2004). Towards culturally relevant preventive interventions: The consideration of racial socialization in parent training with African American families. *Journal of Child and Family Studies, 13*, 277–293.

Cress-Welsing, F. (1990). *The Isis papers: The keys to the colors*. Chicago: Third World Press.

Deater-Deckard, K., Dodge, K. A., Bates, J. E., & Pettit, G. S. (1996). Physical discipline among African American and European American mothers: Links to children's externalizing behaviors. *Developmental Psychology, 32*, 1065–1072.

Ellis, B. J., Bates, J. E., Dodge, K. A., Fergusson, D. M., Horwood, L. J., Pettit, G. S., & Woodward, L. (2003). Does father absence place daughters at special risk for early sexual activity and teenage pregnancy? *Child Development, 74*, 801–821.

Ferguson, R. F. (1998). Teachers' perceptions and expectations and the Black-White test score gap. In C. J., & M. Phillips (Eds.), *The Black-White test score gap* (pp. 273–317). Washington, DC: Brookings Institution Press.

Fields, J. (2003). *Children's living arrangements and characteristics: March 2002. Current Population Reports, P20–547*. Washington, DC: U.S. Census Bureau.

Franklin, A. J., Franklin, N. B., & Draper, C. V. (2002). A psychological and educational perspective on Black parenting. In H. P. McAdoo (Ed.), *Black children: Social, educational, and parental environments* (2nd ed.) (pp. 73–96). Thousand Oaks, CA: Sage.

Gunnoe, M. L., & Mariner, C. L. (1997). Toward a developmental-contextual model of the effects of parental spanking on children's aggression. *Archives of Pediatrics & Adolescent Medicine, 151,* 768–777.

Halle, T. G., Kurtz-Costes, B., & Mahoney, J. L. (1997). Family influences on school achievement in low-income, African American children. *Journal of Educational Psychology, 89,* 527-537.

Henderlong, J., & Lepper, M. R. (2002). The effects of praise on children's intrinsic motivation: A review and synthesis. *Psychological Bulletin, 128,* 774–795.

Jaccard, J., Dodge, T., & Dittus, P. (2003a). Do adolescents want to avoid pregnancy? Attitudes toward pregnancy as predictors of pregnancy. *Journal of Adolescent Health, 33,*(2), 79–83.

Jaccard, J., Dodge, T., & Dittus, P. (2003b). Maternal discussions about pregnancy and adolescents, attitudes toward pregnancy. *Journal of Adolescent Health, 33,* 84–87.

Jackson, S. A. (2002). A study of teachers' perceptions of youth problems. *Journal of Youth Studies, 5,* 313–322.

Johnson, J. D., Adams, M. S., Ashburn, L., & Reed, W. (1995). Differential gender effects of exposure to rap music on African American adolescents' acceptance of teen dating violence. *Sex Roles, 33,* 597–605.

Johnson, J. D., Jackson, L. A., & Gatto, L. (1995). Violent attitudes and deferred academic aspirations: Deleterious effects of exposure to rap music. *Basic & Applied Social Psychology, 16,* 27–41.

Johnson, V. K., Cowan, P. A., & Cowan, C. P. (1999). Children's classroom behavior: The unique contribution of family organization. *Journal of Family Psychology, 13,* 355–371.

Jones, J. (1972). *Prejudice and racism.* Menlo Park, CA: Addison-Wesley.

Kershaw, T. (1992). The effects of educational tracking on the social mobility of African Americans. *Journal of Black Studies, 23,* 152–169.

Kumpfer, K. L., & Alvarado, R. (2003). Family-strengthening approaches for the prevention of youth problem behaviors. *American Psychologist, 58,* 457–465.

Lankford, H., Loeb, S., & Wyckoff, J. (2002). Teacher sorting and the plight of urban schools: A descriptive analysis. *Educational Evaluation & Policy Analysis, 24,* 37–62.

Mandara, J. (2003). The typological approach in child and family psychology: A review of theory, methods, and research. *Clinical Child & Family Psychology Review, 6,* 129–146.

Mandara, J. (2006). The impact of family functioning on African American males' academic achievement: A review and clarification of the empirical literature. *Teachers' College Record, 108*(2), 2006–223.

Mandara, J., & Murray, C. B. (2000). Effects of parental marital status, income, and family functioning on African American adolescent self-esteem. *Journal of Family Psychology, 14,* 475–490.

Mandara, J., & Murray, C. B. (2002). Development of an empirical typology of African American family functioning. *Journal of Family Psychology, 16*, 318–337.

Mandara, J., Murray, C. B., & Joyner, T. (2005). The impact of father's absence on African American adolescents' gender role development. *Sex Roles, 53*, 207–220.

Marcon, R. A. (1999). Positive relationships between parent school involvement and public school inner-city preschoolers' development and academic performance. *School Psychology Review, 28*, 395–412.

Marshall, S. (1995). Ethnic socialization of African American children: Implications for parenting, identity development, and academic achievement. *Journal of Youth & Adolescence, 24*, 377–396.

Massey, G. C., Scott, M. V., & Dornbusch, S. M. (1975). Racism without racists: Institutional racism in urban schools. *The Black Scholar, 7*, 2 –11.

Mattanah, J. F. (2001). Parental psychological autonomy and children's academic competence and behavioral adjustment in late childhood: More than just limit-setting and warmth. *Merrill-Palmer Quarterly, 47*, 355–376.

McDowell, D. J., Parke, R. D., & Wang, S. J. (2003). Differences between mothers' and fathers' advice-giving style and content: Relations with social competence and psychological functioning in middle childhood. *Merrill-Palmer Quarterly, 49*, 55–76.

McLoyd, V. C. (1990). The impact of economic hardship on Black families and children: Psychological distress, parenting, and socioemotional development. *Child Development, 61*, 311–346.

McWayne, C., Hampton, V., Fantuzzo, J., Cohen, H. L., & Sekino, Y. (2004). A multivariate examination of parent involvement and the social and academic competencies of urban kindergarten children. *Psychology in the Schools, 41*, 363–377.

Moynihan, D. P. (1965). *The Negro family: The case for national action.* Washington, DC: U.S. Department of Labor, Office of Policy Planning and Research.

Murray, C. B., & Jackson, J. S. (1997). The conditioned failure model revisited. In R. L. Jones (Ed.), *African American children, youth, and parenting* (pp. 51 – 81). Hampton, VA.: Cobb & Henry.

Murray, C. B., & Mandara, J. (2002). Racial identity development in African American children: Cognitive and experiential antecedents. In H. P. McAdoo (Ed.), *Black children: Social, educational, and parental environments* (2nd ed.) (pp. 73–96). Thousand Oaks, CA: Sage.

Nasir, N. S. (2002). Identity, goals, and learning: Mathematics in cultural practice. *Mathematical Thinking & Learning, 4*, 213–247.

Netzel, D. M., & Eber, L. (2003). Shifting from reactive to proactive discipline in an urban school district: A change of focus through PBIS implementation. *Journal of Positive Behavior Interventions, 5*, 71–79.

Oakes, J. (1985). *Keeping track: How schools structure inequality.* New Haven, CT: Yale University Press.

Pianta, R. C. (1999). *Enhancing relationships between children and teachers*. Washington, DC: American Psychological Association.

Rivers, S. W., & Rivers, F. A. (2002). Sankofa shule spells success for African American children. In H. P. McAdoo (Ed.), *Black children: Social, educational, and parental environments* (2nd ed.) (pp. 73–96). Thousand Oaks, CA: Sage.

Rosenthal, R. (2002). Covert communication in classrooms, clinics, courtrooms, and cubicles. *American Psychologist, 57*, 839–849.

Rosenthal, R., & Jacobson, L. (1968). *Pygmalion in the classroom: Teacher expectation and pupils' intellectual development*. New York: Holt, Rinchart, and Winston.

Schacter, J. (2003). Preventing summer reading declines in children who are disadvantaged. *Journal of Early Intervention, 26*, 47–58.

Smetana, J. G., Crean, H. F., & Daddis, C. (2002). Family processes and problem behaviors in middle-class African American adolescents. *Journal of Research on Adolescence, 12*, 275–304.

Smith, E. P., Prinz, R. J., Dumas, J. E., & Laughlin, J. (2001). Latent models of family processes in African American families: Relationships to child competence, achievement, and problem behavior. *Journal of Marriage & the Family, 63*, 967–980.

Teachman, J., Day, R., Paasch, K., Carver, K., & Call, V. (1998). Sibling resemblance in behavioral and cognitive outcomes: The role of father presence. *Journal of Marriage and the Family, 60*, 835–848.

Turner, K. M. (2003). "Getting it straight": Southern black school patrons and the struggle for equal education in the pre- and post-civil rights eras. *Journal of Negro Education, 72*, 217–229.

Ward, L. M. (2004). Wading through the stereotypes: Positive and negative associations between media use and black adolescents' conceptions of self. *Developmental Psychology, 40*, 284–294.

Widen, S. C., & Russell, J. A. (2004). The relative power of an emotion's facial expression, label, and behavioral consequence to evoke preschoolers' knowledge of its cause. *Cognitive Development, 19*, 111–125.

Woodson, C. G. (1990). *The mis-education of the Negro*. Trenton, NJ: Africa World Press.

Chapter 9

Addressing the Achievement Gap in Education with the Use of Technology

A Proposed Solution for African American Students

Jeffrey G. Sumrall and Ramona Pittman

Recent studies (e.g., Wenglinsky, 1998) have shown that access to and use of technology enhance student achievement. Hoffman, Llagas, and Snyder (2003) reported that African American students fall short in almost every aspect of student achievement (e.g., standardized test scores and grade point averages). Moreover, African Americans tend to be the last ones in their neighborhoods and schools to gain access to computers and networking capabilities such as the Internet (Wenglinsky, 1998). The correlation between those who have computer access and those who do not is closely related to the gap in student achievement. This phenomenon, commonly known as the digital divide, represents the division of those who have and those who do not have access to computers and its many uses. If African Americans and other students of color do not have adequate access to technology, then it can be surmised that there will always be a digital divide. Accordingly, this chapter will focus on technological solutions to the problems associated with the achievement gap that students of color face, with specific recommendations for African American students.

In order to appropriately situate this discourse in the context of education, we must define technology use in schools. The term *technology* elicits various meanings among all involved constituents, as evidenced by Ogle and colleagues, (2000) who state, "The term technology in schools can have several meanings in different context and times" (p. 3). However, within the context of this chapter, technology refers to the complete array of computer and computer-related equipment associated with operating systems, networking, and tool software that provides the infrastructure over which instructional and school management applications of various kinds operate (Ogle et al., 2000).

The use of technology provides students with an alternative method of learning old and new concepts in core and extracurricula classes. With this in mind, the use of technology can serve as a method to help close the achievement gap. In relation to younger children, readiness is an issue with regard to the use of technology. Such issues of readiness can include cognitive development, finger dexterity, eye-hand coordination in using keyboards, comprehension of computer instructions, and integration into content areas (Picciano, 2002). Many times in African American families, children have more access to video games than to computers and educational software (Wenglinsky, 1998). If young children can learn how to maneuver joysticks and game controllers, then surely they can operate a mouse and keyboard.

Nonetheless, technology can be tailored for student learning in an individualized way with the ability to frequently assess and respond to learning needs (Forbus, 2001). Students with different learning styles, prerequisite knowledge, and cultural backgrounds could benefit from a technology-based education, and their performance on standardized achievement measures (e.g., math and sciences scores) can be greatly improved through an integrated technology approach (Goodman, 2001). The fact that by the late 1990s approximately 95% of all elementary schools had acquired microcomputer equipment and were connected to the Internet for instructional purposes suggests that educators believe that children are ready to begin using computer equipment at an early age (Ogle et al., 2000).

CURRENT STATE OF EDUCATIONAL TECHNOLOGY

As a result of the "No Child Left Behind" legislative act, approximately 92% of U.S. public schools had access to the Internet by the fall of 2002. Teachers that were not properly trained for the technology integration were the primary problem that plagued computer use in the classroom, especially for rural and disadvantaged schools (Wenglinsky, 1998). Training teachers to use the computer in the classroom effectively must move beyond basic computer literacy into how to use the technology, when and where to use the technology in current lesson plans, and how to create assessment tools to ensure that the technology is being used to its fullest potential. Due to lack of teacher training in technology, many teachers tend to feel uncomfortable with technology. The introduction of technology always brings great changes and risks to a teaching staff. Even with the appropriate training, many teachers find technology intimidating. These teachers tend to avoid situations in which they distrust their ability to perform successfully (Ashton & Webb, 1986).

Through technology, teachers and staff can promote student achievement in all academic areas (Forbus, 2001). Among the 92% of U.S. schools that have computers and networking capabilities, few teachers use computers to promote higher-order thinking, such as analyzing, synthesizing, and evaluating information, for their students. Many of the teachers use technology as a means of drill and practice. Wenglinsky (1998) found the following:

- Eighth graders whose teachers used computers for "simulation and applications"—both of which are associated with higher-order thinking—performed better on the NAEP than students who had not received that kind of instruction.
- Eighth graders whose teachers used computers for mere "drill and practice" performed worse than other students.
- Eighth graders whose teachers used computers mainly for "math learning games" scored higher than others.
- Students who spent the most time on computers in school did not score any higher than their peers; in fact, they performed slightly worse.

While African Americans do lag behind their counterparts on traditional academic measures, a critical part of the problem has been linked to access to computers. Inner-city schools located in poor districts and larger schools have less computer hardware per student than other schools. These schools are attended by higher percentages of African American and Latino children (Piccano, 2002). In addition, low-income and African American students are the most likely to have teachers who do not use the new technology to its full advantage (Wenglinsky, 1998). Many low-income schools are obtaining the necessary funds to purchase computers. Oftentimes the computers are not being used to the fullest extent, because schools are not spending the funds in the area of teacher technology training (Goodman, 2001). In summation, African American and Latino children have less computer access than do White children (Piccano, 2002). Piccano also indicates that if schools do not find ways for students of color to access computers that will help develop their technical skills, then they will be at a disadvantage, given the continually growing importance of technology skills in employment.

Children from all walks of life and different backgrounds are supposed to gain an adequate education through technology (Cassidy, 2004). However, according to Hoffman, Llagas, and Snyder (2003), 41% of African Americans use a computer at home compared to 42% of Hispanics and 77% of Whites. Overall, White students were more likely than African American and Hispanic students to use computers at home for schoolwork. Of the 40% of African American students who do own computers, just a little over half (28.8%) are using their computers for schoolwork. Concurrently, only 31% of students from families earning less than $20,000 use computers at home, compared to 89% of those from families earning more than $75,000. It would be difficult for teachers to give simulation and application assignments to students to complete as homework when many students do not have access to a computer in the home.

Cassidy (2004) further suggests that another equity issue related to the use of technology is motivation. She also mentions that culturally deprived students would show higher achievement if taught by machines that would neither be judgmental nor discriminatory toward them. Some educators of at-risk students seem to find that their students' achievement improved markedly when students learned through direct contact with computers. Some students prefer computers instead of teachers because they feel that computers are impartial, whereas teachers sometimes are not. In short, African American students have closed the digital divide where it matters least—the amount of time spent on a computer. The gap persists where it matters most—how the computer is used (Archer, 1998).

Due to the academic underachievement of some African American students, we must find different ways to infuse technology into their lives so that they will become lifelong learners (Mills, 2002). Technology, if used properly, is one of the keys that can successfully increase student achievement (Goodman, 2001). In order to make this a reality, we must take the medical stance of early diagnosis of students' strengths and weaknesses. Computers do not get frustrated and tired, as teachers sometimes do, when a student cannot comprehend a certain level of knowledge. Therefore, computers can aid the teacher in the early detection of learning difficulties in individual students. The implementation of technology is a necessity if African American students are going to be competitive for employment in the future. We have to change our way of thinking about the use of computers and all of its entities if we want African American children to succeed. The days of simply using computer technology for lower-order thinking (e.g., drill and practice, playing games, downloading music, and surfing the Web) need to be put behind us, and technology must be integrated into students' daily lives to promote higher-order thinking.

Using Technology to Embrace Learning Styles and Multiple Intelligences

Using students' different multiple intelligences, computer technology can provide them with detailed lessons suited for their appropriate way of learning. Since we know that each child learns differently, we will examine ways to incorporate technology into students' multiple intelligences and how technology can embrace African American students' learning styles through artificial intelligence. Determining learning styles and multiple intelligences is important in order to understand the best practices for teaching students through technology. Technology can be used to assist in each of Howard Gardner's (1993) areas of intelligence:

1. *Verbal/Linguistic*—These students learn best through language, such as speaking, listening, writing, and reading. They are able to verbally or in writing explain, convince, and express themselves. They enjoy writing and creating with words.

2. *Logical/Mathematical*—These students learn best through numbers, reasoning, and problem solving. Students like to figure out problems by questioning, exploring, and experimenting. They are able to create and manipulate visuals and create mental pictures from many perspectives. They like to weigh, measure, calculate, and organize data.

3. *Visual/Spatial*—Students learn best visually and tend to organize their thinking spatially. They like to think and create pictures. They are also drawn to information that is present in the visual form.

4. *Bodily/Kinesthetic*—These students learn best through physical activity such as dance, hands-on tasks, constructing models, and any kind of movement. They are able to manipulate and control objects, as well as express their ideas through movement.

5. *Musical/Rhythmic*—These students learn best through sounds, including listening and making sounds, such as songs, rhythms, patterns, and other types of auditory expression. They are able to use inductive and deductive reasoning and identify relationships in data.

6. *Intrapersonal*—These students learn best through metacognitive practices such as getting in touch with their feelings and self-motivation. They are able to concentrate and be mindful.

7. *Interpersonal*—These students learn best through interaction with other people through discussions, cooperative work, or social activities. They are able to create synergy in a room by being aware of the feelings and motives of others.

8. *Naturalist*—Students learn best through the interactions with the environment, including outdoor activities, field trips, and involvement with plants and animals. They see the subtle meanings and patterns in nature and the world around them. They are able to adapt.

9. *Existentialist*—A new intelligence is existentialist that exhibits the proclivity to pose and ponder questions about life, death, and ultimate realities. These "wondering" people learn best through seeing the "big picture" of human existence by asking philosophical questions about the world.

By examining each of the explanations of Gardner's (2001) multiple intelligences, we can incorporate technological strategies to enhance each student's learning. The key is to discuss each approach and explain how to use technology with that particular intelligence. After identifying a student's individual learning style, a teacher can use technology resources to help develop an appropriate learning strategy. For example, Eduscapes (http://www.eduscapes.com/tap/index.htm) provides "Teacher Tap: Professional Development Resources for Educator," with a wealth of information about integrating technology into the classroom.

No one technology works for all students; therefore, appropriate technologies should be chosen to support a diverse student population to encompass unique learning styles (Pickering, 1999). The method of delivery should therefore parallel unique learning styles. Pickering (1999) revealed that technology has many obvious tangible assets. For instance, it can support students and teachers in various types of information-related activities. Through technology, individuals may extend or enhance their personal productivity. In order for education technology to reach its full potential, educators must continue to investigate student learning patterns that reflect authentic learning and instructional media that enhance their multiple intelligences (Pickering, 1999). If African American students are to be competitive, then they must embrace technology as a lifelong learning experience.

Artificial Intelligence: Cognitive Tutoring Systems

Artificial intelligence is the ability of a digital computer or computer-controlled robot to perform tasks commonly associated with intelligent beings. The term is frequently applied to the project of developing systems endowed with the intellectual processes characteristic of humans, such as the ability to reason, discover meaning, generalize, or learn from past experience (Mills, 2002). We must infuse artificial intelligence into minority communities to diagnose and reinforce educational weaknesses. Along with the cognitive benefits, artificial intelligence has the full functionality that multi-media and digital learning environments offer. Not only can artificial intelligence perform sight, sound, and touch applications, it has the ability to replicate human thinking while diagnosing the weaknesses of each student.

A good example of a research-based cognitive tutoring system is the Pump Algebra Tutor (PAT), designed to demonstrate the potential for dramatic learning gains with the appropriate use of technology (Koedinger, 2001). Koedinger (2001) emphasized that effective technologies for learning and doing mathematics should be based on sound cognitive theory and primarily addressed at mathematics as a modeling language. The PAT was developed under these three very specific guidelines. According to Anderson and Lebiere (1998), cognitive tutors are strongly based on the Advance Cognitive Tutor (ACT), which is a theory of learning and performance. The ACT is a cognition theory for simulating human thought. The overall focus of the theory is to understand how people organize knowledge and produce intelligent behavior.

Newell (1990) stated that the ACT theory is a rather complex comprehensive mathematical model of cognition. Koedinger (2001) also believed that within the field of mathematics, the ACT theory only supports performance knowledge by doing rather than listening or watching. This performance knowledge is demonstrated in Koedinger's small example of if-then production rules associating internal goals and/or external actions.

IF   the goal is to prove two triangles are congruent and the triangles share a side

THEN   check for corresponding sides or angles that may be congruent.

IF   the goal is to solve an equation in X

THEN   graph the left and right sides of the equation and find the intersection between point(s).

IF   the goal is to find the value of quantity Q and Q divided by Num1 is Num2

THEN   find Q by multiplying Num1 and Num2.

The goals of the PAT were to make algebra more accessible to students, to help them make connections between algebra and the world beyond school, and to help them prepare for the "real world" as well as further their academic study. The PAT focused on having students understand and use multiple representations with quantitative relationships. The problem format that students are given usually includes reading a problem, constructing multiple representations, comparing alternatives, and providing a numeric answer. Students must read a description of a situation and a series of questions about it. They then investigate the situation by representing it in graphs, tables, and symbols, and by using these representations to answer the questions, students learn to model with algebraic symbols using today's powerful calculation tools such as graphic and symbolic calculators, programming, and spreadsheets. The crucial point with the PAT is that students not only need to develop mathematical concepts, but they also learn a fluency or mastery with mathematical modeling languages such as algebraic symbols, statistics notation, dynamic geometry tools, and programming languages (Forbus, 2001).

CONCLUSION AND SUMMARY

It is clearly defined, by previous research, that a significant achievement gap exists between African American and White students. The integration and implementation of technology into the educational equation is the key to closing the achievement gap for African American students. African American students tend to lag behind White students in access and ability to use technology. Even when African American students have access to computers, they are not being exposed to technology in a significant way (Howe, 2002). Oftentimes that technology is used for entertainment purposes (e.g., video games) only. In prescribing the use of technology as a partial solution to the epidemic problems that plague African Americans in education, there is indeed cause for optimism. The main focus surrounding this school of thought is early-stage technological curriculum infusion, coupled with artificial intelligence. It is quite apparent that African American students possess the unique ability to learn via unorthodox teaching and learning methodologies (Hoffman, Llagas, & Snyder, 2003). Therefore, educators need to somehow harness and cultivate students' unique learning styles in order to build solid educational foundations. Early technological infusion means that each African American student has the potential ability to begin the educational process with a solid foundation. If by chance a student slips through the cracks, then artificial intelligence can target identified "weak educational areas" and fill the gaps. Developing a thorough and comprehensive learning system that directly identifies with individual learning styles and/or abilities will be the start of closing the achievement gap.

REFERENCES

Anderson, J. R., & Lebiere, C. (1998). *The atomic components of thought.* Hillsdale, NJ: Lawrence Erlbaum.

Archer, J., (1998). Technology counts. http://www.edweek.org/tm/articles/1998/11/01/03compute.h10.html

Ashton, P. T., & Webb, R. B. (1986). *Making a difference: Teacher sense of efficacy and student achievement.* New York: Longman.

Cassidy, M. (2004). *Bookends: The changing media environment of American classrooms.* Cresskill, NJ: Hampton Press.

Forbus, K. D. (2001). Exploring analogy in the large. In D. Gentner, K. H. Holyoak, & B. K. Kokinov (Eds.), *The analogical mind: Perspectives from cognitive science* (pp. 23–58). Cambridge, MA: MIT Press.

Gardner, H. (1993). *Multiple intelligences: The theory in practice.* New York: Basic Books.

Goodman, P. S. (2001). *Technology enhanced learning.* Mahwah, NJ: Lawrence Erlbaum.

Hoffman, K., Llagas, C., & Snyder, T. D. (2003). *Status and trends in the education of Blacks.* Washington, DC: National Center for Educational Statistics.

Howe, A. C. (2002). *Engaging children in science.* Upper Saddle River, NJ: Merrill Prentice Hall.

Jagers, R. J., & Carrol, G. (2002). Issues in educating African American children and youth. In S. Stringfield & D. Land (Eds.), *Educating at-risk students* (pp. 49–88). Chicago: National Society for the Study of Education.

Koedinger, K. R. (2001). Cognitive tutors as modeling tools and instructional models. In K. D. Forbus & P. J. Feltovich (Eds.), *Smart machines in education* (pp. 37–70). Menlo Park, CA: American Association for Artificial Intelligence.

Mills, D. W. (2002). Applying what we know—Student learning styles.http://www.csrnet.org/csrnet/articles/student-learning-styles.html

The national and economic importance of improved math-science education and H.R. 4272. The National Science Education Enhancement Act Hearing before Committee on Education and the Workforce, House of Representatives, 106th Congress 2nd Session, September 2001.

Newell, A. (1990). *Unified theories of cognition*. Cambridge, MA: Harvard University Press.

Ogle, T., Branch, M., Canada, B., Christmas, O., Clement, J., Fillion, J., Goddard, E., Loudat, N. B., Purwin, T., Rogers, A., Schmitt, C., & Vinson, M. (2000). *Technology in school: Suggestions, tools, and guidelines for assessing technology in elementary and secondary education*. Washington, DC: National Center for Educational Statistics.

Picciano, A. (2002). *Educational leadership and planning for technology* (3rd ed.). Upper Saddle River, NJ: Pearson Education.

Pickering, J. C. (1999). Teachers in technology initiative. http://www.ri.net/RITTI_Fellows/Carlson-Pickering/MI_Tech.htm

Reksten, L. (2000). *Using technology to increase student learning*. Thousand Oaks, CA: Corwin Press.

Schank, R., & Neaman, A. (2001). Motivation and failure in educational simulation design. In K. D. Forbus & P. J. Feltovich (Eds.), *Smart machines in education* (pp. 37–70). Menlo Park, CA: American Association for Artificial Intelligence.

Wenglinsky, H. (1998). *Does it compute? The relationship between educational technology and student achievement in mathematics*. Princeton, NJ: Educational Testing Service.

Conclusion

Reconceptualizing the African American Educational Pipeline

New Perspectives from a Systematic Analysis

Jerlando F. L. Jackson

The history of African American education in the United States has several defining moments, in which social, political, and legal forces demanded reform and equity (Anderson, 1988). Prior to the mid-1900s, the education system in the United States was segregated by law. African Americans and Whites were educated in separate systems based on the premise that "separate but equal" educational experiences were best for both parties. With the rise of social unrest with regard to the "separate and unequal" education systems for African Americans, demands for equal opportunity for a quality education increased. By 1954, the *Brown* decision provided the legal basis and platform for a desegregated education system in the United States (Grant, 1995). For some time afterward, orchestrated efforts were needed to ensure that the "letter and spirit" of the law was enforced.

Fifty years beyond the *Brown* decision, today's education system has yet another defining moment. With legal segregation no longer in place, African Americans continue to struggle in their pursuit of education (Hoffman, Llagas, & Snyder, 2003). The achievement gap between African American students and their counterparts is well documented in this book and elsewhere. Instead of the legal segregation that existed prior to the *Brown* decision, African Americans subsequently experience de facto segregation in the form of tracking by virtue of attending programs and schools deemed as low performing (Ogbu, 2003). Therefore, while the United States is 50 years beyond a monumental decision to change the course of education for African Americans, many contemporary reform efforts are aimed at achieving the same goals.

The role of education is broader than simply providing educational experiences for students. It also acts as an enterprise, inasmuch as it trains professionals and, in turn, employs them (Jackson, 2004; Pollard, 1997). Be-yond consideration of the educational foundation for students and future professionals and preparation for the workplace, America's education system creates knowledge through research and enriches civic and community life by service learning and other noneconomic outcomes (e.g., family roles, use of leisure time, and faith development). Therefore, while a great deal of at-tention has been placed on increasing the participation of African American students in education, the same attention must be geared toward diversify-ing the education workplace. Thus a clear connection among all of the parts of the educational infrastructure emerges. In order to improve the African American experience in the education system, a holistic plan that connects the participation of African American students in pre-K–12 to postsec-ondary education, and in turn students' participation in postsecondary edu-cation to the workforce as professionals, is needed. Hence, this approach requires a look at the "life cycle" of the contemporary education system in the United States (Havinghurst, 1947, 1968, 1972). This would allow for a better understanding of how to strengthen the educational pipeline for African Americans.

This book attempts to address these disconnects by establishing inte-grated systems linking all levels of education from pre-K–12 to the higher education workplace and the influence of the surrounding community (see Figure 1). Such an integrated system can provide researchers, policy makers, and practitioners with a framework to help improve the educational pipeline for African Americans. The ultimate goal of this book was to reflect on the challenges associated with strengthening the educational pipeline for African Americans based on the premise that researchers, policy makers, and educators must conceptualize the critical stages within the educational

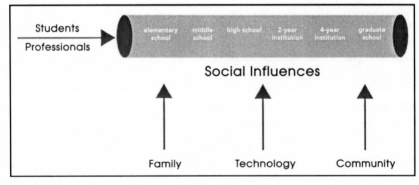

Figure 1 African American Educational Pipeline Framework

process that constitute the pipeline in order to implement interventions. More importantly, the book was anchored in the proposition that education does not work independently of families, communities, and social influences. In short, the individual insights and collective results of this book suggest that a thorough analysis of the educational pipeline not only requires examining the education experiences of student but also the work experiences of education professionals and the role of social influences (e.g., family, community, and technology).

The sections that follow highlight implications from the book that can be used to improve the African American educational pipeline based on the findings from each chapter and examine the efficacy of the pipeline metaphor for use considering the education experiences and outcomes for African Americans.

SYSTEMIC LEVEL IMPLICATIONS

African American Pre-K–12 Students

Data continues to confirm the unique predicament that African American students face with the pending choice between academic prowess and cultural competence (e.g., Ford, 1996; Miron & Lauria, 1998). Research referred to in chapter 1 argued that culturally responsive teaching is one method to ease this tension for African American students. Significantly, African American students tend to put forth more effort when their learning environment is linked to their daily sociocultural realities. In sum, classroom environments and school curricula that are reflective of African American culture can improve the performance of African American students.

African American Schoolteachers

Scholars (e.g., King, 1993; Ware, 2002; Wilson, 1988) have found that low prestige, low salary, and poor working conditions are among the factors that detract African Americans from pursing careers in teaching. Data in chapter 2 recommended that aggressive recruitment strategies be employed, just like in other professions. For example, other professions have developed creative methods to ensure that as early as junior high, and definitely by high school, students are exposed to their professions as an option. A key element in efforts to increase the participation of African Americans in teaching is school-based initiatives aimed at improving feelings of efficacy among aspiring and current African American teachers.

African American School Leaders

For the most part, school leaders are credentialed through university preparation programs, as discussed in chapter 3. In turn, any efforts to increase the participation of African American school leaders will begin with diversity initiatives by these programs. Aspiring African American school leaders should be encouraged to participate in professional development activities, such as leadership academies, to increase their competitiveness in the job market. Lastly, purposeful mentoring relationships with current school leaders are essential for preparing potential African American school leaders for the challenges of the workplace.

African American College Students

For approximately 3 decades, the level and quality of college student involvement has been one of the key measures of student outcomes (Pascarella & Terenzini, 1991). Data discussed in chapter 4, demonstrated that student involvement levels were moderate to low for African American students. In an effort to increase student involvement for African American students, a conceptual model was developed to assist practitioners to design programs to improve on-campus experiences. Further, at colleges and universities, a campus-wide effort to increase African American student awareness of various activities on campus was advised.

African American Faculty

Data discussed in chapter 5 showed that graduate school preparation programs are the main targets for increasing African American faculty representation. To assume faculty ranks, graduate-level training of some kind is generally needed. Therefore, the recruitment and retention practices of graduate preparation programs are key from the perspective of increasing the pool of candidates. Once hired, African Americans should be able to draw on two sets of support systems: internal support and external support. Internal support comes primarily from the academic department through mentoring relationships, financial support, and a respect for the scholarly contribution that the African American faculty can provide. External support refers to the need to develop a professional network that contains both senior and junior faculty for advice.

African American College Administrators

As a result of the changes in U.S. demographics, workforce needs are shifting in higher education. As the student population becomes more ethnically diverse, the need to have individuals in key decision-making roles on campus becomes paramount, as shown in chapter 6. In order to achieve a more diverse administrative workforce, institutions will need to develop a strategic hiring plan to ensure that diversity goals are being met. In addition to recruitment efforts, institutions will have to make serious attempts to address workplace conditions for African Americans. Difficult discussions will have to occur on campuses to address the "silent discrimination" that still exists today.

Community Involvement

As evidenced in chapter 7, school-community partnerships can play a significant role in the education of African American students. The fundamental principle behind school-community partnerships is that the education of a student is a holistic process. More specifically, student learning occurs outside of the classroom, and these partnerships provide additional avenues for interventions. By increasing the avenues to improve student performance in education, the overall opportunities for African American student success are increased.

Family-Based Interventions

Just as learning occurs in the classroom setting and surrounding community, students learn while at home. Chapter 8 data revealed that regardless of the identified problems with student learning, parents have the primary responsibility for the academic achievement of their children. These data showed that African American children perform best in school when their parents are actively involved in their educational process. Moreover, students with parents who instill in them racial pride perform better in school.

Technology As an Intervention

The appropriate use of technology in education can serve as a promising approach to addressing the achievement gap for African American students. Technology can be used to provide an alternative learning method for standard pre-K–12 curricula. Moreover, learning plans can be tailored to individual learning styles. Chapter 9 provided an argument on how artificial intelligence can be used to alleviate any teacher bias that may occur in the classroom due to racial perceptions. The possibility of employing technology as an intervention relies on the computer literacy of teachers, thus training initiatives would have to be implemented to fully realize this possibility.

Extending the Pipeline
Metaphor for Use in Education:
Knowledge Derived from Applied Science

The pipeline metaphor in education has received vast criticism, both in written text and undocumented discourse. As noted in the introduction of this book, critics suggest that the pipeline metaphor does not capture the dynamic nature or the multiplicity of the educational process in general, and the African American experience in particular. Conventional wisdom does suggest that a pipeline is straight; therefore, on the surface, these criticisms find understandable support throughout the field of education. However, a closer examination of the knowledge base derived from applied science, from which the metaphor is borrowed, responds to most, if not all, of these criticisms. Applied science is the exact science of applying knowledge from one or more natural scientific fields to practical problems. It is closely related or identical to engineering. Applied science can be used to develop technology. Moreover, educational researchers and policy makers have provided evidence for the use of the pipeline metaphor to examine the experiences for underrepresented groups (e.g., Kazis, Pennington, & Conklin, 2003).

Accordingly, this section of the book attempts to extend the pipeline metaphor for potential use within the context of education. This discussion explains the pipeline in two parts: structure and materials transported. In so doing, discussed are the materials transported, the supply system, the types of pipes, pipe fittings, and pipe problems.

Materials Transported

Pipes are used to transport and/or protect various types of materials. In turn, a material can be transported for various outcomes. The properties of the transported material determine the type (e.g., water) of pipe used. Types of materials traditionally transported by pipelines include, but are not limited to, water, sewage, conduit/ducting (e.g., electrical and communication wire), oil, and gas. While it is clear that various types of materials can be transported within a pipeline, a single material can be transported for various reasons (i.e., outcomes). To illustrate this point, I will use water as an example. Hot water is transported for washing, cold water for cooking, filtered water for drinking, and treated water for laundry and showers.

I hasten to draw the crude comparison between materials and humans, but the pipeline metaphor requires it. In doing so, I simply describe a basic product and outcome variation as provided above. A great deal of variation exists among African Americans who pass through the educational pipeline. The variation has at least two dimensions: status and ability group. The status refers to whether the individual passes through as a student or professional (e.g., faculty and principal). While the majority of the discourse related to the educational pipeline focuses on the former, the latter receives little attention. Oftentimes the discussion of the educational pipeline neglects to mention or provide equal attention to the challenges associated with African American professionals' active participation in the pipeline. Needless to say, regardless of the status level considered, a variation in ability level and preparedness to engage in the educational pipeline exists.

Supply System

The supply system disperses water throughout the house. The system primarily includes three functions: (1) brings water into the house; (2) divides the water into hot and cold water lines; and (3) distributes the water to various fixtures (e.g., sinks) and appliances (e.g., washing machine). Likewise, the educational process has filters throughout the pipeline. First, prior to entering the educational pipeline, both as students and professionals, pre-entry characteristics (e,g., human and social capital) affect the overall experience (Hoffman, Llagas, & Snyder, 2003). For example, students whose parents and community help ensure kindergarten readiness are more likely to be successful in kindergarten (Federal Interagency Forum on Child and Family Statistics, 2005). Further, students who participate in pre-kindergarten learning experiences (e.g., preschool) are more likely to be successful as well. It is at this initial stage of the pipeline that multiple pathways emerge. Second, within the educational pipeline, students, based on their academic abilities and sometimes other characteristics (e.g., bad behavior), are divided into low, average, and high ability groups (Horn, 1997; Horn & Chen, 1998). The learning experiences for each group vary considerably and in turn impact the type and quality of institution that the member of each group can attend at later stages in the pipeline (Martinez & Klopott, 2003). Third, the prechool experiences and individual assessment (i.e., ability group) may influence whether the student attends a low-, average-, or high-performing institution. Likewise, professionals within the educational pipeline are channeled accordingly by ability group and institution type, based on undergraduate and graduate education (Cole & Barber, 2003).

Types of Pipes

The types of pipes that construct the pipeline vary considerably in material type, cost, usage, and size. *Cast iron pipes*, used mostly before the 1960s, are strong and generally durable. In good condition, a cast iron pipe can last for decades; however, it may rust. *Plastic pipes* are inexpensive and easy to install. Most commonly used for drain pipes, plastic pipes are strong, long lasting, and impermeable to most chemicals. Older homes may have *steel pipes* for supply and drain lines. While steel pipes are strong, rarely, if ever, do they last more than 50 years. They rust like cast iron pipes but may also become clogged with mineral deposits, thus causing low water pressure. *Copper pipes* resist corrosion and are extremely long lasting; they are the prime candidates for supply lines. While reasonably priced, copper pipes are more expensive than plastic pipes. Generally, cast iron pipes are viewed as the highest quality, followed by steel, copper, and plastic pipes.

Equally so, the educational pipeline varies along the same four lines. First, as mentioned in the previous section, students with various backgrounds and abilities are filtered into various pipelines based on quality of experience. Previous research (e.g., Bell, 2004) indicates that educational experiences for students vary considerably across the United States. Second, often the variance in quality of an educational pipeline can be linked to funding. More often than not, low-performing educational pipelines lack the necessary funding to provide students with adequate learning resources and to attract high-performing teachers and staff (e.g., Ferguson, 1991; Ferguson & Ladd, 1996). Likewise, well-funded educational pipelines are able to provide the resources to increase student performance. Third, usage of educational pipelines varies based on perceived and actual outcomes. These usages may include education to work (e.g., career and armed forces) and postsecondary education (e.g., two-year institution and professional degree). Lastly, in many ways the size of the educational pipeline is linked to its quality. For example, high-performing systems tend to be smaller, while lower-performing systems tend to be larger (Commission on Chapter 1, 1992).

Pipe Fittings

A pipe fitting is any connector (except a valve) that allows one to join pipes of similar or dissimilar size or material in a straight run or at an angle. Regardless of material (e.g., copper, steel, plastic, or iron), most fittings fall into four categories: (1) couplings; (2) elbows; (3) tees, Ys, and crosses; and (4) caps (see Figure 2). Couplings are fittings used to join pipes in a straight line. Elbows permit pipes to turn corners. Tees, Ys, and crosses allow pipes to branch into multiple lines. And finally caps are used to seal the ends of pipes. The educational pipeline is equally dynamic, as described earlier. There are many areas within the educational pipeline where couplings would describe the straight nature of movement. For the most part, however, the educational pipeline has bends and curves that are

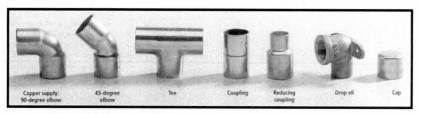

Figure 9.2 Various Types of Pipe Fittings

better explained by elbow fittings. While the educational pipeline is often discussed as a unified system, it consists of multiple lines, which makes understanding it complex. Many of these bends, curves, and multiple lines can be explained by alternative educational routes such as charter schools, voucher schools, alternative schools, and online colleges. Lastly, the end point of a line may not be "free flowing" to permit exit; in turn, a cap may be present to cause stoppage. Therefore, exiting may be very difficult, or close to impossible. In many ways, this could explain stages in the educational pipeline where African Americans experience problems moving through and out (e.g., undergraduate degree completion and doctoral education).

Pipe Problems, Symptoms, Repairs, and Solutions

Considering the level of daily activity and strain placed on pipelines, it is inevitable that problems arise and repairs are needed. With any repair job, one must figure out the problem to determine a repair or solution. Small exposed repairs can be easily tackled by a practitioner with no special knowledge or skills. The work becomes more challenging when the problems get larger and less transparent, thus requiring skills that general practitioners may not possess. What makes these repairs more difficult may not be the actual work but rather obstacles to the job. As stated before, the pipeline is not simply straight—it has multiple lines and curves, requiring some maneuvering to locate the problem.

The nature of the repair is further complicated, in that the pipeline material dictates the kind of tool and repair options. In other words, one cannot repair all pipeline materials the same way. As mentioned earlier in this chapter, due to the material, certain pipes are predisposed to specific types of problems (e.g., rust). Therefore, educational pipelines too must be approached differently, according to the properties (e.g., cast iron, steel, copper, and plastic) of the system. For example, some educational pipelines are armed with adequate funding, high-performing staff, and high achievers (e.g., cast iron and steel pipes), while the opposite is true for other educational pipelines (e.g., copper and plastic pipes). Regardless of the type of educational pipe, common challenges and problems are faced by all (see Figure 3).

Problem	Symptom	Repair	Solution
Clogged Pipe	Stages within the educational pipeline where African Americans are stopped from moving forward (e.g., two-year institutions and doctoral studies)	↑	↑
Cracked Pipe	Stages within the educational pipeline where African American students may become damaged in the learning process (e.g., being told that they are not smart and being placed in low-ability groups without appropriate opportunity to perform)		
Leaky Pipe	Stages within the educational pipeline where African Americans frequently exit prematurely (e.g., high school and college dropout)	Perform an evaluation to determine factors, both institutional and individual, that lead to marginal academic performance at identified stage of the educational pipeline.	Implement an educational intervention based on the findings of the evaluation.
Noisy Pipe	Stages within the educational pipeline where African Americans start to experience significant problems and are slowed down (e.g., proficiency concerns in reading and math classes)		
Frozen Pipe	Stages within the educational pipeline where African Americans experience challenges (e.g., chilly climate) related to institutional culture and/or climate (predominantly White college or university)	↓	↓

FIGURE 3   Common African American Educational Pipeline Problems and Repairs Chart

An increasingly competitive global market and the health of the U.S. workplace demand the educational system to fully develop all available human talents. To achieve this goal, the system can no longer overlook groups that have not performed well. In this book, the group examined was African American. A systemic effort between pre-K–12, higher education, and social influences (e.g., community and family) needs to be developed to address America's competitiveness in the global market, thus, repairing its educational pipeline framework. A framework of this nature builds lines of communication between each sector discussed within this book and others yet to be explored.

In closing, John W. Gardner once noted, "The society which scorns excellence in plumbing as a humble activity and tolerates shoddiness in philosophy because it is an exalted activity will have neither good plumbing nor good philosophy: neither its pipes nor its theories will hold water." This book takes one step toward providing direction for addressing systemic problems in the educational pipeline for African Americans in the United States. While the expanded pipeline metaphor serves as a useful heuristic tool, it has limitations like any other framework attempting to explain such a complex system. The pipeline metaphor is just one of many frameworks available to help explain the systemic nature of the education system in the United States. Whether electing to use the pipeline metaphor or some other framework, the selection of a framework is necessary to enable educators to improve the conditions and experiences of African Americans in education.

NOTE

I would like to thank Clifton F. Conrad, L. Allen Phelps, and Alan B. Knox of the University of Wisconsin, Ruben Anthony Jr. of the Wisconsin Department of Transportation, and Barbara J. Johnson of the Jackson State University for their feedback on previous drafts of this chapter.

REFERENCES

Anderson, J. A. (1988). *The education of Blacks in the South, 1860–1935.* Chapel Hill: University of North Carolina Press.

Bell, D. (2004). *Silent covenants: Brown v. Board of Education and the unfulfilled hopes for racial reform.* New York: Oxford University Press.

Cole, S., & Barber, E. (2003). *Increasing faculty diversity: The occupational choices of high-achieving minority students.* Cambridge, MA: Harvard University Press.

Commission on Chapter 1. (1992). *High performance schools: No exceptions, no excuses.* Washington, DC: Author.

Federal Interagency Forum on Child and Family Statistics. (2005). *America's children: Key national indicators of well-being 2005.* Washington, DC: Government Printing Office.

Ferguson, R. F. (1991). Paying for public education: New evidence on how and why money matters. *Harvard Journal on Legislation, 28*(2), 465–498.

Ferguson, R. F., & Ladd, H. F. (1996). How and why money matters: An analysis of Alabama schools. In H. F. Ladd (Ed.), *Holding schools accountable* (pp. 265–298). Washington, DC: Brookings Institute.

Ford, D. Y. (1996). *A study of underachievement among gifted, potentially gifted, and talented students.* Storrs: University of Connecticut, National Research Center on the Gifted and Talented.

Grant, C. A. (1995). Reflections on the promise of *Brown* and multicultural education. *Teachers College Record, 96*(4), 707–721.

Havinghurst, R. J. (1947). *Who shall be educated? The challenges of unequal opportunities.* New York: Harper.

Havinghurst, R. J. (Ed.). (1968). *Comparative perspectives on education.* New York: Little and Brown.

Havinghurst, R. (1972). *Developmental tasks and education* (3rd ed.). New York: David McKay.

Hoffman, K., Llagas, C., & Snyder, T. D. (2003). *Status and trends in the education of Blacks.* Washington, DC: National Center for Educational Statistics.

Horn, L. (1997). *Confronting the odds: Students at risk and the pipeline to higher education.* Washington, DC: U.S. Department of Education, National Center for Education Statistics (NCES, 98–084).

Horn, L., & Chen, X. (1998). *Toward resiliency: At-risk students who make it to college.* Washington, DC: U.S. Department of Education, Office of Educational Research and Improvement.

Jackson, J. F. L. (2004). Engaging, retaining, and advancing African Americans to executive-level positions: A descriptive and trend analysis of academic administrators in higher and postsecondary education. *Journal of Negro Education, 73*(1), 4–20.

Kazis, R., Pennington, H., & Conklin, K. D. (2003). *Ready for tomorrow: Helping all students achieve secondary and postsecondary success.* Washington, DC: National Governors Association.

King, S. H. (1993). Why did we choose teaching careers and what will enable us to stay?: Insights from one cohort of the African American teaching pool. *The Journal of Negro Education, 62*(4), 475–492.

Martinez, M., & Klopott, S. (2003). *Improving college access for minority, low-income, and first-generation students.* Boston: Pathways to College Network.

Miron, L. F., & Lauria, M. (1998). Student voice as agency: Resistance and accommodations in inner-city schools. *Anthropology & Education Quarterly, 29*(2), 189–213.

Ogbu, J. U. (2003). *Black Americans in an affluent suburb: A study of academic disengagement*. Mahwah, NJ: Lawrence Erlbaum.

Pascarella, E. T., & Terenzini, P. T. (1991). *How college affects students: Findings and insights from twenty years of research*. San Francisco: Jossey-Bass.

Pollard, D. (1997). Race, gender, and educational leadership: Perspectives from African American principals. *Educational Policy, 11*(3), 353–374.

Ware, F. (2002). Black teachers' perceptions of their professional roles. In J. J. Irvine (Ed.), *In search of wholeness: African American teachers and their culturally specific classroom practices* (pp. 33–45). New York: Palgrave.

Wilson, R. (1988). Recruiting and retaining minority teachers. *The Journal of Negro Education, 57*(2), 195–198.

Contributors

Tracy Buenavista is a doctoral student in the division of Higher Education and Organizational Change at the Graduate School of Education and Information Studies at UCLA.

Tamitha F. Campbell is a doctoral student in the department of Teacher Development and Leadership/Graduate Division of Education at Johns Hopkins University and former assistant principal for Montgomery County Public Schools. Her professional interests include community-based educational supports for African American students and the use of data in educational decision making.

Brandon D. Daniels is currently a Ph.D. student and research assistant in the Department of Educational Leadership and Policy Analysis, focusing on higher and postsecondary education at the University of Wisconsin-Madison. He received his bachelor's degree in English from the University of North Texas and masters degree in higher education administration from Florida State University.

Lamont A. Flowers, distinguished professor of educational leadership, received a bachelor of science degree in accounting from Virginia Commonwealth University, a master of arts degree in social studies education from the University of Iowa, and a doctorate in higher education from the University of Iowa. Flowers is the director of the Charles H. Houston Center for the Study of the Black Experience in Education in the Eugene T. Moore School of Education at Clemson University. The center addresses the breadth of social circumstances and conditions impacting African Americans in today's educational setting. Flowers also served as an associate director of the Institute of Higher Education in the College of Education at the University of Florida. He has written more than 60 scholarly publications in the areas of academic achievement, student retention, and educational leadership and serves as editor in chief of the *Journal of the Professoriate* and as senior associate editor for the *College Student Affairs Journal.*

R. Evely Gildersleeve is a doctoral student in the division of Higher Education and Organizational Change at the Graduate School of Education and Information Studies at UCLA. He graduated from Occidental College and has worked in a variety of urban school outreach initiatives, including students' academic empowerment, college access, and mentoring. He also worked in higher education student affairs at Iowa State University.

Tyrone C. Howard is an associate professor at UCLA in the Graduate School of Education and Information Studies Urban Schooling Division. His primary responsibilities involve the preparation and mentoring of in-service and pre-service teachers in urban school settings. Prior to entering the professoriate, Howard was an elementary schoolteacher in Compton, California, where he was born and raised. While working as a teacher, he completed his master's degree in education from California State University, Dominguez Hills. In addition to his teaching experience in Los Angeles, he has 2 years of teaching experience in Seattle, Washington. He received his Ph.D. from the University of Washington in 1998.

Jerlando F. L. Jackson is interested in the study of administrative diversity, executive behavior, and the nexus between administrative work and student outcomes in higher and postsecondary education. He is an assistant professor of higher and postsecondary education in educational leadership and policy analysis and a faculty associate for the Wisconsin Center for the Advancement of Postsecondary Education at the University of Wisconsin-Madison. In addition, he serves as a research associate for the Center for the Study of Academic Leadership, which is developing and publishing a new generation of research on academic administrators. His central interest has been to contribute to administrative science, with a focus on the impact of administrators on higher and postsecondary education. Recently he was appointed executive director of the Center for African American Research and Policy, whose mission is to engage in scholarly research in order to advance critical discourse and promote informed decisions pertaining to policy issues confronting African Americans in both the academy and the society at large.

Barbara J. Johnson is an associate professor at Jackson State University. Her research interests include the experiences of faculty and students at historically Black colleges and universities, the recruitment, development, and retention of students and faculty in a variety of postsecondary institutions, and student affairs administration. Her recent publications have appeared in the *Review of Higher Education, Urban Education, Faculty in New Jobs, Black College Review* and *Education and Society*. She received her Ph.D. from Vanderbilt University, an MBA from Ohio State University, and her BS from Winston-Salem State University.

Peter Kim is a doctoral candidate in the Urban Schooling Division of the Graduate School of Education and Information Studies at UCLA. He completed his master's degree in history at California State University at Northridge. In 1996, he served as an intern with the U.S. Department of Education. He is a former Rena L. Vassar Scholar, Picard Lurman Scholar, and Graduate Equity Fellow. He is also the recipient of the University Honors Achievement Medallion and the National Academy of Science Award.

Jelani Mandara is a social/personality psychologist with a focus on family and child development, person-centered research methods, and systems science. His primary research agenda is a person-centered analysis of the effects of family functioning (e.g., do parents have control over their children?), family structure (e.g., is a dad at home?), and other factors such as gender, family, SES, and race on child and adolescent social and personality development (e.g., do their children behave at school?). His other research interests include the synthesis of general systems and cybernetic theories with basic psychological constructs such as self-control, depth of processing, nonconscious perception, and cognitive resources. He also has done some Monte Carlo work on cluster analysis and other person-centered methods.

Tyson Marsh received his master's degree in higher education and organizational change at UCLA and is currently a doctoral candidate in the Urban Schooling Division at UCLA. He is a graduate of the University of Washington and has worked in the development and implementation of outreach recruitment and retention programs designed to improve educational opportunities and college access for students of color.

Carolyn B. Murray is currently a full professor in the Psychology Department at the University of California, Riverside. She received her Ph.D. from the University of Michigan, Ann Arbor, and was awarded a 4-year grant from the National Institute of Child Health and Human Development, National Institute of Mental Health (NIMH) to conduct a pioneer longitudinal study of the socialization processes of African American families and their children. The study assessed normal development processes of African American children and socialization techniques used by their caregivers. Her earlier research and published work was in attribution and the affective consequences of negative stereotypic expectations for academic achievement. In addition, she has investigated social support among older persons.

Jennifer E. Obidah is an associate professor in the Graduate School of Education and Information Studies at UCLA. She completed her doctorate in education at the University of California, Berkeley. In 1995 she received a National Institute of Mental Health (NIMH) postdoctoral fellowship. Her area of research is the sociocultural contexts of economically disenfranchised African American students' educational achievement. She focuses specifically on the sociocultural contexts of teacher-student interactions in urban classrooms, youth violence in communities and schools, and urban school reform. She has published articles and research papers on violence among youth in distinguished journals such as the *Harvard Educational Review Journal* and *The Journal of Negro Education*. Her paper, published in the *Harvard Educational Review Journal*, was selected as part of an edited volume for a Critics Choice Award by the American Educational Studies Association in November 2000. She is also the first author of the book *Because of the Kids: Facing Racial and Cultural Differences in Schools*, published by Teachers College Press. This book received the 2001 Gustavus Myers Outstanding Book Award, which "recognizes works that increase understanding of intolerance and bigotry, and most importantly, that inspire and inform strategies and actions that can lead to greater equity in our society."

Henrietta Pichon is an assistant professor in the Educational Leadership Department at Rowan University. She earned her Ph.D. in education administration (higher education) from the University of New Orleans and her master of education and bachelor of arts degrees from Louisiana Tech University. She has over 11 years of experience as a student affairs professional and instructor, and her research interests include access and persistence of students and faculty.

Ramona Pittman is currently a doctoral student in the College of Education at Texas A&M University in College Station, Texas. Her degree will be in curriculum and instruction, with an emphasis on reading and language arts education. Her research interests include multicultural and adolescent literacy and literature. She received a bachelor of science degree in elementary education from the University of Southern Mississippi and a master of education degree from William Carey College. She has taught in Mississippi and Texas for 7 years.

Mavis G. Sanders holds a Ph.D. in education from Stanford University and a joint appointment as research scientist at the Center for the Social Organization of Schools (CSOS) and associate professor in the Teacher Development and Leadership/Graduate Division of Education at Johns Hopkins University.

Her research and teaching interests include school reform, parent and community involvement, and African American student achievement.

Jeffrey G. Sumrall is an assistant professor at the University of Houston, College of Technology. He holds a master's degree in computer engineering technology from the University of Southern Mississippi as well as a Ph.D. in educational technology from Louisiana State University. He currently teaches various courses in information systems, including Integrated Systems, Client/Server Technology Computer Systems Security, and Principles of Information System Networks. His research agenda involves concepts related to distributed high performance computing applications, specifically medical image (fMRI) data mining.

Linda C. Tillman is associate professor in the Educational Leadership Program at the University of North Carolina at Chapel Hill. Her research interests include mentoring teachers and principals, culturally sensitive research approaches, parental involvement, and leadership theory. Her current research investigates the role of the principal in mentoring first-year African American teachers in an urban school district. She is a member of the American Educational Research Association (AERA) Annual Meeting Policies and Procedures Committee, and chairperson of the Division A Mentoring Committee and serves as a mentor for the University Council for Educational Administration Jackson Scholars Program. Tillman is also a Fellow of the National Institute on Leadership, Disability, and Students Placed at Risk at the University of Vermont. Her recent publications include "African American Principals and the Legacy of Brown" in the *Review of Research in Education* and "Mentoring New Teachers: Implications for Leadership Practice in an Urban School" in *Educational Administration Quarterly*. In 2004, she received the AERA Scholars of Color Education Early Career Contribution Award.

Index

Adams v. Richardson, 5, 98
Administrators: in student affairs, 125–28
Advance Cognitive Tutor (ACT), 192;
    See also research-based cognitive
    tutoring system
Affirmative action: policies, 5, 20;
    programs, 117; regulations, 116
African American faculty: stress, 102;
    racism, 103
African American family: mother-headed,
    169
African American females: in adminis-
    trative positions, 10; in faculty
    positions, 10, 99; as student affairs
    administrators, 125
African American males: in adminis-
    trative positions, 10; in faculty
    positions, 10; salary, 99; special
    education, 19; as student affairs
    administrators, 125
African American students: pre-k
    education, 17, 18–32 passim;
    special education, 19, 142, 150
African Free School, 3
American Association of University
    Professors (AAUP): tenure and
    promotion guidelines, 105
American Council of Education, 6
American Negro Academy, 3

Artificial intelligence, 190, 192–4
Ayers v. Fordice, 5.
Ayers v. Waller. See *Ayers v. Fordice.*

Black land-grant institutions, 4
Black Mississippians' Council of Higher,
    The, 5
Bouchet, Edward A., 3
*Brown v. Board of Education, Topeka,
    Kansas,* 5, 23, 40, 46, 47, 55, 66
Brown v. Fordice, 12

California School Leadership Academy,
    60
California State Department of
    Education. *See Williams v. State
    of California.*
Children's Defense Fund (CDF), 156;
    summer freedom school, 156
Chronicle, 108
Civil Rights Act of 1964, 2, 5, 66, 402
Cognitive tutoring systems. *See* research-
    based cognitive tutoring systems.
Coleman Report. See *Equality of
    Educational Opportunity.*
College Board, 21
College Student Experiences
    Questionnaire (CSEQ), 74, 76–7
Computer literacy, 188

217

Condition of Education, The, 21
Cooper v. Aaron, 5
Council of Graduate Schools (CGS), 100
Crummel, Alexander, 3
Cultural production, 41
Cultural taxation, 102

Danforth Educational Leadership
     Program, 60
Developmental appropriateness, 26
Digital divide, 187
Discrimination, 20
Diversity, 6, 26: administrative, 117, 119;
     ethnic, 115, 116, 132; structural,
     110; workplace, 115, 134
Dreamkeepers, The (Ladson-Billings), 25

Early Recognition program. See
     Rochester public school system.
Educational Opportunity Programs
     (EOP), 117
Educational pipeline, 6, 7, 18; African
     Americans, 19, 21, 27, 32, 41, 47,
     198–99; opponents of, 100; in pre-
     K–12, 19, 21; and socialization, 109
Elementary and Secondary Education
     Act (ESEA), 159
Empirical research, 143
Engagement, Retention, and Advance-
     ment Model, (ERA), 130–131
Equality of Educational Opportunity, 2, 5
Equal Protection Clause, 5
Executive Order 11246, 5
Extended-family academic group, 104

Four Corner Sharp program, 156–7, 159
Frazier v. UNC Board of Trustees, 5

Gardner's multiple intelligences: exis-
     tentialist, 191; intrapersonal, 191;
     interpersonal, 191; naturalist, 191
Geimeinshaft, 158

Handbook on Research on Educational
     Administration, 56
Harvard Principals Center, 60

Head Start programs, 5
Higher Education Act (Title III), 5
Historically Black colleges and universities
     (HBCU), 4, 5, 64, 97, 100
Howard Street Tutoring Programs, 144
Howard University Upward Board, 154
Hundred Book Challenge program,
     151; See also school-community
     partnerships.

Individuals with Disabilities Education
     Act (IDEA), 160

Jeanes Foundation, 4
Johnson, Lyndon B., 5
Journal of Blacks in Higher Education,
     The, 98

Kansas City Freedom School, 156

Lincoln University (Pennsylvania), 3

Manumission Society, 3
Marshall, Thurgood, 5
McLaurin v. Oklahoma State Regents for
     Higher Education, 4
Mentoring, 61, 64–5, 109, 131
Mentoring programs: national commu-
     nity-based, 145; school and commu-
     nity-based, 144; Four Corner Sharp
     Program, 157
Missouri ex rel. Gains v. Canada, 4
Morrill Act II, 4
Mount Olivet after-school program,
     The, 144

Nation At Risk Report, A, 48
National Alliance of Black School
     Educators (NABSE), 61
National Assessment of Educational
     Progress (NAEP), 20, 22
National Association for the Advancement
     of Colored People (NAACP), 5
National Association for Equal Opportu-
     nity in Higher Education
     (NAFEO), 5

National Association for Student Person-
nel Administrators (NASPA), 118
National Center for Educational Statis-
tics (NCES), 21, 97–100
National Education Association, 58
National Study of Postsecondary Faculty
(NSOPF), 118–24
National Urban League, 155
Negro Rural School Fund (Anna T.
Jeanes Fund), 4
New York State Education Department,
38
No Child Left Behind Act (NCLB), 30,
48, 60, 63, 160,188

Oberlin College (Ohio), 3
Office of Economic Opportunity
(OEO), 5, 154
Office of Minorities in Higher Education,
6
Ohio State University's College of
Education, 144

Partnership in Education program,
151; *See also* school-community
partnership.
Pathway to Teaching program, 58
Patterson, Frederick D., 4
Pedagogical approach, 47
Pedagogical practices, 18, 24
Pedagogical principles, 26
Pedagogy, 23–6, 38, 44, 48; African
Americans students, 44, 46; cultur-
ally responsive (relevant), 24–5, 28,
38, 44; engaged, 31; multicultural, 26
Pipeline: academic, 98; at historically
Black colleges and universities
(HBCU), 103–4; at predominately
White Institutions (PWI), 101
Pipes: cast iron, 204–6; copper, 204–6;
plastic, 204–6; steel, 204–6
Plessy v. Ferguson, 4, 40
Policy tools, 4–6
Praxis-based information, 1
Pre-Kindergarten-schools (pre-K), 17–32
passim

*Preparing School Principals: A National
Perspective on Policy and Program
Innovations,* 54
Project Raise, 144
Project Talent, 2
Public policy designs, 4
Pump Algebra Tutor (PAT), 192–3;
See also research-based cognitive
tutoring system.

RAND Education, 54
Racism, 20
*Regents of the University of California v.
Bakke,* 6
Research-based cognitive tutoring
system: Advance Cognitive Tutor
(ACT), 192–3; Pump Algebra Tutor
(PAT), 192–3
Rochester Public School System: Early
Recognition program, 155
Rochester Urban League: Black Scholars
program, 155; Black Scholars
Mentor program, 155
*Rolling Up Their Sleeves: Superintendents
and Principals Talk About What's
Needed to Fix Public Schools,* 54

*Scholarship Reconsidered: Priorities of the
Professoriate,* 105
School administration. *See* school
leadership.
School-community partnership,
146–152, 158–9; Hundred Book
Challenge program, 151;Partnership
in Education program, 151
School, Family, and Community
Partnership Program of the
National Network of Partnership
Schools (NNPS), 149–52
School leadership, 54–66 passim
Segregation: *Brown v. Board of Education,*
40, 55, 197; Coleman Report, 5;
de facto, 6, 46; de jure, 46; *Plessy v.
Ferguson,* 40; racial, 5; resegregation,
5; school, 45, 47
Slavery, 3, 41

Slosson Oral Reading Test, 144
Social Economic Status (SES), 170, 174
Socialization: direct academic, 173–7, 181; general, 166; gendered, 169; racial, 171–3, 181–2
Souls of Black Folk, The (DuBois), 41
Special education, 19; African Americans receiving, 142, 150; placements, 19; programs, 44
Status of the Public Schools. See National Education Association.
Supreme Court, 5, 6
Sweatt v. Painter, 4

Teach for America program, 58
Teaching: of African American teachers, 24; culturally responsive, 18, 28–9; in "hard to teach in", 37–49 passim; pedagogical approach to, 47; through technology, 190; unorthodox, 194
Technology, 187–94 passim
Technology-based education, 188
Texas Southern University, 5
Texas State University for Negroes (TSUN) School of Law, 5
Tokenism, 102
Tracking, 177–8, 180
21st Century Community Learning Centers, 160
TRIO Programs, 1
Tuskegee Institute, 4

United Negro College Fund (UNCF), 4
United States Congress, 4
United States Constitution, 5
United States Current Population Survey, 37
United States Department of Education, 21, 48, 63
United States Department of Health, Education, and Welfare (HEW), 5, 6
United States Freedman Bureau, 4
United States v. Fordice, 6
Universal literacy, 26
University Council for Educational Administration, 57
University of Texas Law School, 5
Urban League: Four Corner Sharp Program, 156; National, 155; Rochester. *See* Rochester Urban League. Black Scholars Early Recognition program. *See Rochester* Public School System.

Voting Rights Act of 1870, 41

Who Is Leading Our Schools?: An Overview of School Administrators and Their Careers, 54
Williams v. State of California, 39
Wyant v. Jackson Board of Education, 6

Yale University, 3